AF600326

THE SACRED CONGREGATION FOR THE ORIENTAL CHURCH

THE CATHOLIC UNIVERSITY OF AMERICA
CANON LAW STUDIES
No. 214

THE SACRED CONGREGATION FOR THE ORIENTAL CHURCH

BY

REV. MICHAEL W. DZIOB, J.C.L.
PRIEST OF THE DIOCESE OF PROVIDENCE

A DISSERTATION

SUBMITTED TO THE FACULTY OF THE SCHOOL OF CANON LAW OF THE CATHOLIC UNIVERSITY OF AMERICA IN PARTIAL FULFILLMENT OF THE REQUIREMENTS FOR THE DEGREE OF DOCTOR OF CANON LAW

THE CATHOLIC UNIVERSITY OF AMERICA PRESS
WASHINGTON, D. C.
1945

Nihil Obstat:
HIERONYMUS D. HANNAN, A.M., LL.B., S.T.D., J.C.D.,
Censor Deputatus.
Washingtonii, D. C., die 20 maii, 1945.

Imprimatur:
✠ FRANCISCUS P. KEOUGH, D.D.,
Episcopus Providentiensis.
Providentiae, R.I., die 20 maii, 1945.

MURRAY & HEISTER—WASHINGTON, D. C.

PRINTED IN THE UNITED STATES OF AMERICA

 9

TO
HIS EXCELLENCY
THE MOST REVEREND FRANCIS P. KEOUGH, D.D.
BISHOP OF PROVIDENCE

TABLE OF CONTENTS

PART II

THE SACRED CONGREGATION FOR THE ORIENTAL CHURCH SINCE THE PROMULGATION OF THE *CODEX IURIS CANONICI*

FOREWORD

It is the purpose of this dissertation to trace the development of the Sacred Congregation for the Oriental Church through its various stages of formation up to the present time both as to its historical and canonical aspects. At the more important stages of this evolution an indication of and a commentary on the powers of the Sacred Congregation are given in order to present a rather complete picture of its function and organization at those times.

All the sources within reach of the writer have been used. Unfortunately some of the requisite reference books and documents have not been available. Wherefore, in instances where the necessary documents were not obtainable and historical data were lacking, the opinions and assertions of other authors are narrated. If no conclusion is drawn in those cases, it is only because the writer does not wish to form conjectures on uncertain or unknown facts, but rather hopes that such gaps will be filled by those who have access to the primary documents and historical records.

It is to be noted that all references to the Code in this work pertain to the *Codex Iuris Canonici,* and not to the Code of Canon Law of the Oriental Church, which as yet has not been published.

The writer wishes to acknowledge his sincere gratitude to His Excellency, the Most Reverend Francis P. Keough, D.D., Bishop of Providence, for the privilege of advanced study in Canon Law; to Professor Willibald Plöchl under whose supervision this dissertation was written; to the Faculty of the School of Canon Law of the Catholic University of America for their generous assistance in the preparation of this dissertation; and to his fellow-priests in the School of Canon Law for their aid and encouragement.

PART I

THE EVOLUTION OF THE SACRED CONGREGATION FOR THE ORIENTAL CHURCH PRIOR TO THE PROMULGATION OF THE *CODEX IURIS CANONICI*

CHAPTER I

STAGES OF FORMATION PRIOR TO POPE URBAN VIII

Article I. Short Introductory Survey of the History of the Sacred Roman Congregations

During the second half of the fifteenth century and the first half of the sixteenth the reigning popes occasionally appointed various commissions of cardinals to act in a definite capacity, such as, to carry on consultations with certain envoys concerning particular matters,[1] to deliberate on all measures necessary for the prosecution of the Crusades,[2] to make proposals both for carrying out the war and for providing the means therefor,[3] to deliberate on means of reform in the Church,[4] to draw up proposals with regard to the Leonine appointments which had been recently made,[5] and to consider the question of reopening the Council of Trent.[6] These Congregations of cardinals, created when pressing problems arose, lacked stability;[7] they were named to cover an assignment, and they ceased to exist when their mission was performed. The transition from this temporary basis to a more stable, permanent, organized cardinalitial Congregation assigned to definite matters appeared for the first time under Pope Paul III (1534–1549) with the establishment of the *Congregatio pro sancta Inquisitione*[8] (also referred to as the Congregation of the

---

[1] Pastor, *The History of the Popes* (34 vols., Vols. I–VI edited by Frederick Ignatius Antrobus; Vols. VII–XXIV by Ralph Francis Kerr; Vols. XXV–XXXIV by Dom Ernest Graf, St. Louis: B. Herder, 1898–1941), III (2. ed.), 327.

[2] *Op. cit.*, IV, 80.

[3] *Op. cit.*, VII, 220.

[4] *Op. cit.*, V, 512, 515.

[5] *Op. cit.*, IX, 107.

[6] *Op. cit.*, XIII, 78.

[7] *Op. cit.*, XIX, 59.

[8] *Loc. cit.; Bullarum Diplomatum et Privilegiorum Sanctorum Romanorum*

Inquisition)[9] in 1542. Following this precedent, Pope Pius IV (1559–1565) formed the *Congregatio pro executione et interpretatione concilii Tridentini*[10] (also known as the Congregation of the Council);[11] and Pope Pius V (1566–1572) established the *Congregatio pro Indice librorum prohibitorum*[12] as well as the *Congregatio pro consultationibus episcoporum et aliorum praelatorum*[13] (for the sake of brevity called the Congregation of Bishops).[14] However, it is to be noted that these four Congregations had not suppressed the employment of the temporary, provisional type, for Pope Pius IV himself used the latter whenever an important question called for special consideration, such as, the reconciliation of heretics, the conversion of infidels, the war against the Turks.[15] In fact, the succeeding popes continued to make more and more use of these temporary Congregations, so that a report of February, 1574, concerning Pope Gregory XIII's pontificate (1572–1585) listed thirteen such bodies existing at the same time.[16]

The need of successive, independent commissions, as well as frequent consistorial assemblies, was greatly diminished by Pope Sixtus V (1585–1590) when he re-arranged the whole system of ecclesiastical administration through a complete elaboration and methodical organization of stable, cardinalitial Congregations; for he realized that a systematic, logical, speedy discharge and dispatch of the complicated business brought to Rome from all parts of the world, as well as the papal management of the temporal States of the Holy See, would best be procured by its being

---

Pontificum Taurinensis Editio (24 vols. et Appendix, Neapoli 1857–1872), VIII, 986, footnote 1; Vol. VI, p. 344, Const. XLIII "*Licet ab.*" Hereafter this collection will be cited as *Bull. Rom.*

9 Pastor, *op. cit.*, XVII, 203; XIX, 59; XXI, 245.

10 *Bull. Rom.*, VIII, 991, footnote 1; Vol. VII, p. 300, Const. XCIX "*Alias nos;*" Pastor, *op. cit.*, XXI, 250.

11 Pastor, *op. cit.*, XVII, 203; XIX, 59; XXI, 245, 251.

12 *Bull. Rom.*, VIII, 990–991; Pastor, *op. cit.*, XVII, 203; XIX, 59; XXI, 250.

13 *Bull. Rom.*, VIII, 994; Pastor, *op. cit.*, XIX, 59; XXI, 250.

14 Pastor, *op. cit.*, XVII, 204; XXI, 245.

15 *Op. cit.*, XIX, 59.

16 *Loc. cit.*

entrusted to an orderly, constant organization.[17] Accordingly, by means of the Constitution "*Immensa,*"[18] of January 22, 1588,[19] he instituted fifteen such bodies,[20] which he called Congregations,[21] to execute his program for a more facile and adequate handling of the manifold and complex work heaped upon the Holy See.[22] Each individual, stabilized Congregation underwent changes in the course of the following centuries—several disappeared entirely, others were established; the affairs formerly considered by one Congregation were transferred to the jurisdiction of another; the number of cardinals in a Congregation varied, etc.—but the system of fixed cardinalitial administrative bodies as organs of the Roman Curia continued to the present day.

Among the original fifteen Congregations of Pope Sixtus V there was not included a Congregation to treat of matters pertaining to the Oriental Church or any of its divisions.[23] The first permanent Congregation of the Roman Curia to whose care the Orientals were to be entrusted was the Sacred Congregation *de Propaganda Fide* (1622). Within that Sacred Congregation various adaptations preceded the founding of an official Sacred Congregation established exclusively for the Oriental Church. The history of its progressive formation follows.

Article II. First Steps towards the Founding of the Sacred Congregation for the Oriental Church

From the very beginning the authoritative members of the

---

[17] *Op. cit.*, XXI, 5, 245.

[18] *Bull. Rom.*, VIII, 985–997.

[19] "Constit. '*Immensa*' habet revera datam 22 Ianuarii 1587, at, quia ante Pium X anni computabantur in datatione bullarum a die 25 Martii, seu a die Incarnationis non Nativitatis Domini, inde fit ut revera annus quo illa constitutio edita est non fuerit in communi computatione annus 1587 sed 1588."—Coronata, *Institutiones Iuris Canonici* (5 vols., Taurini [Italia]: Marietti, 1928–1936), I, 385, footnote 5. Cf. also Simier, *La Curie Romaine* (Paris: Editions de la "Revue Augustinienne," 1909), p. 128, footnote 2.

[20] *Loc. cit.;* Pastor, *op. cit.*, XXI, 249–261.

[21] Monin, *De Curia Romana* (Lovanii: Josephus Van Linthout, 1912), p. 9.

[22] *Bull. Rom.*, VIII, 986, § 2.

[23] *Ibid.*, pp. 986–987.

Sacred Congregations have been cardinals,[24] even though they have been assisted in their work by others not of their dignity, and to this very day they have maintained that same position in the Sacred Congregations. Therefore in the reviewing of the stages leading to the formation of the Sacred Congregation for the Oriental Church, attention must be focused upon a group composed entirely of cardinals, or at least a body whose principal members in authority were cardinals, appointed by the pope to conduct in his name and with his authority some transaction or negotiation with or concerning the Catholics of the Oriental Rite or their separated brethren.

Instances of the functioning of just such a group occurred at the reunion council held at Florence. At this council in the early days of April, 1439, the Emperor John VII (Palaiologos, 1425–1448) sent the pope a message in which he declared that all discussions were leading nowhere, for neither the Latins nor the schismatic Greeks would yield to the other, and that if the Supreme Pontiff knew of another way to bring about the union he should indicate it; otherwise, the Greeks would return home. The pope replied that he would entrust the dissolution of the barrier to a group of cardinals who would be sent to them. Four days later, on the Wednesday after the Sunday *in albis,* April 15, 1439, three cardinals, Nicola Albergati of Fermo, Francesco Condolmerio, Giulio Cesarini, arrived at the house of the Patriarch of Constantinople, Joseph II (1416–1439), where the Emperor also awaited them. The ensuing meeting finally resulted in an agreement that ten representatives should be selected from each side, and these should look for the proper way to lead to the desired union.[25]

On May 21 the Emperor once more besought the pope to conclude the affair. Pope Eugene IV (1431–1447) commissioned three cardinals to obtain from the Greeks a more precise explanation of their dogmatic declaration regarding the *Filioque.* The

[24] *Bull. Rom., loc. cit.;* Pastor, *op. cit.,* XXI, 250; V. Martin, *Les Congrégations Romaines* (Paris: Librairie Bloud & Gay, 1930), pp. 6–7.

[25] Hefele-Leclercq, *Histoire des Conciles* (10 vols. in 19, Paris: Letouzey et Ané, 1907–1938), Vol. VII, Part II, n. 706, pp. 997–998; nn. 709–710, p. 1001.

Greeks refused, and the parleys between the two factions on the following day were also in vain.[26]

Then, at a later date, when the Emperor saw that the union was nearing a successful end, he hastened through the intermediation of Isidore of Kiev (ca. 1380/90–1463) to negotiate with the Vicar of Christ concerning the material aid that the Greeks would receive after the union. It was three cardinals who on June 1, 1439, made them promises in the name of His Holiness.[27]

On June 28, when the Emperor objected to two of the expressions of the decree of union, Pope Eugene IV sent some cardinals to him. They resumed their conference on June 30, but that afternoon ended with no results. In the evening of the same day the cardinals again attempted to clarify the issue. After the departure of the Pontiff's commission, the Greeks' deliberations among themselves terminated in a formula which they presented to Pope Eugene IV. Another formula, which was a modification of this first, also was submitted, although there is no account of *why, how,* or *when* it was altered. The next day the cardinals returned to the Emperor and submitted to him the chosen decree of union, informing him that the Holy Father had received the two formulas of the Greeks and had charged the cardinals to select one of them.[28]

Thus, even though the amount of work allotted was small, its duration short, and its assignments few in number, nevertheless these small groups of cardinals (whether they were always one and the same is undetermined) were invested by the pope with authority to act in matters pertaining to the separated brethren, the Greeks. It is true that they functioned merely at a council; but it is equally true that they were appointed for these particular tasks in preference to any of the mixed commissions which operated during this same council. It is conceivable, therefore, that these groups may be placed on a basis similar to that of the first provisional commissions[29] which preceded the formation of the

[26] *Ibid.*, n. 714, n. 1005.

[27] *Ibid.*, nn. 717–718, p. 1009.

[28] *Ibid.*, n. 737, pp. 1028–1029; n. 738, p. 1029.

[29] Such as, the Congregation of cardinals to draw up proposals with regard

subsequent, more developed temporary commissions, which latter in turn led to the fixed, stable Sacred Congregations. Regardless of whether the above explanation is accepted or not, it seems proper nevertheless to mention in this type of work this association of cardinals with matters concerning the Oriental Rite.

Article III. The Congregation during the Pontificate of Gregory XIII

The narrations of various authors evince the existence of a forerunner of the Sacred Congregation for the Oriental Church in the form of a transitory commission of cardinals during the pontificate of Pope Gregory XIII (1572–1585). It is not clear whether their accounts are incomplete, describing one and the same body at various phases of its formation; or whether they are complete and designating distinct, either co-existing or successive, commissions, to which some of the same cardinals were attached.

Wernz-Vidal,[30] Monin [31] and V. Martin [32] refer to the formation of a commission of three cardinals by Pope Gregory XIII, which was constituted for the two-fold purpose of: (a) preserving unsoiled the purity of the Faith among the Catholics of the Greek rite; and (b) reuniting the dissident Oriental Christians with the Roman Catholic Church. With the exception of Monin's assertion that the commission seems to have been engaged in several matters pertaining to the general propagation of the Faith [33] and Martin's association of it with the Congregation *de rebus Graecorum*,[34] the above mentioned authors provide no further details of its existence during this pontificate—they neither name its cardinals nor state the year of its constitution, they simply

to the Leonine appointments, and that for the case of the Archbishop of Toledo. For the latter, see Pastor, *op. cit.*, XIX, 59.

[30] Wernz (1842–1914)-Vidal (1867–1938), *Ius Canonicum* (7 vols. in 8, Romae: apud Aedes Universitatis Gregorianae, 1923–1943), II (3. ed., recognita A. P. Philippo Aguirre, 1943), n. 495. Cf. also Wernz, *Ius Decretalium* (6 vols., Romae et Prati, 1898–1905), II, 764.

[31] *De Curia Romana*, p. 66.

[32] *Les Congrégations Romaines*, p. 136.

[33] *De Curia Romana*, p. 66.

[34] *Les Congrégations Romaines*, compare pp. 136 and 191.

relate in a general way that Pope Clement VIII (1592–1605) confirmed it, increased its cardinal members, improved the rules governing its sessions and set it to active work. Wernz-Vidal, for instance, after reporting the founding of the commission by Gregory XIII, continue in the very next sentence thus: "*Quae*[35] commissio a Clemente VIII compluribus Cardinalibus aucta in perfectiorem formam redacta est."[36] Monin links Pope Clement VIII with the commission in a similar way: "*Hanc*[37] commissionem confirmavit, membris pluribus auxit, ipsiusque sessiones melius ordinavit Clemens VIII; . . . ."[38] V. Martin does likewise: "Cette seconde commission [the commission under discussion], dont Clement VIII renforça les attributions et activa les travaux, ..."[39] Their manner of expression leaves unanswered the query whether this commission of three (even though perhaps not the original three) persisted through the reigns of Pope Sixtus V (1585–1590), Urban VII (September 15, 1590–September 27, 1590),[40] Gregory XIV (1590–1591), Innocent IX (October 29, 1591–December 30, 1591),[41]—all of whom had preceded Pope Clement VIII,—or whether it ceased to function during that time either by merely remaining inactive or by disbanding completely until Pope Clement VIII revivified or re-established the organization.

Petrani affirms that Pope Gregory XIII under the inspiration of the Cardinal of Santa Severina, Giulio Santorio,[42] who at that time was cardinal protector of the Orientals, instituted in 1573 a particular Congregation to reform the Basilian Order[43] and to

---

35 Italics supplied by the writer.

36 *Ius Canonicum,* II (1943), n. 495.

37 Italics ours.

38 *De Curia Romana,* p. 66.

39 *Les Congrégations Romaines,* pp. 136 and 191.

40 He died before his coronation.

41 His coronation was on November 3, 1591.

42 Sometimes spelled "Santori." Cf. Pastor, *op. cit.,* XX, 486; XIX, 60, footnote 1; also spelled "Sanctorius."

43 It has been associated with the Orientals from the beginning of the Rule of St. Basil, a pattern of Oriental monasticism. The name "Ordo S. Basilii Magni" arose in Italy only in the 14th century (?), where Greek monasticism was conceived according to the analogy of the Occidental Orders.

promote the return of the dissident Orientals; it was commonly known as the *Congregatio Graeca* or simply *de rebus Graecorum.* He neither names the cardinals nor gives the number of cardinal members. After the death of Gregory XIII Petrani would have this Congregation commence languishing and afterwards become extinct.[44]

Pastor, in speaking of Pope Gregory XIII's aim for the restoration of the Greek schismatics, at first mentions Cardinals Sirleto (1514–1585), Santorio (+ 1602), and Savelli (+ 1587) as his advisers in this matter; and then "in 1573 he formed these into a special Congregation to deal with the affairs of the Greeks. By their advice the Roman Catechism was translated into modern Greek, and in 1576 no less than 12,000 copies were sent to the Levant, together with a like number of copies of the decrees of the Council of Trent."[45] A check upon Pastor's indicated reference to Cardinal Santorio's consistorial diary under the date of June 10, 1573,[46] reveals that on that day *four* cardinals—Savelli,[47] Sirleto, Santorio, and A. Carafa (1538–1591)[48] were appointed to a *congregatio Graeccorum* (in the margin in another hand is written "*De Graecis*"), a Congregation for the reformation of the Greeks and of the monks and monasteries of the Order of St. Basil. Furthermore, on another occasion when Pastor states that a report of February, 1574, "makes no mention of the so-called 'Greek' congregation, established by Pope Gregory XIII in 1573, which was first engaged upon the reform of the Basilian monasteries in Italy and afterwards with the propaga-

---

Cf. *Lexikon für Theologie und Kirche* (10 vols., edited by Michael Buchberger, Frieburg im Breisgau, 1930–1938), II, 18; *Archiv für katholisches Kirchenrecht* (Innsbruck, 1857–1861; Mainz, 1862–), XLVIII (1882), 99–102; Besse, "Rule of St. Basil"—*The Catholic Encyclopedia* (15 vols., and 2 supplements, New York, 1907–1922), II, 324.

[44] Petrani, "De Sacra Congregatione pro Ecclesia Orientali eiusque facultatibus"—*Apollinaris* (Romae, 1928–), X (1937), 28.

[45] Pastor, *op. cit.*, XX, 486.

[46] Tacchi Venturi, "Diario Concistoriale di Giulio Antonio Santori di S. Severina"—*Studi e Documenti di Storia e Diritto* (Roma, 1880–), XXIV (1903), 135.

[47] In Latin this name is sometimes written "Sabellum."

[48] Also spelled Caraffa or Carrafa by others.

tion of the faith in the East,"[49] he evidently is referring to this very Congregation under consideration. This conclusion is confirmed by the fact that the author in his footnote to the above excerpted quotation has a reference to the very same place in the *Diario Concistoriale* as is mentioned above. Yet, in this same footnote[50] Pastor himself avers: (a) that according to Santorio's *Autobiografia* five cardinals belonged to that Congregation, namely, Savelli, Sirleto, A. Carafa, Filippo Boncompagni (+ 1586),[51] and Santorio; and (b) that Coquelines[52] mentions other names in *Annali di Gregorio XIII*.[53] Unfortunately the writer could not procure the text of the last reference to obtain the names listed. However, a check upon the autobiography[54] shows that still another person, though not a cardinal, was nevertheless a member; he was the Archbishop of Corfù[55] who had written very learnedly against the errors of the Greeks.

On the other hand, according to Moroni (1801–1883)[56] and

---

49 *The History of the Popes,* XIX, 57–60.

50 *Ibidem,* p. 60, footnote 1.

51 Also known as "San Sisto" from his title: Cardinal of San Sisto.

52 Also spelled Cocquelines. Cf. Moroni, *Dizionario Di Erudizione Storico-Ecclesiastica* (103 vols., Venezia: Della Tipografia Emiliana, 1840–1861), XVI, 241. Hereafter cited *Dizionario.*

53 G. P. Maffei (1533–1603), *Annali di Gregorio XIII* (2 vols., Roma, 1742), I, V. Cf. Pastor, *The History of the Popes,* XIX, p. 60, and p. XVIII.

54 Cugnoni, "Autobiografia del Card. G. A. Santori"—*Archivio della R. Società Romana di Storia Patria* (Roma, 1877–), XII (1889), 355.

55 S. Congregazione Orientale, *Statistica con Cenni Storici della Gerarchi e dei Fedeli di Rito Orientale* (Tipografia Poliglotta Vaticana, 1932), p. 11. Hereafter cited *Statistica.*

Antonius Caucus was Archbishop of Corfù from May 29, 1560 to Nov. 29, 1577—Eubel, *Hierarchia Catholica Medii Aevi sive Summorum Pontificum, S. R. E. Cardinalium, Ecclesiarum Antistitum Series* (4 vols., Vols. I [1913] and II [1914] in 2. ed., edited by Conradus Eubel; Vol. III [1910] edited by Gulielmus Van Gulick-Conradus Eubel; Vol. IV [1935] edited by Patritius Gauchat under the title of *Hierarchia Catholica Medii et Recensioris Aevi sive Summorum Pontificum, S.R.E. Cardinalium, Ecclesiarum Antistitum Series;* Monasterii: Sumptibus et Typis Librariae Regensburgianae), III (1910), 194. Hereafter cited *Hierarchia.*

Corfù (Corcyren, Corcyra, Corfien) is a Greek island in the Ionian Sea.

56 *Dizionario,* XVI, 241–242.

others [57] Pope Gregory XIII gave special instructions to Cardinals Carafa, Medici and Santorio to concern themselves with all things connected with the propagation and maintenance of the Faith of the Oriental Christians (Maronites, Slavs, Greeks, Ethiopians, Egyptians). For this purpose they were to hold meetings at the house of Cardinal Santorio. In this enumeration the change in the trio of cardinals should be noticed.

Still another version may be added. It seems to combine the preceding accounts. The first beginnings of a special Congregation for Christians of the Oriental rite go back to Pope Gregory XIII, who a year after his election [58] instituted the *Congregatio de rebus Graecorum,* to which he entrusted not only the treatment of the causes and affairs concerning Catholics of the Byzantine or Greek rite, but also the promotion of the maintenance and propagation of the Faith among other Christians of the Orient. Cardinals Savelli, Sirleto, Boncompagni, Carafa, and Santorio composed this commission; Cardinal Medici [59] and Antonio Cauco, Latin Archbishop of Corfù, were added later.[60]

When Pope Gregory XIII decided to found a Greek college for the education of ecclesiastics and laymen belonging to the Greek rite, who he hoped would help bring about the reunion of the Greek schismatics,[61] he assigned four cardinals well known

---

[57] Schmidlin, "Die Gründung der Propagandakongregation"—*Zeitschrift für Missionswissenschaft* (Münster: Aschendorffsche Verlagsbuchhandlung, 1911–), XII (1922), 2, and also footnote 4; Benigni, "Sacred Congregation of Propaganda"—*The Catholic Encyclopedia,* XII, 456.

[58] I. e., 1573.

[59] Probably Ferdinando de Medici, who was made a Cardinal Deacon on May 15, 1565; he resigned from the cardinalate on November 28, 1588.—Van Gulik-Eubel, *Hierarchia,* III (1910), p. 44, n. 24. The only other "de Medici" who could possibly be considered was Alessandro de Medici, who was a cardinal on January 9, 1584; but all indications point rather to Ferdinand, for A. Cauco was Archbishop of Corfù from 1560 to 1577.

[60] *Statistica,* p. 11.

[61] "Quocirca, cupientes antiquam et celebrem nationem ab huiusmodi ignorantiae et errorum caligine ad veritatis lucem et salutis viam revocare, nullum ad id aptius remedium a nobis existimavimus posse adhiberi, quam si in alma hac Urbe nostra collegium erigatur, in quo pueri et adolescentes Graeci ex ipsa Graecia et aliis provinciis ac locis, ubi commorantur, conquisiti, alantur, et Graecis litteris, liberalibus disciplinis ac scientiis, sacra praesertim theo-

for their interest in the Orient to accomplish its realization. They were Cardinals Savelli, Santorio, A. Carafa, and Sirleto; Gaspare Viviani, at that time Bishop of Sithia in Crete,[62] was included. It was the work of this commission that produced the Greek college,[63] which was officially established by the Constitution "*In apostolicae Sedis*," of January 13, 1577.[64]

Article IV. The Congregation between 1585–1607

In the next decade and a half no word is had about any Congregation dealing with the Greeks or any of the Orientals; in fact, during the quick succession of four popes from 1585–1592 no mention of it is made. Is there any indication at all concerning the existence or non-existence of any such group during that period? Petrani, after proposing his statement of the ultimate extinction of the Congregation *de rebus Graecorum* after Pope Gregory XIII's death, relates that in 1588 Antonio Lombardi, Archbishop of Messina, as a result of a diocesan synod had some doubts about the rites of the Greeks, and did not hesitate to present these to the Supreme Pontiff on his *ad limina* visit to Rome. Pope Sixtus V sent the Archbishop to Cardinal Santorio, who, having heard the prelate, wrote his *Responsio* probably at the end of 1588 or in the beginning of 1589. This response, consisting of ten parts, was a study of the greatest value, and was to serve as a guide for many years at meetings[65] summoned for

---

logia, ecclesiasticis praeterea ritibus . . . instituantur, ut, . . . ad eorum patriam et loca redeuntes, . . . alii autem qui in clerum adscribentur, nationis suae populis prodesse et praeesse, animarum curam exercere, verbum Dei sincere praedicare, populos ab erroribus et schismate removere, et ad salutarem orthodoxae fidei veritatem reducere possint; reliqui vero qui in laicali lita permanserint, publice per civitates aliorum Graecorum filios eiusdem fidei rudimenta et veritatem litterasque et artes liberales edocere . . . ."—*Bull. Rom.*, Vol. VIII, p. 159, § 2, const. LXIII "*In apostolica Sedis.*"

[62] Gaspar Vivianus, bishop from July 17, 1556–August 3, 1579. Van Gulik-Eubel, *Hierarchia*, III (1910), 320.

[63] *Revues des Questions Historiques* (Paris, 1866–), XLV (1889), 180.

[64] *Bull. Rom.*, Vol. VIII, pp. 159–162.

[65] Some were held from 1593–1595.

the discussion of the rites of the Greeks.[66] Even though Korolevskij,[67] a priest of the Greek-Slavonic rite, does not specify a definite year for the appearance of these interrogations, *written* by the same Archbishop a few months after he had celebrated the diocesan synod, he rather indicates the last years of the sixteenth century before the Instruction of Clement VIII *Super aliquibus ritibus Graecorum* in 1595. Korolevskij says that the style of the reply is too prolific to be that of a Congregation whose juridical decisions are very concise; this is rather the work of a consultor whose identity is not known by this priest of the Greek-Slavonic rite.[68] In either case whether the answer was given in 1588–1589 or before 1595, if any one of the previously existing Congregations was still active, would it not have been mentioned and consulted in such a grave matter?

There is no sign of any Congregation for Greeks or Orientals in the first year of Pope Clement VIII's assumption of the papal tiara. However, this pope did manifest his interest in the missions and the dissident Orientals by a partial application of the proposal of Bishop Vendeville (+ 1592) of Tournai in Belgium. The latter desired the establishment of special seminaries under the direction of religious for training men for the missions: his idea was to found in the Roman States—in such cities as Rome, Bologna, or Perugia—one or two Franciscan seminaries, a Dominican seminary, and a Jesuit seminary, where aged and experienced religious would prepare a certain number of young men for the missions.[69] There is no doubt that his plan regarding the missions included the Orthodox Orientals, for in each of these seminaries there were to be four sections: the first would prepare the students to work for the conversion of the Moham-

[66] Petrani, "De Sacra Congregatione pro Ecclesia Orientali eiusque facultatibus"—*Apollinaris,* X (1937), 28–29.

[67] *Statistica* spells his name "Korolevskij"; after the articles attributed to him in *Bessarione,* his name is given as "Karalevskij."

[68] Korolevskij, "L'Istruzione di Clemente VIII 'Super Aliquibus Ritibus Graecorum' (1595) e le Congregazioni per la Riforma dei Greci (1593)"—*Bessarione* (Roma, 1896–), Anno XVII (1913), Vol. XXIX, pp. 466–467. Hereafter, cited "L'Istruzione."

[69] Goyau, "Les Initiatives Belges dans la Fondation de la Propagande"—*La Revue Générale* (Bruxelles, 1865–). Vol. CXII (1924), pp. 11, 19, 20.

medans and idolators; the second, for the conversion of the Jews; the third, for the conversion of the schismatics and heretics of the Levant and of India; the fourth, for the conversion of the heretics of Europe.[70] Moreover, their training would equip them for their future work; for instance, if they were trained to fast, this would not be merely that they should draw personal benefit from the mortification, but also because (as Vendeville said) the Greeks and schismatics were very exact in their fasting, and consequently the clerics of the Roman Church by not fasting with them would diminish the impression of edification that they could produce.[71] He also expressed his opinion that, of the various assignments, the missionaries who would go to the schismatics and heretics of the Orient would have *la partie belle* inasmuch as the separated Christians did not have very learned men, and so the latter would not be unresponsive at the sight of the efforts which the missionaries would be expending for the instruction of the heathens.[72] After having heard the bishop's plea, the pope ordered the Congregation of four cardinals and two consultors, which had previously been charged by his predecessor Pope Gregory XIV to study the proposition of the Bishop of Tournai,[73] to bring forward their conclusions.[74] Thereupon Cardinal Mathieu, protector of the Franciscans, was immediately charged to communicate without delay to the Promotor General of the Order of St. Francis the program planned by the Flemish prelate. The pope wished to initiate the plan in a partial application of it with the Franciscans.[75] Indeed, the pope was interested in the missions and the separated Oriental brethren.

But Goyau's statement that the pope a little after his accession to the throne had held a meeting at the palace of Cardinal Santorio, and presided at this reunion of the three cardinals, who from the time of Pope Gregory XIII formed the commission *de*

---

[70] *Ibid.*, p. 13.
[71] *Ibid.*, p. 12.
[72] *Ibid.*, p. 15.
[73] *Ibid.*, p. 17.
[74] *Ibid.*, p. 19.
[75] *Loc. cit.*

propaganda fide,[76] cannot be affirmatively supported by the writer. That there was such a commission under the title *de propagande fide* cannot be verified by any documents within the writer's reach. If Goyau constructs or formulates this title from the fact that a Congregation appointed by Pope Gregory XIII was concerned with the propagation of the Faith, then he most likely refers to one of the groups of three cardinals mentioned at the beginning of this work. If this supposition be true, then certainly he cannot mean that the very same original three cardinals of that commission were reunited, for only Cardinals Santorio and Medici[77] of those groups were still alive;[78] if Goyau means that this commission had been kept at three in its numbers by means of substitutions for the deceased and had assembled on this occasion, the writer can neither confirm nor deny it from records.

In the following year, on February 10, 1593, which was the Wednesday before Septuagesima Sunday of that year, occurred the first of several congresses called *Congregationes super reformatione graecorum*.[79] These *Congregationes* are not to be taken in the sense of Sacred Congregations of the Roman Curia, nor as one of the transient Congregations foreshadowing the Sacred Congregation for the Oriental Church, for both of these demand cardinals as their principal members.[80] Only one cardinal participated in these conferences;[81] namely, Cardinal Santorio; his associates were Ludovico di Torres, Archbishop of Monreale (1584–1609) in Sicily,[82] Gaspare Viviani,[83] Bishop of Anagni

---

76 *Loc. cit.*

77 Cf., *infra*, p. 17, footnote 89.

78 Cardinal Sirleto died in 1585; Cardinal Savelli in 1587; Cardinal A. Carafa in 1591. Cf. Heteren, "Progetto di fondazione di un Collegio di rito greco nell' isola di Candia verso la fine del XVI secolo"—*Bessarione*, Anno IV (1899-1900), Vol. VII, p. 603, footnotes 1, 2, 4.

79 Staffa, "De Sacrae Congregationis pro Ecclesia Orientali competentia" —*Apollinaris*, XI (1938), 360; Korolevskij, "L'Istruzione"—*Bessarione*, Anno XVII (1913), Vol. XXIX, 345.

80 Cf. *supra*, p. 6.

81 Staffa, *loc. cit.*; Korolevskij, *loc. cit.*

82 Monreale is a town overlooking the beautiful Val d'Oro adjacent to Palermo.

(1579–1605) in Latium (Italy,)[84] and Owen,[85] Bishop of Cassano in Calabria (Italy).[86] They were joined at the fourth assembly by Carlo Conti,[87] Bishop of Ancona (1585–1616) in the Marches (Italy).[88] The *Congregationes super reformatione graecorum,* therefore, were the meetings of these competent dignitaries to discuss, weigh, and decide the doubts concerning the rites of the Greeks and other problems pertaining to the people of the Greek rite. The existence of this selected committee strongly points to the non-existence at that time of a Congregation for Greek questions. Would this group or committee have been chosen if a cardinalitial Congregation was available? Hardly. Moreover, of all the cardinals previously listed as associated with the Congregations for Greeks Cardinal Santorio alone was still active:[89] Savelli died in 1587;[90] Sirleto in 1585;[91] A. Carafa in 1591;[92] and Filippo Boncompagni in 1586.[93]

On August 31, 1595, Pope Clement VIII issued a special instruction, the *Instructio super aliquibus ritibus Graecorum,*[94] which dealt exhaustively with the controversy that had arisen about the rites and usages of the Greeks. He made great use of

---

[83] Also spelled Viviano. He was formerly connected with the cardinalitial commission for the founding of the Greek College in Rome.

[84] A town in the region of the former Pontifical States. Cf. Haine, *De La Cour Romaine* (Louvain: Typographia de Vanlithout et Cie, 1859), p. 249.

[85] He was an Englishman who was driven from England during the Protestant persecution and took refuge in Italy.—Korolevskij, *ibid.*, p. 345, footnote 3.

[86] Cf. Haine, *loc. cit.*

[87] Staffa, *loc. cit.;* Korolevskij, *ibid.*, p. 351.

[88] Also within the former Pontifical States. It was an ancient seaport town in the north of this district, situated on a promontory forming a remarkable curve or elbow, as the name implies.

[89] Ferdinando de Medici resigned from the cardinalate in 1588.—Van Gulik-Eubel, *Hierarchia,* III (1910), p. 44, n. 24. However, if it was Alessandro de Medici who was connected with the Congregation, he was still alive at that time, for he died in 1605.—Van Gulik-Eubel, *Hierarchia,* III, p. 52, n. 17.

[90] Van Gulik-Eubel, *op. cit.*, III, p. 29, n. 38.

[91] *Ibid.*, p. 46, n. 45.

[92] *Ibid.*, p. 48, n. 5.

[93] *Ibid.*, p. 50, n. 1.

[94] Korolevskij, *ibid.*, p. 344.

the results of the *Congregationes super reformatione graecorum.*[95] When Pastor writes: "The publication of this document had been preceded by a detailed inquiry by a Congregation expressly intended for the reform of the Greeks," [96] he has in mind the *Congregationes.* Also when he says that the pope established a Congregation for the Italo-Greeks in 1595,[97] it is to be understood that he again means the *Congregationes,* and not a Sacred Roman Congregation in the canonical sense as is used throughout this work.[98]

Finally, Pope Clement VIII re-established a special Congregation of nine cardinals to care for the affairs of the Greeks and other Orientals as well as for the propagation of the Faith in the region of the Occident.[99] On Tuesday evening, August 10, 1599,[100] the cardinals appointed to this work [101]—the Cardinal of Santa Severina [Santorio], the Cardinal of Florence,[102] Cardinals Federigo Borromeo (1564–1631), Cæsare Baronius (1538–1607), Alfonso Visconti (1552–1608), Silvio Antoniani (1540–1603), Roberto Bellarmin (1542–1621) and Pietro Aldobrandini (1571–

---

[95] Pastor, *The History of the Popes,* XXIV, 263; Korolevskij, "L'Istruzione"—*Bessarione,* Anno XVII (1913), Vol. XXIX, 344, footnote 1. Compare with Petrani, "De Sacra Congregatione pro Ecclesia Orientali eiusque facultatibus"—*Apollinaris,* X (1937), 29.

[96] *Loc. cit.*

[97] *Op. cit.,* XXIV, 266.

[98] Cf. *supra,* p. 6.

[99] Staffa, "De Sacrae Congregationis pro Ecclesia Orientali competentia"—*Apollinaris,* XI (1938), 360; *Statistica,* p. 11.

[100] Lemmens, *Acta S. Congregationis de Propaganda Fide pro Terra Sancta, Biblioteca Bio-Bibliograficà della Terra Sancta e dell' Oriente Francescano* (14 vols., edited by Girolamo Golubovich, Quaracchi presso Firenze, 1921–1936), I, p. 1, footnote 2. Hereafter cited *Acta.*

[101] *Loc. cit.; Schmidlin,* "Eine Vorläuferin der Propaganda unter Klemens VIII"—*Zeitschrift für Missionswissenschaft,* XI (1921), 233; Pastor, *op. cit.,* XXIV, 266.

[102] Alessandro de Medici (1535–1605), who became Pope Leo XI (April 1, 1605–April 27, 1605). That the Cardinal of Florence referred to was Alessandro de Mèdici is concluded from comparing this list of names with that of Pastor, *op. cit.,* XXIV, 266. Cf. also Van Gulik-Eubel, *Hierarchia,* III (1910), p. 52, n. 17, where the date of his death is given as April 27, 1605.

1621),[103] and the Cardinal of St. George[104]—were informed in the presence of His Holiness that on the following day at twelve-thirty o'clock the Congregation would meet.[105] Accordingly, on August 11, the Congregation assembled before the pope;[106] thereafter, however, the meetings were scheduled to take place at Santorio's palace—the first meeting being held on August 16.[107] Pastor asserts that at the first assembly—whether he alludes to August 11 or to August 16 is not clear to the writer—it was decided to hold meetings twice a month. He likewise declares that after each meeting Cardinal Santorio went to the pope to relate the decisions of the meetings. At the next gathering the pope's replies were communicated to the Congregation and executed in accordance with his wishes.[108] According to others[109] the cardinals were to meet weekly in order to prepare the matters which were to be reported to the Pontiff every second week. Unfortunately the necessary documents are not within reach of the writer, and so it is impossible at present to settle the doubt. At any rate the meetings did not proceed according to plan, since the *acta*[110] which are available up to August 14, 1600,[111] reveal only twelve meetings during that entire period—a whole year.[112]

---

[103] Petrus Aldobrandinus, nephew of Pope Clement VIII, died Feb. 10, 1621. Gauchat, *Hierarchia,* IV (1935), p. 4, n. 3.

[104] Cincio Aldobrandini (Cinthius Aldobrandinus [1551-1610]), nephew of Pope Clement VIII, was cardinal of the title *S. Giorgii* from Oct. 11, 1593, till his transfer to the title *S. Petri ad Vincula* on June 1, 1605. Died Jan. 1, 1610.—Gauchat, *Hierarchia,* IV, p. 4, n. 4.

[105] Lemmens, *Acta,* I, p. 1, footnote 2.

[106] *Loc. cit.;* Moroni, *Dizionario,* XVI, 242; Schmidlin, *ibid.,* p. 232; Pastor, *The History of the Popes,* XXIV, 266.

[107] Schmidlin, *ibid.,* p. 233; Pastor, *loc. cit.*

[108] Pastor, *ibid.,* p. 267. Cf. Schmidlin (*loc. cit.*) for further details on procedure.

[109] Moroni, *Dizionario,* XVI, 242; Schmidlin, *ibid.,* p. 232. Cf. also Benigni, "Sacred Congregation of Propaganda"—*The Catholic Encyclopedia,* XII, 456.

[110] Found in the miscellaneous codex of the archives "S. Congregationis de Propaganda Fide." Cf. Lemmens, *ibid.,* p. 1; Schmidlin, *loc. cit.*

[111] Lemmens, *loc. cit.;* Schmidlin, *ibid.,* p. 233, footnote 7; Pastor, *The History of the Popes,* XXIV, 266-267.

[112] Lemmens, *loc. cit.*; Schmidlin (*ibid.,* p. 233, footnote 7) enumerates the dates as follows: in the year 1599—(he omits August 11 in his footnote,

Schmidlin does mention that the records and minutes of the special meetings of this Congregation should be found in the Vatican archives.[113] To determine the object of these special meetings, the time at which they were held, and the number of assemblies, the documents must be consulted.

These *acta* give the Congregation three names: first, "*super negotiis sanctae fidei et religionis acatholicae*" (folio 4);[114] then, "*de propagatione s. fidei*" (folio 19); finally, "*de propaganda fide*" (folio 39). Moreover, of the 475 folios, the first section of 60 folios narrates the "*Pertinentia ad S. C. de Propaganda Fide*" (folios 3–62); the next 227 folios, "*Super nonnullis ritibus vel abusibus Graecorum*" (folios 63–289); and the remainder "*De reformatione monialium Neopolitanarum*" (folios 290–475).[115] Therefore this Congregation devoted a good share of its time during that year to the Greeks. Even within the first 60 folios mention of Oriental matters is found. On July 3, 1600 (folio 39), the following was related in the Congregation:

> de Turcarum persecutione in christianos orientales, de poena pali illati archiepiscopo Jacobitarum, vicario patriarchae, et suspendio locumtenentis sangiacchi, qui erat in Hierusalem, . . . de persecutione in patriarcham Sophronium Hierosolymitanum nationis graecae et in archiepiscopum Armeniae, vicarium patriarchae Armeniae Minoris, . . . et de auxilio et de eleemosinis, quae petunt pro eis eorumque redemptione.[116]

No record of its *acta* after August 14, 1600, is had, although

---

since he starts this list from the first meeting in Santorio's house), August 16, August 30, September 20, November 24, December 13; in the year 1600—January 17, January 31, February 28, July 3, July 17, August 14. This demonstrates contrary to the assertion of Pastor (*op. cit.*, XXIV, 266: "Unfortunately only the notes of the first 10 meetings have been preserved.") that the acts of the first twelve meetings are preserved.

[113] Schmidlin, *ibid.*, p. 232.

[114] There is a slight difference in the reference to the numbering of the folios in Lemmens, *Acta*, I, p. 1, footnote 2, and Schmidlin, *ibid.*, p. 232, footnote 10, and p. 233, footnote 1. The numbering as found in the former is transcribed here.

[115] Lemmens, *loc. cit.*

[116] Lemmens, *Acta*, I, 2.

the Congregation continued to exist. The death of Cardinal Santorio in 1602 caused an interruption in its activities. Pastor states: "As the presidency, and therefore the *Acta* now passed into the hands of another Cardinal, this explains their disappearance." [117] An indication that this Congregation (which foreshadowed the Sacred Congregation of the Propagation of the Faith (1622) not only in name, in purpose, and in procedure,[118] but even in having under its care the colleges founded by Pope Gregory XIII) [119] resumed its labors and was functioning in 1604 is obtained from a letter of December 11, 1604.[120] But, according to some of the authors, after the death of Pope Clement VIII, its inspiring promoter, on March 3, 1605, the Congregation did not meet any more.[121] On the other hand, Benigni writes: "The death of Clement VIII revealed an essential weakness of the institution. It was a personal commission, depending for its very existence on the energy of its few members. Eventually the meetings of the three cardinals ceases; . . . ." [122] Surely he cannot mean that the Congregation at its beginning was composed of only three members, or that after the pope's death only three

[117] *The History of the Popes,* XXIV, 268, footnote 1. Pastor adds: "But perhaps it will still be possible to find them."

[118] Schmidlin ("Eine Vorläuferin der Propaganda unter Klemens VIII" —*Zeitschrift für Missionswissenschaft,* XI [1921], 233) describes it as follows: First of all, reference was made to the letters received; then, to the letters sent out and circulated; next came the reports or letters of petition; after this, a council was held which ended in a vote and resolution; finally, as a rule of Santorio, the question was put before the pope for a decision. Pastor (*ibid.,* p. 267) adds: "The *acta* were written by a secretary, and in the margin Cardinal Santori wrote with his own hand the Pope's replies to the decisions of the Congregation."

[119] Pastor, *ibid.,* p. 268.

[120] Pastor (*op. cit.,* XXIV, p. 575, n. 23) gives an extract of this letter of Francesco Maria Vialardo to the Duke of Mantua: ". . . Il card[le] di Perone sarà qui questa sera. Gioiosa è ammalato di lieve puntura, il Papa fa sborsare 50[m] duct[i] per il negotio dell' acqua di Ferrara, vuole che si rimetta la congregatione de propaganda fide . . ."

[121] V. Martin, *Les Congrégations Romaines,* pp. 191, 136; Moroni, *Dizionario,* XVI, 242; Petrani, "De Sacra Congregatione pro Ecclesia Orientali eiusque facultatibus"—*Apollinaris,* X (1937), 29; Monin, *De Curia Romana,* p. 66.

[122] *The Catholic Encyclopedia,* XII, 456.

of the cardinal commission survived him, for both these assertions are contrary to open evidence: (a) there is no doubt that nine cardinals formed the Congregation;[123] (b) six of these—Cæsare Baronius,[124] Alfonso Visconti,[125] Cincio Aldobrandini,[126] Pietro Aldobrandini,[127] Roberto Bellarmin,[128] Federigo Borromeo[129]—outlived the pope. But, if Benigni means that of these cardinals three kept up the meetings for a while but eventually stopped, the writer can neither confirm nor deny it.

Although the activity of the Congregation may have fallen into abeyance, nevertheless, from a document which Pastor quotes,[130] it is evident that a Congregation named "*de Fide Propaganda*" existed under Pope Paul V (1605–1621); the document further relates that in this Congregation discussions were held and resolutions taken concerning the plan to be followed in those places where there is reason to believe that the Catholic Faith has some beginning and where there is some one trying to instruct and spread it. Moreover, some of the members of Pope Clement VIII's Congregation are in the list of cardinals of this Congregation: the Cardinal of Ascoli, the Cardinal of St. Cecelia, Aldobrandino (Pietro Aldobrandini), San Giorgio (Cincio Aldobrandini), Paravicino,[131] Arigonio,[132] Visconti (Alfonso),[133] Spinelli,[134]

---

[123] Cf. *supra*, pp. 18–19.

[124] Died June 30, 1607—Gauchat, *Hierarchia,* IV (1935), p. 5, n. 13.

[125] Died September 19, 1608—*ibid.*, p. 6, n. 24.

[126] Died January 1, 1610—*ibid.*, p. 4, n. 4.

[127] Died February 10, 1621—*ibid.*, p. 4, n. 3.

[128] Died September 17, 1621—*ibid.*, p. 6, n. 30.

[129] Died September 21, 1631—Van Gulik-Eubel, *Hierarchia,* III (1910), p. 58, n. 26.

[130] *Op. cit.*, XXVII, p. 130, footnote 2: "It is clear, from B. Ceci that it still existed in the time of Paul V, *Relazione di Roma,* etc., in whch it is specifically mentioned: 'La Congregazione detta de Fide Propaganda. Qui si discorre e risolve del modo che si de' tenere in quei luoghi ove si sente che la fede cattolica habbia qualche principio e che vi sia chi cerchi istruirla e propagarla. Vi sono questi cardinali: Ascoli, S.ta Cecilia, Aldobrandino, San Giorgio, Paravicino, Arigonio, Visconti, Spinelli, Monopoli, Serafino, San Caesario' . . . For its ends through lack of means, which had always been the great difficulty, see P. A. Santorii, *Annales,* in Cod. K. 7, of the Vallicelliana Library, Rome."

[131] Octavianus Paravicinus. Paravicinus was the name attached to the

Monopoli,[135] Seraphino,[136] San Cesario.[137] Thus the Congregation did exist even though it may not have been very active. From the death of Anselmo Marzati (Monopoli) on August 17, 1607, it is deduced that the Congregation existed before this date; how long "before" is not revealed; how it met its end can be ascertained by those to whom the *Annales* (see footnote quoted from Pastor) are available.

The establishment of one Congregation to expedite the affairs of both Latins and Orientals, as was the case with the above mentioned Congregation founded by Pope Clement VIII, was to appear again in the establishment of the Sacred Congregation *de Propaganda Fide* (1622) in the Roman Curia.

Article V. Persons Influencing the Establishment of the Sacred Congregation of the Propagation of the Faith

Pope Paul V (1605–1621) maintained his interest and connections with the missions, the Orientals, and the Orthodox. He proceeded cautiously in the negotiations with the Patriarch of the dissident Armenians in 1610, and made use of the Sacred Congregation of the Roman Inquisition in pointing out errors of the Nestorians to the Patriarch of the Chaldean Nestorians of Babylon, whose residence was at Mosul; he also manifested his solicitude for Moldavia and Walachia; he maintained his interest in the activities of the missionaries in the midst of the Orientals.[138]

---

cardinal of the title of St. John before the Lateran Gate. Octavianus was cardinal there from 1591. He died in 1611.—Van Gulik-Eubel, *op. cit.*, III (1910), p. 60, n. 2.

[132] Pompeius Arrigonius (Arrigoni, Arigonus). Died April 4, 1616. Gauchat, *op. cit.*, IV (1935), p. 5, n. 19, and footnote 1.

[133] Died September 19, 1608—*ibid.*, p. 6, n. 24.

[134] Philippus Spinellus (Spinelli). Died May 25, 1616—*ibid.*, p. 7, n. 39.

[135] Anselmus Marzatus (Marzati), Monopolitanus. Died August 17, 1607—*ibid.*, p. 8, n. 51.

[136] Seraphinus Olivarius—Razalius (Oliver-Razali). Died February 10, 1609—*ibid.*, p. 7, n. 36, and footnote 3.

[137] Silvester Aldobrandinus called the Cardinal of S. Cesario from his title *S. Caesarei in Palatio.* Died January 28, 1612—*ibid.*, p. 6, n. 35, and footnote 7.

[138] Pastor, *The History of the Popes,* XXV, 372–379.

In the meantime Tommaso a Jesu [139] was preparing to present in book form his ideas about the need of a Sacred Congregation for the propagation of the Faith. In 1613 appeared his thousand-page volume on the missions known as *De procuranda salute gentium,*[140] although originally the complete, cumbersome title read: "*De procuranda salute omnium gentium, schismaticorum, haereticorum, judaeorum, sarracenorum, coeterorumque infidelium libri XII, quibus impiissimarum sectarum, maxime orientalium, ritus ad historiae fidem narrantur, errores ad veritatis lucem confutantur. Accedit pro laborantibus inter infideles brevis casuum resolutio, gratiarum ac privilegiorum compendium, et pro conversis Catechismus, cum indicibus rerum et materiarum copiossimis.*" [141]

From the title it is clear that the dissident Orientals were considered a part of the mission problem and were treated as such in this manual. The heading of the first chapter of the third book is: *De erigenda Congregatione pro fide propaganda.* The author, as he begins the systematic exposé of his method for the mission apostolate, gives the first place in this project to the necessity of a governing Congregation of a few zealous, eminent,

---

[139] Diaz Sanchez of Avila whose name in the Order of Discalced Carmelites in Spain was Tommaso a Jesu (Thomas of Jesus, Thomas de Jésus). Cf. Salaville, "Un Théoricien de l'Apostolat Catholique au XVIIe Siècle" —*Échos d'Orient,* XIX (1920), 129–152; Pastor, *op. cit.,* XXIV, p. 264, footnote 6.

[140] Salaville (*ibid.,* pp. 130–131) notes that this book in the citations of different editions of the work is also referred to as *Thesaurus sapientiae divinae in gentium omnium salute procuranda;* it was re-edited in 1652, then published a third time at Cologne in 1684 in the three volume collection of *Opera omnia homini religioso et apostolico utilissima.* This last edition is the best according to Hurter, *Nomenclator Literarius Recentioris Theologiae Catholicae Theologos Exhibens qui inde a Concilio Tridentino Floruerunt Aetate, Natione, Disciplinis Distinctos* (2. ed., 3 vols., Oenipotente: Libraria Academica Wagneriana, 1892–1895), I, 272–273.

A more recent critical edition has been made under the care of the Rev. Thomas de Jésus [Pammoli], O.C.D., (Roma: Collegio Internazionale S. Teresa, 1940). Cf. Gérin, *Le Goüvernement des Missions,* Les Thèses Canoniques de Laval, n. 1 (Québec, Canada: Université Laval, 1944), pp. XXI and 32, footnote 8.

[141] Salaville, *ibid.,* p. 130.

prudent men at Rome who will meet on set days seriously to contemplate the practical means of aiding all people and, moreover, will execute all necessary measures in the name of the pope.[142]

The functioning of this institution was to depend in a special way upon the secretaries—four or five in number—who would be of uncontested competence: men of piety and knowledge, well-versed in the languages and usages of the countries with whose affairs they would be connected. Their duties were outlined thus: "quorum munus esset cuncta ordine Congregationi proponere, constituta exsequi, orthodoxos et pios libellos pro ratione uniuscujusque provinciae variis linguis conscriptos habere; regesta litterarum, episcoporum etiam, parochorum, concionatorum, familiarum, illustrium catholicorum sive aliorum, a quibus posset huic negotio aliquod auxilium adferri, catalogos asservare." [143]

Each secretary was to be assigned for the care of a definite region. Of course, one undoubtedly would have the office of general secretary; the second would be charged with the northern countries of England, Scotland, Ireland, France, Germany, Denmark, and Sweden; the third would care for Dalmatia, Bosnia, Greece with the adjacent islands, and Thrace; the fourth would have Cyprus, Asia Minor, Syria, Palestine, Egypt, Algiers, Poland, Lithuania, Russia, Hungary, and Transylvania; the fifth would be concerned with "les Indes occidentales et orientales." [144] That plan in the assignment of regions shows beyond a doubt that the Orientals and their Orthodox brethren fitted into the entire program for the mission apostolate, and its importance is further evidenced in the devotion of the seventh book of the manual to the question of the union of the Greeks and the Russians with the Catholic Church.[145] Thus did Tommaso a Jesu contribute his share towards keeping alive throughout the pontificate of Pope Paul V the idea of a Sacred Congregation for the Orientals, their

[142] *Ibid.*, p. 136.

[143] Salaville, "Un Théoricien de l'Apostolat Catholique au XVIIe Siècle" —*Echos d'Orient*, XIX (1920), 137.

[144] *Loc. cit.*

[145] Salaville, *Ibid.*, p. 132.

Orthodox brethren, and the propagation of the Faith in general.[146]

Another discalced Carmelite who worked unflinchingly throughout Pope Paul V's reign for this cause was Dominicus a Jesu-Maria (1559–1630).[147] So great was his contribution and so sincere his effort in behalf of this undertaking that he was later nominated by the pope to the Sacred Congregation of the Propagation of the Faith itself, though he was not a cardinal. Still another religious, Girolamo (Jerome) of Narni (1562–1632), of the Capuchin Order, zealously labored with the same end in view.[148] Gifted, according to the testimony of his contemporaries,[149] with an eloquence comparable to that of St. Paul, this devout Capuchin, who was Preacher of the Apostolic Palace under Popes Paul V (1605–1621) and Gregory XV (1621–1623),[150] influenced Allesandro Cardinal Ludovisi (the future Pope Gregory XV) in favor of the Propagation of the Faith Congregation. In fact, Schmidlin attributes the immediate occasion of the founding of the Sacred Congregation of the Propagation of the Faith (the last impetus, as it were) to his fiery talk.[151] According to Moroni [152] acknowledgment also must be rendered to two others; namely, Msgr. Juan Baptista Vives [153] and the priest Giovanni Leonardi (1543–1609) of Lucca in Italy,[154] whose enthusiasm and discussions in this

---

[146] Pastor, *The History of the Popes,* XXVII, 130.

[147] Schmidlin, "Die Gründung der Propagandakongregation"—*Zeitschrift für Missionswissenschaft,* XII (1922), p. 4, footnote 2; Moroni, *Dizionario,* XVI, 243; Pastor, *op. cit.,* XXVII, 130.

The family name of Dominicus a Jesu-Maria was Urrusolo.

[148] Pastor, *loc. cit.*

[149] Pastor, *op. cit.,* XXV, 280.

[150] Pastor, *op. cit.,* XXVII, 128, 130–131.

[151] Schmidlin, *ibid.,* p. 4.

[152] *Dizionario,* XVI, 244.

[153] Great benefactor of the Urban College.

[154] Since Giovanni Leonardi died in 1609, his influence upon Pope Gregory XV antedated the latter's ascendance to the papal throne.

Giovanni Leonardi was canonized a Saint on April 17, 1938—*Acta Apostolicae Sedis,* Commentarium Officiale (Romae, 1909–), XXX (1938), 149. Hereafter cited *AAS.* He was founder of the "Congregatio Clericorum saecularium a Beata Virgine" (September 1, 1574), whose title was changed by Pope Paul V after Leonardi's death to the "Congregatio Clericorum Regularium a Matre Dei."—*AAS,* XXX (1938), 122.

regard had some effect upon Gregory XV in disposing him favorably toward the need of such a Sacred Congregation. Finally, credit must be given to the centralized organization of the Jesuits, which likewise exercised an influence on Pope Gregory XV.[155]

Article VI. The Sacred Congregation of the Propagation of the Faith as a Foundation of the Future Sacred Congregation for Oriental Matters

It was not surprising, therefore, that Pope Gregory XV gave an early consideration to so important a matter, especially since at that time there appeared to be "doors opening wide for the conversion of unbelievers and heretics." [156] The Sacred College also agreed that the time was opportune to do something for the missions. Naturally, their minds searched for the most efficacious means and procedure; the cardinals made their suggestions, and as Pastor relates: "Some of the Cardinals laid particular stress on the rôle of the national Colleges which Gregory XIII had supported with so much enthusiasm; others were of the opinion that the propagation of the gospel should be made the care of the nuncios." [157] Pope Gregory XV and Cardinal Lodovico Ludovisi [158] finally arrived at a decision which previously was indicated and advocated by Tommaso a Jesu as being of prime importance, i.e., the need of a Sacred Congregation to supervise the mission apostolate. In its aims and general organization this institution was to be a revival of that which was begun under Pope Clement VIII in 1599.[159] Such a Sacred Congregation could employ and direct

---

[155] Pastor, *The History of the Popes,* XXVII, 131; Schmidlin, *ibid.,* p. 4.

[156] Pastor, *The History of the Popes,* XXVII, 131.

[157] *Loc. cit.*

[158] Nephew of Pope Gregory XV and his competent Secretary of State. Cf. Pastor, *ibid.,* pp. 50–52, 54.

[159] Pastor, *The History of the Popes,* XXVII, 131, and footnote 5: "That Gregory XV had the Congregation, instituted by Clement VIII, before him as a model, appears from a note not hitherto utilized, though printed by Lämmer, Zur Kirchengesch, 130. It occurs in the Instruction for the Polish nuncio, Lancellotti, December 14, 1622: 'E noto a V. S. che la S.tà di N. S. rinnovando o di nuovo instituendo La Congregazione de Propaganda Fide tanto importante per ampliare la fede, ordinata già da Clemente VIII di f. mem. e poco appresso tralasciata, ha eccitato tutti i nuntii,' etc."

the use of the other above mentioned suggestions of the cardinals. It was just such a firm central governing body that was needed to determine the field of work for the various missionaries and to settle their disputes and problems.

On January 6, 1622,[160] Pope Gregory XV founded the Sacred Congregation *de Propaganda Fide*,[161] which consisted of thirteen cardinals, two bishops, and a secretary.[162] This newly appointed group held their first meeting on January 14, 1622,[163] at the house of Cardinal de Saulis,[164] and decreed among other things that a Bull of the erection of this Sacred Congregation with its faculties and privileges should be composed just as was done by other popes in the erection of the other Sacred Congregations.[165] Evidently there had not been issued any Bull of erection on January 6th when the personnel of this Sacred Congregation was designated. Nevertheless, the group eagerly commenced working.[166] It was in the Constitution "*Inscrutabili divinae providentiae*," of June 22, 1622, that Pope Gregory XV officially confirmed the erection of the Sacred Congregation of the Propagation of the Faith, publishing the names of the members and detailing the work of the Sacred Congregation.[167] It should be noted here that in the

---

160 Schmidlin, "Die Gründung der Propaganda Kongregation (1622)"—*Zeitschrift für Missionswissenschaft*, XII (1922), 5, and footnote 1; Pastor, *ibid.*, p. 132.

161 According to Benigni in *The Catholic Encyclopedia*, XXI, 456, the official title is "sacra Congregatio christiano nomini propagando." Cf. also Lega, *Praelectiones in Textum Iuris Canonici de Iudiciis Ecclesiasticis* (4 vols., Romae, 1896–1901), II, 129. Authors frequently refer to this Sacred Congregation as the *Propaganda*.

162 *Collectanea S. Congregationis de Propaganda Fide seu Decreta Instructiones Rescripta Pro Apostolicis Missionibus* (2 vols., Romae: Ex Typographia Polyglotta S. C. de Propaganda Fide, 1907), I, p. 1, n. 1. Hereafter cited *Collectanea*; Schmidlin, *loc. cit.*; Pastor, *loc. cit.*

163 Collectanea, *loc. cit.*; Schmidlin, *loc. cit.*; Pastor, *The History of the Popes*, XXVII, 133; Moroni, *Dizionario*, XVI, 243.

164 Schmidlin, *loc. cit.*; Pastor, *loc. cit.*

165 *Collectanea, loc. cit.*

166 Pastor, *op. cit.*, XXVII, 138; *Collectanea*, I, pp. 1–2, nn. 1–2.

167 *Codicis Iuris Canonici Fontes cura Emi Petri Card. Gasparri editi* (9 vols., Romae [postea Civitate Vaticana]: Typis Polyglottis Vaticanis, 1923–1939), I, n. 200. Hereafter cited *Fontes*. *Bullarium Pontificium Sacrae*

meantime another non-cardinal member, the Carmelite Dominicus a Jesu-Maria, was added to the afore-mentioned number of two prelates and a secretary. Of this select body three of the thirteen cardinals were Cardinal Bishops: Antonio de Saulis,[168] Odoardo Farnese,[169] Ottaviano Bandini;[170] the remaining ten members were Cardinal Priests: François de Sourdis,[171] Maffeo Barberini,[172] Giovanni Millini,[173] Gaspare Borgia,[174] Roberto Ubaldini,[175] Scipione Cobelluzio,[176] Pierre Valier,[177] Eitel von Hohenzollern,[178] Ludovico Ludovisi,[179] Francesco Sacrati;[180] the

---

Congregationis de Propaganda Fide (Romae: Typis Collegii Urbani, 1859–), I, 26–30. Hereafter cited *Bull. Pontificium.*

[168] Antonius Ostiensis Saulius (also spelled Sauli by some authors)—*Fontes,* n. 200, § 10; *Bull. Pontificium,* I, 29. He died August 24, 1623. Cf. Van Gulik-Eubel, *Hierarchia,* III (1910), p. 57, n. 20.

[169] Odoardus Sabinensis Farnesius—*Fontes, loc. cit.; Bull. Pontificium, loc. cit.* He died February 21, 1626. Cf. Van Gulik-Eubel, *ibid.,* p. 60, n. 4.

[170] Octavius Praenestinus Bardinus—*Fontes,* n. 200, § 10; *Bull. Pontificium,* I, 29. He died August 1, 1629. Cf. Gauchat, *Hierarchia,* IV (1935), p. 4, n. 8.

[171] Franciscus S. Praxedis de Sourdis d'Escobleau (also Surdis). He died February 8, 1628. Cf. Gauchat, *ibid.,* p. 6, n. 32.

[172] Maphaeus S. Honuphrii Barberinus, the future Pope Urban VIII (1623–1644). Cf. Gauchat, *ibid.,* p. 10, n. 4.

[173] Joannes Garzias SS. Quatuor Coronatorum Millinus. He died October 2, 1629. Cf. Gauchat, *ibid.,* p. 10, n. 5.

[174] Gaspar Sanctae Crucis in Hierusalem Borgia. He died November, 1645. Cf. Gauchat, *ibid.,* p. 12, n. 29.

[175] Robertus S. Alexii Ubaldinus. He died April 22, 1635. Cf. Gauchat, *ibid.,* p. 12, n. 33.

[176] This conclusion is drawn from a comparison of the *Fontes,* n. 200, § 10, and *Bull. Pontificium,* I, 29, with Pastor's *The History of the Popes,* XXVII, 132, and the information from Gauchat, *ibid.,* p. 13, n. 47, that Scipio Cobelluzio was made Cardinal of the title of St. Susanna on October 17, 1616; he died on June 29, 1626.

[177] Petrus S. Salvatoris in Lauro Valerius (also Valiero). He died April 5, 1629. Cf. Gauchat, *ibid.,* p. 14, n. 53.

[178] Itelius Fridericus S. Laurentii in Panisperna a Zollern (de Zolleren). He died September 19, 1625. Cf. Gauchat, *ibid.,* p. 14, n. 54.

[179] Ludovicus S. Mariae trans Pontem Ludovisius. He died November 18, 1632. Cf. Gauchat, *ibid.,* pp. 15–16, n. 1.

[180] Franciscus S. Matthaei in Merulana Sacratus. He died September 6, 1623. Cf. Gauchat, *ibid.,* p. 16, n. 3.

prelates were Bishop Juan Baptista Vives [181] and Bishop Gion Battista Agucchi; [182] the Carmelite Dominicus a Jesu-Maria [183] and the priest Francesco Ingoli [184] completed the group.

According to the constitution it was the pope's wish that the cardinals, to whose special solicitude the work of the Sacred Congregation was entrusted, having assembled together and employing the aid of some prelates of the Roman Curia, religious men, and a secretary after the pattern which he himself had established at its beginning, should take counsel together, give much care dedicating themselves diligently together with him to so great a task, and apply themselves to the limit of their ability to a work so holy and pleasing to the Divine Majesty. In order that this might be done more efficiently and adequately, they were to assemble once a month in the presence of the pope, and twice a month at the house of the senior member,[185] and they were to take cognizance of and treat all and every kind of business (*omnia et singula negotia*) pertaining to propagating the Faith in the whole world; the more serious, more important matters (*graviora*), after having been treated by them at their assemblies at the house of the senior member, were to be referred to the pope; they themselves, however, were to decide all other matters and expedite them according to their own prudence. They were to supervise the preaching and teaching of the gospel and Catholic doctrine for all the missions, and they were to appoint and to transfer the missionaries when they judged it necessary. The pope by his apostolic authority conceded and imparted to them the full, free and ample faculty, authority, and power to perform,

---

[181] "In utraque Signatura nostra Referendarius." Cf. *Fontes*, n. 200, § 11, *Bull. Pontificium*, I, 29; *Collectanea*, I (1907), 4.

[182] Io. Baptista Aguchius (also spelled Aguchi, Agucci). The pope's secretary, and notary of the Apostolic See. Cf. *Fontes, loc. cit.; Bull. Pontificium, loc. cit.; Collectanea, loc. cit.*

[183] Not mentioned in Pastor's list (*The History of the Popes*, XXVII, 132), but found in Moroni, *Dizionario*, XVI, 243.

[184] Franciscus Ingolus, secretary of this Sacred Congregation, was a priest from Ravenna, and a Doctor of both laws (U.I.D.).

[185] "In domo antiquioris eorum"—*Fontes*, n. 200, § 8; *Bull. Pontificium*, I, 28; *Collectanea*, I (1907), 3. The senior member was Cardinal de Saulis, who was the first prefect.

manage, treat, do, and execute the foregoing as well as all and everything else necessary or opportune for that purpose, even if they be such that they require a special, specific and express mention.[186] This concession of powers was protected by the abrogation of all existing legislation to the contrary.[187]

What was the extent of its competency in regard to matters and causes to be treated by this Sacred Congregation? There is a divergence of opinion among the authors. One group places no limitations except for the one limitation that is expressly stated in the constitution, i. e., the *graviora* cannot be decided unless it has been referred to the Supreme Pontiff. In positive terms they attribute to the Sacred Congregation an exclusive competence in all affairs which regard the land of the missions,[188] and a most ample (*amplissima*) power as to the kinds of matters and causes so that all ecclesiastical causes, of whatever species they may be, belonging to these regions are subject to the Sacred Congregation *de Propaganda Fide.*[189] This position is aptly summarized by M. Martin, a pre-Code author: " Hence what the various Con-

---

186 *Fontes, loc. cit.; Bull. Pontificium, loc. cit.; Collectanea, loc. cit.*

187 " Non obstantibus quibusvis Constitutionibus et ordinationibus Apostolicis, privilegiis quoque, indultis, et literis Apostolicis, quibusvis Ordinibus, Congregationibus, Societatibus et Institutis, sub quibuscunque tenoribus et formis, ac cum quibusvis, etiam derogatoriarum derogatoriis, aliisque efficacioribus, et insolitis clausulis ac irritantibus, et aliis decretis, in genere vel in specie, ac alias in contrarium praemissorum quomodolibet concessis, confirmatis, et innovatis. Quibus omnibus et singulis, eorum omnium tenores praesentibus pro plene et sufficienter expressis, et ad verbum insertis habentes, illis alias in suo robore permansuris hac vice dumtaxat specialiter, et expresse derogamus caeterisque contrariis quibuscumque."—*Collectanea,* I (1907), 4; *Bull. Pontificium,* I, 29.

188 De Meester, *Juris Canonici et Juris Canonico—civilis Compendium* (nova ed., 3 vols. in 4, Brugis: Desclée, De Brouwer & S^{i}, 1921–1928), II (1923), n. 590.

189 Bouix, *Tractatus de Curia Romana seu de Cardinalibus, Romanis Congregationibus, Legatis, Nuntiis, Vicariis et Protonotariis Apostolicis* (Parisiis, 1859), p. 232 (hereafter cited *Tractatus de Curia Romana*); Cappello, *De Curia Romana Juxta Reformationem a Pio X Sapientissime Inductam* (2 vols., Romae, Ratisbonae, Neo-Eboraci, Cincinnati: Fridericus Pustet, 1911–1912), I, 232 (hereafter cited *De Curia Romana*); Meehan, *Compendium Juris Canonici* (Roffae: Ex Typographia Joannis P. Smith, 1899), p. 66.

gregations were accustomed to do for those countries subject to the common law of the Church, the same the Propaganda Congregation has done for those countries placed under its jurisdiction. It has been therefore a common saying regarding the Propaganda that 'ceteras Congregationes habet in ventre.' In other words, this Congregation takes cognizance within the territory assigned to it of all the ecclesiastical affairs of which the other Congregations take cognizance in regard to the rest of the Church. All business relating to the supreme government of missionary countries has been transacted by the *Propaganda; . . . .*" [190] Then he goes beyond the generalities of the above mentioned authors in order to stress an important point: " When questions of doctrine were proposed to the Propaganda for solution, it was the general practise of this Congregation to refer them to the Holy Office. *There was not, however, any obligation of this kind imposed upon the Propaganda Congregation, since no prohibition was issued to prevent it from giving a decision on doctrinal matters.*" [191] Sipos, a post-Code author, likewise explicitly affirms that the jurisdiction of the Sacred Congregation of the Propagation of the Faith up to the reform of Pope Pius X included matters of Faith.[192] Goyau—Peraté—Fabre, pre-Code authors, also declare that difficulties which arose in the territories subject to the Sacred Congregation of the Propagation of the Faith were judged by this Sacred Congregation so that it supplied the functions of the other Sacred Congregations, the Holy Office included.[193] However, at

---

190 M. Martin, *The Roman Curia* (New York: Benziger Brothers, 1913), p. 70.

191 *Ibid.*, pp. 70–71. Italics ours.

192 Sipos, *Enchiridion Iuris Canonici* (3. ed., Pécs: Ex Typographia "Haladás R. T.", 1936), p. 212, footnote 24: "Ante const. 'Sapienti consilio' etiam in his causis [in negotiis quae fidem, causas matrimoniales, et causas rituum attingunt] competens fuit haec C., i. e., in regionibus missionum locum tenuit omnium aliarum congregationum."

193 "Les congrégations que nous avons étudiées [Congregations other than the Sacred Congregation of the Propagation of the Faith] prennent tantôt des décisions générales, applicables au monde chrétien, et tantôt, constituées en tribunaux, elles jugent les difficultés spéciales qui leur sont déférées. Dans le vaste royaume de la Propaganda cette dernière juridiction n'a point lieu de s'exerçer; la Propaganda elle-même y supplée. Un

another time they assert that the Sacred Congregation *de Propaganda Fide* fulfilled in regard to the countries of the missions the rôle of *almost* all the Sacred Congregations, and that it was the necessary intermediary of its subjects as to those Sacred Congregations whose work it was not able to do.[194] But they do not explain this last statement nor do they name any specific Sacred Congregation whose work was beyond the jurisdiction of the Sacred Congregation *de Propaganda Fide.* Perhaps by the expression " whose work it was not able to do " they had in mind matters which the Sacred Congregation used to send to the other Sacred Congregations for solution, as is mentioned by Simier, another pre-Code author. Simier also states that the competency of the Sacred Congregation of the Propagation of the Faith extended to all affairs without distinction which ordinarily were referred to the other dicasteries of the Curia, and that these other dicasteries possessed no direct and immediate jurisdiction for territories of the Sacred Congregation of the Propagation of the Faith because the latter Sacred Congregation had all the rights which the Sacred Congregation of the Holy Office, the Sacred Congregation of the Council, the Sacred Congregation of Sacred Rites, etc., possessed for all other countries. But, frequently for certain more delicate questions demanding a particular adeptness or competence, for instance, when it was a question of rites, indulgences, points of dogma, difficulties relative to the administration of sacraments, it had recourse to the particular Sacred Congregations respectively concerned with those affairs.[195]

Choupin, however, avers that for the countries under its jurisdiction the Sacred Congregation of the Propagation of the Faith

---

missionnaire est-il taxé d'indignité: elle fait, à son égard, fonction de Saint-Office. Est-il nécessaire, en un pays infidèle, de déroger à la liturgie: elle y autorise, faisant fonction de congrégation de Rites; . . ."—Goyau-Pératé-Fabre, *Le Vatican, les Papes et la Civilisation* (Paris: Librairie de Firmin-Didot et Cie, 1895), p. 351.

[194] *Ibid.*, pp. 351–352: ". . . la Propagande remplit, à leur égard, le rôle de presque toutes congrégations; elle est, auprès de celles dont elle ne peut faire la besogne, l'intermédiaire nécessaire des requérants; . . ."

[195] Simier, *La Curie Romaine,* pp. 46–47.

was in itself an ensemble of all the other Sacred Congregations with the sole exception of the Holy Office.[196]

Thus far no direct reference to the Sacred Penitentiaria has been made in connection with the Sacred Congregation of the Propagation of the Faith. The following group of authors mention it explicitly. Wernz states that all ecclesiastical matters which concerned the supreme and universal rule of the missions were subject to the Sacred Congregation of the Propagation of the Faith; wherefore, this Sacred Congregation had exclusive jurisdiction in those regions and in regard to them took the place of all the other Sacred Congregations with the exception of the Sacred Penitentiaria.[197] In the footnote to this assertion he cites Bangen.[198] The same view is presented by Forget [199] and Ojetti.[200] Monin and V. Martin express themselves in another way: they say respectively that questions of conscience [201] or of the internal forum [202] were excluded from the competency of the Sacred Congregation of the Propagation of the Faith and had to be referred to the Sacred Penitentiaria. Moreover, V. Martin adds that for certain particularly delicate questions demanding a special experience, e.g., matters of dogma, rites, and sacraments, the Sacred Congregation of the Propagation of the Faith rather often had recourse to the other Sacred Congregations; but [and this is to be noted] it did so spontaneously, freely, *à titre de service* so to speak.[203] Thus, it was not compelled to do so by law. Monin also remarks that the Sacred Congregation was accustomed to remit doubts and questions to the other dicasteries of the Roman Curia according to their competence.[204] Here again it is to be

---

[196] Choupin, "La Constitution 'Sapienti consilio' de Pie X et la Réorganisation de la Curie Romaine"—*Etudes Religieuses,* CXVII (1908), p. 647.

[197] Wernz, *Ius Decretalium,* II (1899), 765.

[198] *Ibid.,* footnote 288.

[199] Forget, "Congrégations Romaines"—*Dictionnaire de Théologie Catholique* (14 vols. in 26, Paris: Letouzey et Ané, 1903-1939), III, 1113.

[200] Ojetti, *De Romana Curia* (Romae: Ex Cooperativa Typographia Manuzio, 1910), n. 76.

[201] Monin, *De Curia Romana,* p. 68.

[202] V. Martin, *Les Congrégations Romaines,* p. 142.

[203] *Loc. cit.*

[204] Monin, *loc. cit.*

noticed that it was accustomed to do so, though there was no such obligation attached. Deshayes attributes most ample (*amplissima*) power to the Sacred Congregation *de Propaganda Fide* for all matters which concerned the clergy and the faithful in mission lands except for matters pertaining to Faith and the forum of conscience.[205]

On the other hand Bargilliat states that the power of the Sacred Congregation of the Propagation of the Faith as to the species of matters and causes was most ample for all ecclesiastical causes, *of whatever species they may be*,[206] in the regions of the missions. Then he explains that the Sacred Congregation of the Propagation of the Faith was accustomed ("*solet*") to remit to the Holy Office matters which directly concerned Faith, and that it requested ("*exposcit*") from the Sacred Penitentiaria the opportune remedy or solution of a question directly concerned with the forum of conscience.[207] Lega [208] and Santi-Leitner [209] offer exactly the same explanation. Whence according to their writing it can be maintained that there was no obligation to remit such matters to the Holy Office—the "solet," moreover, indicates that it did not necessarily always do so; but it is not clear whether there was an

---

[205] Deshayes, *Memento Juris Ecclesiastici* (Parisiis: Apud Berche et Tralin, 1895), n. 564.

[206] Italics ours.

[207] "Quod si agatur de negotio quod *materiam fidei directe* respicit, S. Congregatio illud ad S. Officium remittere solet. Si vero negotium *conscientiae forum* directe attingat, a S. Poenitentiaria opportunum remedium vel solutionem quaestionis exposcit."—Bargilliat, *Praelectiones Juris Canonici* (22. ed., 2 vols., Parisiis: Apud Berche et Tralin, 1905), I, n. 465b, 2°. Baart (*The Roman Court* [4. ed., New York: Fr. Pustet & Co., 1899], p. 214) omits the word "*solet*": "It may be noted that whenever a matter is sent to the Propaganda which directly concerns faith, this Congregation sends it to the Congregation of the Holy Office. Likewise if a matter pertains directly to the forum of conscience, it requests a proper remedy or solution of the question from the Sacred Penitentiary. In each case, however, the answer is usually returned through the Propaganda."

[208] *Praelectiones in Textum Iuris Canonici de Iudiciis Ecclesiasticis,* II (1898), 140–141.

[209] *Praelectiones Juris Canonici* (4. ed., 3 vols., Ratisbonae, Romae, Neo-Eboraci & Cincinnati: Sumptibus et Typis Friderici Pustet, 1904–1905), I, 313.

obligation to recur to the Sacred Penitentiaria—even though the "*exposcit*" seems to indicate that it had recourse in every case, yet it may simply mean that it was the practise of the Sacred Congregation of the Propagation of the Faith to do so without being obliged just as in its recourses to the Holy Office. In fact, Sebastianelli employs the "*solet*" for the S. Penitentiaria also, and holds that the Sacred Congregation of the Propagation of the Faith was accustomed to remit (a) to the Holy Office the affairs directly concerned with Faith, (b) to the Sacred Penitentiaria cases and petitions for the internal forum, (c) to the Sacred Congregation of the Council or to another competent Sacred Congregation the solution of doubts which touch the common law.[210] From this it would be concluded that since the Sacred Congregation of the Propagation of the Faith was certainly not bound to have recourse to the Sacred Congregations mentioned in (c), so also it was not bound to have recourse in matters of (a) and (b).

Finally, Laurentius contends that the Sacred Congregation of the Propagation of the Faith considered all business of the external forum to be in its jurisdiction, and he seemingly limits its jurisdiction to that forum.[211] Craisson, on the contrary, cites Lequeux who asserted that it solved questions and the cases of conscience which were proposed by the missionaries.[212]

What is to be concluded? According to the Constitution "*Inscrutabili divinae providentiae*" Pope Gregory XV conferred very extensive authority upon the Sacred Congregation of the Propagation of the Faith: it was to take cognizance of and treat all and every kind of business pertaining to propagating the Faith in the whole world; it was to perform, manage, treat, do, and

[210] "At solet haec Congregatio remittere ad S. Officium negotia directe ad fidem spectantia, ad S. Poenitentiariam casus et petitiones pro foro interno, ad S. Cong. Concilii, aut aliam competentem, solutionem dubiorum, quae jus commune attingunt."—Sebastianelli, *Praelectiones Juris Canonici* (3 vols., *Romae, Ratisbonae, Neo-Eboraci,* Cincinnati: Fridericus Pustet, 1905–1906), Vol. I (*De Personis,* 2. ed., 1905), 87.

[211] Laurentius, *Institutiones Iuris Ecclesiastici* (Friburgi Brisgoviae: Sumptibus Herder, 1903), n. 155.

[212] Craisson, *Manuale Juris Canonici* (5. ed., 3 vols., Pictavii: Ex Typis H. Oudin, 1877), I, n. 780.

execute all and everything necessary or opportune for that purpose. He demanded only that the *graviora* matters, after having been treated by them at their assemblies, were to be referred to him; but he definitely did not exclude any species of business from its jurisdiction. In fact, he safeguarded these powers by the abrogation of any previous enactments contrary to his concessions.[213] Hence, all ecclesiastical causes, no matter what their species, which arose from the designated missionary regions were subject to the Sacred Congregation of the Propagation of the Faith. In all cases the affairs from these territories were to be addressed to this Sacred Congregation.[214] However, it is to be remarked that this Sacred Congregation did not in practise decide all these matters by itself since it could and was accustomed to remit doubts, questions and problems to the other Sacred Congregations for resolution;[215] in such cases, the answer was gratuitously returned to the Sacred Congregation, and the latter in turn forwarded it gratuitously to the party concerned[216]—such was the usual practise in regard to matters concerning Faith (which were sent by the Sacred Congregation of the Propagation of the Faith to the Sacred Congregation of the Holy Of-

[213] *Supra*, p. 31.

[214] Smith (*Elements of Ecclesiastical Law* [3 vols., New York, Cincinnati, Chicago: Benziger Brothers, 1877-1888], Vol. I [9. ed., 1893], n. 508) states: ". . . [ecclesiastical matters] from missionary countries must be referred *exclusively* to, and are arranged *solely* by, the Propaganda. Hence, of this congregation it is said: *Caeteras congregationes habet in ventre—i. e.*, for missionary countries the Propaganda is the *sole* congregation, combines in itself the powers and discharges the duties or functions not merely of several, but of all the other congregations; so that while the priests and bishops of countries where canon law obtains must refer matters to the respective congregations, the priests and bishops of missionary countries must, *in all cases*, address themselves to the Propaganda, but to no other congregation."

[215] Simier, *La Curie Romaine*, pp. 46-47; V. Martin, *Les Congrégations Romaines*, p. 142; Monin, *De Curia Romana*, p. 68; Bargilliat, *Praelectiones Juris Canonici*, I (1905), n. 465 b, 2o; Baart, *The Roman Court*, p. 214; Lega, *Praelectiones in Textum Iuris Canonici de Iudiciis Ecclesiasticis*, II (1898), 140-141; Santi-Leitner, *Praelectiones Juris Canonici*, I (1904), n. 99; Sebastianelli, *Praelectiones Juris Canonici*, I, 87.

[216] Constitution "*Cum inter multiplices*"—*Bull. Rom.*, XII, 766-768. Cf. also Monin, *De Curia Roma*, p. 68.

fice).[217] It must be pointed out that this latter procedure was a prudent use of a practise, and by no means an obligation imposed upon the Sacred Congregation *de Propaganda Fide* to act in that way exclusively. Furthermore, from the Acts of the Sacred Congregation of the Propagation of the Faith it is readily apparent that the Sacred Congregation itself also treated matters on Faith.[218] Moreover, that the Sacred Congregation of the Propagation of the Faith enjoyed such powers over matters of Faith is definitely established by the explicit curtailment of this right by the Constitution "*Sapienti consilio*" in 1908.[219] Of course, it is understood by all that whenever the Holy Office issued a doctrinal pronouncement, it bound all Catholics both Latin and Oriental, for there is no exception of place or of persons in pronouncements of the Holy See in matters of Faith.

In regard to the Sacred Penitentiaria it is recalled that Pope Pius V (1566–1572) by the Constitution "*Ut bonus paterfamilias,*" of May 18, 1569, confined its jurisdiction to matters of the internal forum: [220] among its faculties it had the power to absolve and to order others to absolve from certain grave sins and from reserved censures, to dispense and to order others to dispense in the forum of conscience from certain irregularities, in cases involving contracted marriages to dispense from certain impediments provided they are occult, to commute certain vows into other works of piety, and to solve doubts in matters of sin or in matters which otherwise in any way at all concerned the penitential forum.[221] These faculties of the tribunal were increased little by little by Pope Pius V himself and his successors,[222] and a

[217] M. Martin, *The Roman Curia*, p. 70.

[218] *Collectanea*, I (1907), Pars III—De Fide et Moribus.

[219] "Nihilominus, ut unitati regiminis consulatur, volumus ut Congregatio de Propaganda Fide ad peculiares alias Congregationes deferat quaecumque aut fidem attingunt, aut matrimonium aut sacrorum rituum disciplinam."—*Fontes*, n. 682 (I, 6º, 4).

[220] *Bull. Rom.*, VII, 750–752.

[221] Constitution "*Ut bonus paterfamilias,*" § 8, (*Bull. Rom.*, VII, 751) prescribes: "Dubia quoque in materia peccatorum seu forum poenitentiale alias quomodolibet concernentia, cum consilio doctorum et theologorum suorum, declarare."

[222] Monin, *De Curia Romana*, p. 90; Ojetti, "Roman Curia"—*The Cath-*

number of these new concessions were made by word of mouth.[223] Among the faculties listed by Pope Innocent XII in the Constitution "*Romanus Pontifex,*" of September 3, 1692,[224] and by Pope Benedict XIV in the Constitution "*Pastor bonus,*" of April 13, 1744,[225] was the power to absolve in both forums Regulars from certain offences and from censures.[226] Moreover, at a later date when the Dataria was impeded in the exercise of its offices on account of the civil disturbances of the eighteenth century,[227] the Sacred Penitentiaria supplied its function of granting matrimonial dispensations in the external forum; and even when the Dataria resumed its office of dispensing in the external forum, the Sacred Penitentiaria retained the power of dispensing in the external forum public matrimonial impediments for the poor and the quasi-poor (*fere pauperes*).[228]

It is difficult to determine whether the jurisdiction of the Sacred Penitentiaria in all these matters also extended to those under the jurisdiction of the Sacred Congregation of the Propagation of the Faith to such an extent that the latter *was obliged* to defer all such cases to the Sacred Tribunal. In the above enumerations of the opinions of the various authors it was shown that some authors mentioned that the Sacred Congregation of the Propagation of the Faith was merely accustomed to refer matters

---

olic Encyclopedia, III, 148; Ojetti, *De Romana Curia,* p. 167; Phillips (1804–1872), *Kirchenrecht* (7 vols., Regensburg, 1845–1872, Vol. VIII, Part I, ed. by Friedrich Vering [1833–1896], Regensburg, 1889), VI, 525.

223 Ojetti, *loc. cit.; Benedicti XIV Pont. Opt. Max. olim Prosperi Cardinalis De Lambertinis Bullarium* (commencing with tome III the title is *Bullarii Romani Continuatio Summorum Pontificum Benedicti XIV, Clementis XIII, Clementis XIV, Pii VI, Pii VII, Leonis XII et Pii VIII*) (9 tomes in 14, Prati: in Typographia Aldina, 1845–1856), I, p. 535, § 3. Hereafter this work will be referred to as *Bullarii Romani Continuatio.*

224 *Bull. Rom.,* XX, 450–461.

225 *Bullarii Romani Continuatio,* I, 334–363.

226 *Bull. Rom.,* XX, 453, § 9; *Bullarii Romani Continuatio,* I, 356, § 6.

227 Kubelbeck, *The Sacred Penitentiaria and Its Relations to Faculties of Ordinaries and Priests,* The Catholic University of America Canon Law Studies, n. 5 (Washington, D. C.: The Catholic University of America, 1918), p. 27.

228 Kubelbeck, *loc. cit.;* Monin, *De Curia Romana,* p. 90; Ojetti, *De Romana Curia,* p. 168.

pertaining to the Sacred Penitentiaria to that tribunal, while others actually limited the competence of the Sacred Congregation in this respect. The writer, due to a lack of source material on this point, is not able to make a definite assertion in favor of either side. Unfortunately the writer was not able to procure the text of Lequeux's remark and thus evaluate the real meaning of his assertion concerning the solution of questions and cases of conscience by the Sacred Congregation of the Propagation of the Faith. If these cases of conscience were really cases of conscience and not merely questions dealing with the explanation of the existing law, this might be indeed a strong indication that perhaps in such matters the Sacred Congregation of the Propagation of the Faith had full competence without the necessity of recurring to the Sacred Penitentiaria. Perhaps in support of Lequeux's statement one might refer to the Acts of the Sacred Congregation of the Propagation of the Faith wherein it is recorded that the latter answered questions pertaining to the internal forum.[229] If the Sacred Penitentiaria had competence over all the faithful in this matter, it would seem as though such questions should have been answered by it according to its faculties, i. e., "Dubia quoque in materia peccatorum seu forum poenitentiale alias quomodolibet concernentia, cum consilio doctorum et theologorum suorum, declarare." [230]

In favor of the jurisdiction of the Sacred Penitentiaria over subjects of the Sacred Congregation of the Propagation of the Faith from the time of the Constitution "*Romanus Pontifex,*" of September 3, 1692, and the Constitution "*Pastor bonus,*" of April 13, 1744, are the following: (a) the statement at the beginning of the Constitution "*Pastor bonus*" about the wish of the Roman Pontiffs from early times for an Office of the Apostolic Penitentiaria to which all the faithful from all over the world might have recourse;[231] (b) both the Constitution "*Ro-*

[229] *Collectanea,* I (1907), nn. 14 and 16; *Collectanea,* I (1893), nn. 973, 975.

[230] Constitution "*Ut bonus paterfamilias,*" § 8—*Bull. Rom.,* VII, 751, and Constitution "*Pastor bonus,*" § 48—*Bullarii Romani Continuatio,* I, 362.

[231] "Ideo, praeter alia plura pro variis causarum generibus constituta Romanae Curiae Tribunalia, voluerunt [Romani Pontifices] imprimis jam

manus Pontifex" and the Constitution "*Pastor bonus*" conclude with the confirmation of the powers of the Sacred Penitentiaria notwithstanding any other Constitutions and Apostolic Ordination to the contrary.[232]

What was the nature of the power which the Sacred Congregation of the Propagation of the Faith possessed at this time over the matters it treated? Again authorities are not in complete accord in all respects. They do not question the fact that this Sacred Congre-

---

inde a vetustissimis usque temporibus exstare in ea . . . Apostolicae Poenitentiariae Officium ad quod universi Fideles ex omni Christiani Orbis regione pro suis quisque spiritualibus morbis quamlibet occultis, sive per se, sive per arcanas literas, propriis etiam suppressis nominibus, tuto confugere possent, et convenientem vulneribus medicinam, secreta et gratuita curatione (qualis ab omnibus optanda foret) protinus consequerentur. Cujus tam praeclari, tamque salutaris instituti ratio Romanis pro tempore Pontificibus magnopere cordi fuit; tantamque ex hujus Officii ministerio in Ecclesiae administratione utilitatem experti sunt; ut olim eidem Officio non modo causas ad interius poenitentiae forum, sed alias etiam complures ad gratiam, et justitiam externi fori pertinentes, expediendas committere non dubitarent." —*Bullarii Romani Continuatio,* I, p. 355, § 1.

[232] "Non obstantibus praemissis, et aliis quibuscumque constitutionibus et ordinationibus apostolicis, et dictae Poenitentiariae, etiam iuramento, confirmatione apostolica, vel quavis alia firmitate roboratis, statutis et consuetudinibus quibuscumque, ac quibusvis vivae vocis oraculis, privilegiis, indultis et literis apostolicis, eiusdem Poenitentiariae officio, illiusque maiori poenitentiario, ac officialibus et ministris, et quibusvis aliis, sub quibuscumque tenoribus et formis, ac cum quibusvis etiam derogatoriarum derogatoriis, aliisque efficacioribus et insolitis clausulis et decretis, in genere vel in specie, etiam motu proprio, et alias quomodolibet per praedecessores nostros Romanos Pontifices ac etiam nos concessis, innovatis, confirmatis et approbatis; quibus omnibus et singulis, etiamsi pro illorum sufficienti derogatione de illis eorumque totis tenoribus specialis, specifica, individua et expressa, ac de verbo ad verbum, non autem per clausulas generales idem importantes, mentio seu quaevis alia expressio habenda aut aliqua alia exquisita forma ad hoc servanda foret, tenores huiusmodi, ac si de verbo ad verbum nihil penitus omisso, et forma in illis tradita observata insererentur, iisdem praesentibus pro plene et sufficienter expressis et insertis habentes, ad effectum praesentium, illis alias in suo robore permansuris, harum serie derogamus; ceterisque contrariis quibuscumque."—Constitutio, "*Romanus Pontifex,*" of September 3, 1692—*Bull. Rom.,* XX, 460–461, § 51; Constitution "*Pastor bonus,*" of April 13, 1744—*Bullarii Romani Continuatio,* I, 363, § 57.

gation exercised administrative, judicial, coercive power.[233] In regard to its judicial power Cardinal De Luca related in one paragraph that it was accustomed to handle and decide some forensic or contentious matters with the summary and extrajudicial style of the Sacred Congregations,[234] and in the next paragraph he made reference to the fact that after the pattern of the Sacred Congregation of the Holy Office it also judged contentious and criminal causes which concerned the Sacred Congregation.[235] This second paragraph of Cardinal De Luca does seem to indicate that a strict judicial process was used in contrast to the preceding reference of a summary and extrajudicial style.

That criminal causes belonging to ecclesiastical tribunals, as well as contentious affairs seemingly demanding a strict judicial proceeding, were treated by the Sacred Congregation of the Propagation of the Faith is verified in the exhaustive study of the Sacred Roman Congregations in the *Analecta Juris Pontificii* of 1857.[236] Monin with reference to the judicial power of this Sacred Congregation stated that it took upon itself to judge both the contentious and the criminal causes of the missionaries and others, and this even in the first instance as often as it was concerned

---

[233] Baart, *The Roman Court,* p. 213; Forget, " Congrégations Romaines "—*Dictionnaire de Théologie Catholique,* III, 1113; Monin, *De Curia Romana,* p. 68; Wernz, *Ius Decretalium,* II (1899), 765; Wernz-Vidal, *Ius Canonicum,* II (1943), n. 495 III.

[234] " Adhuc tamen, ad instar praesertim Congregationis Regularium, ab aliquo tempore, aliqua forensia, vel contentiosa negotia peragere, ac decidere, cum eodem Congregationum summario, et extrajudiciali stylo, consuevit . . ." —De Luca, *Theatrum veritatis et Justitiae sive Decisivi Discursus, ad Veritatem Editi in Forensibus, Controversiis, Canonicis, et Civilibus, in Quibus, in Urbe Advocatus, pro Una Partium Scripsit, vel Consultus Respondit* (16 tomes in 9, Coloniae Agrippinae: Apud Henricum Rommerskirchen, 1706), tome VII, disc. XXIII, n. 7.

[235] " Ac etiam (ad instar Cong. S. Officii) forensem, prophanam cognitionem habet civilium, criminalium, et mixtarum causarum eiusdem Congregationis, vel Collegii ministrorum et operariorum, seu quae respiciunt bona temporalia eiusdem operis vel Collegii, ex quorum fructibus missionum sumptus . . . erogantur."—De Luca, *ibid.,* n. 8.

[236] " Des Congrégations Romaines et de Leur Pratique "—*Analecta Juris Pontificii* (Rome, 1855–1869, Paris, 1872-1891, and under the title *Analecta Ecclesiastica,* 1893–1911), II (1857), col. 2394, n. 113; col. 2413, n. 138.

with regions where there was not as yet an episcopal tribunal.[237]

As to the existence of legislative power of the Sacred Congregation of the Propagation of the Faith the following may be noted. In a general session of this Sacred Congregation in the presence of the pope on July 30, 1652, a report was read to the effect that in the Philippine Islands there were Religious who, making light of the decrees of the Sacred Congregation *de Propaganda Fide,* with very great harm to souls were spreading that the "*resolutiones*" and "*decreta*" of this Sacred Congregation had the value only of a probable opinion, as a pure and simple declaration of the cardinals, and whence even the contrary could be defended. Thereupon Pope Innocent X (1644–1655) confirmed the decree of Pope Urban VIII, namely, that the "*decreta*" of the Sacred Congregation *de Propaganda Fide,* as often as they were properly signed by the prefect and undersigned by the secretary and affixed with the seal, had the force and value of an Apostolic Constitution, and were to be observed inviolably by all and by each and every one,[238] i. e., by those in the territories of the missions for which they were given.[239] This decree was again affirmed by this Sacred Congregation on May 15, 1779.[240] Hence, it cannot be denied that the Sacred Congregation of the Propagation of the Faith had at least some legislative power.[241] Even though such decrees of this Sacred Congregation properly signed and affixed with the

---

[237] Monin, *De Curia Romana,* p. 68; Vromant, *Ius Missionariorum* (Louvain: Librairie E. Desbarax, 1929), p. 9.

[238] *Collectanea,* I (1907), n. 10; Lega, *op. cit.,* II, 143; Wernz-Vidal, *Ius Canonicum,* I (1938), 283, footnote 43.

[239] Wernz-Vidal, *loc. cit.*

[240] *Collectanea,* I (1907), p. 6, n. 11.

[241] Wernz-Vidal, *loc. cit.* Others who attributed legislative power to this Sacred Congregation are: Baart, *The Roman Court,* p. 213; Bouix, *Tractatus de Curia Romana,* pp. 232–233; Hilling, *Procedure at the Roman Curia* (New York: Joseph F. Wagner, 1907), p. 83; Lega, *Praelectiones in Textum Iuris Canonici de Iudiciis Ecclesiasticis,* II, 142–143, 363–370; Laurentius, *Institutiones Iuris Ecclesiastici,* p. 124, n. 155.

Monin, *De Curia Romana,* p. 68, footnote 1, stated: "Hinc concluserunt quidam hanc S. C. habere etiam potestatem *legislativam.*" Similarly Vromant, *Ius Missionariorum,* p. 9, after indicating the decree of July 30, 1652, continued: ". . . quidem concluserunt hanc S. C. habere etiam potestatem *legislativam* pro universis terris missionum."

seal had the same force as if they had come immediately from the Roman Pontiff, they were not to be considered general laws on this account alone, for the pope also can make laws which are not general.[242] Moreover, Bouix indicated that these "*decreta*" had their force from the authority which Pope Gregory XV conceded to the Sacred Congregation in the Constitution "*Inscrutabili divinae providentiae,*" of June 22, 1622,[243] whereas Monin stated that it is rightly doubted whether it had such power "*jure proprio et ordinario.*"[244]

Lega carefully points out that the above decree of Pope Innocent X did not demand as necessary the consultation with the pope, but only that the signs of authenticity be present—the signatures of the prefect and secretary, and the seal. Hence, when it was evident through such signs that the "*decreta*" came from the Sacred Congregation, they had the value of an Apostolic Constitution.[245] However, some authors [246] claim that the general decrees were considered as *graviora negotia.* If this were true, then it must be admitted with them that the pontifical approbation was required for such decrees, since according to the Constitution "*Inscrutabili divinae providentiae*" the more serious matters were to be referred to the pope.[247]

Another decree worthy of note was that of September 19, 1671; according to this, from a command of Pope Clement X it was enjoined that, whenever resolutions of doubts by the Sacred Con-

---

[242] Ojetti, *De Romana Curia,* p. 12.

[243] *Tractatus de Curia Romana,* p. 233.

[244] *De Curia Romana,* p. 68, footnote 1.

[245] *Praelectiones in Textum Iuris Canonici de Iudiciis Ecclesiasticis,* II, 366.

[246] Monin, *loc. cit.;* Vromant, *Ius Missionariorum,* p. 9; Wernz-Vidal, *Ius Canonicum,* II (1943), 597.

[247] *Fontes,* n. 200, § 8; Monin, *loc. cit.;* Vromant, *loc. cit.* The writer wonders whether Sipos (*Enchiridion Iuris Canonici,* p. 211, footnote 23) means that even general decrees had the force of law without being referred to the pope, when he says: "Antea decret huius C.—is etiam sine relatione facta Papae vim legis habebant (decr. huius C.—is 30 jul. 1652). Nunc [with the Constitution "*Sapienti consilio*" of 1908] decreta generalia condere potest sub conditionibus supra dictis (in § 20 nr. 7., § 41 I. nr. 4.)." If so, was it because he didn't consider the general decrees as *graviora negotia?*

gregation of the Holy Office and the Sacred Congregation of the Propagation of the Faith were sent to missionaries and other ministers of the latter Sacred Congregation, they were to be sent not as Definitions but as simple Instructions, by which the missionaries and ministers could and ought to be governed in the solution of practical doubts.[248]

The final aspect of the Sacred Congregation of the Propagation of the Faith which is to be mentioned is its connection with the Oriental Church. With the establishment of the Sacred Congregation of the Propagation of the Faith it is to be noted that once again Catholics of the Oriental Rite and their dissident brethren came to fall within the orbit of the missions. Not only were countries inhabited by them included in the division of the territories subjected to the Sacred Congregation of the Propagation of the Faith,[249] but in the beginning the Sacred Congregation of the Propagation of the Faith busied itself less with the missions to the pagans than with those to the Oriental Church [250] and the

[248] *Collectanea,* I (1907), n. 5: "De mandato Sanctissimi (Clementis X) iniunctum fuit, quotiescumque missionariis ceterisque S. C. de Prop. Fide ministris mittuntur resolutiones dubiorum factae a S. C. S. Off. et Propag. Fidei, non mittantur tamquam Definitiones, sed tamquam simplices Instructiones, quibus in occurrentibus dubiis gubernari valeant et debeant."

[249] In the meeting of March 8, 1622 (before the issuance of the Constitution "*Inscrutabili divinae providentiae*") they divided the provinces of the world, arranging them under nuncios: "South-West Germany and Austria, Hungary, Transylvania, Moldavia and Walachia to the nuncio of Vienna. The Polish nuncio looked after Poland, Prussia, Pomerania, Sweden, and Russia; the southern Slav countries were under the nuncio of Venice . . . Special patriarchal Vicars were appointed for the Balkans, Asia Minor and Northern Africa with residence, respectively, in Constantinople, Jerusalem, and Alexandria. These territories, in this same order, were later assigned to individual Cardinals of the Congregation."—Pastor, *The History of the Popes,* XXVII, 135. Catholics and dissidents of the Oriental Rite did not exclusively occupy these territories, but they did inhabit some of them and in places formed a large part of the population. The missions established in these places were greatly concerned with them.

[250] The following data, taken from Attwater, *The Catholic Eastern Churches* (revised ed., Milwaukee, Wisconsin: The Bruce Publishing Company, 1937), p. 282 reveal the Churches of the Oriental Rite which were reunited and those which were in schism at the time of the foundation of the Sacred Congregation of the Propagation of the Faith in 1622:

very difficult missions in the Protestant countries where the care of souls met with even greater obstacles than in the schismatic East.[251] Schmidlin [252] asserts that letters and petitions still extant of this first year deal only with Europe and the near Orient, and not a single one with the far East or the pagan missions proper. He concludes that for this early period the heavy weight of the mission problems rested on the Protestant and Schismatic districts. That this special interest of the Sacred Congregation of the Propagation of the Faith in Catholics and dissidents of the Oriental Rite was well justified is apparent from the startling

Church	Date of Schism of Original Church	Date of Catholic Reunion
Alexandrian Rite		
1. Copts	451 A. D.	1741 A. D.
2. Ethiopians	c. 550	1839
Antiochene Rite		
1. Syrians	543	1656
2. Maronites	?	1182
[It is disputed whether the Maronites really did fall into schism.]		
3. Malankarese	1653	1930
Armenian Rite		
1. Armenians under the patriarch	c. 525	1198:1742
Byzantine Rite		
1. Bulgars	1054	1860
2. Greeks	1054	1860
3. Hungarians	1054	c. 1595
4. Italo-Greek-Albanians	never separated	[This is disputed]
5. Melkites	1054	1439:1724
6. Rumanians	1054	1701
7. Russians (a) in Poland	19th century	1920
(b) elsewhere	1054	1905
8. Ruthenians (a) in Polish Galicia	c. 1200	1595
(b) Podcarpathian	1054	1652
9. Yugoslavs	1054	1611
Chaldean Rite		
1. Chaldeans	431	1551
2. Malabarese (India)	?	before 1599

[251] Pastor, *The History of the Popes*, XXVII, 138.

[252] "Die Gründung der Propagandakongregation (1922)"—*Zeitschrift für Missionswissenschaft*, XII (1922), 8–9, and footnotes 1 and 2 on p. 9.

reports in 1623 of the bishops specially delegated to Hungary, Serbia, Bulgaria, Bosnia and Albania.[253] Yet, in spite of the adverse circumstances in those countries, the Latin missionaries of the Franciscan, Dominican, Capuchin, Carmelite, and Jesuit Orders, continued to strengthen those who had remained in communion with Rome, to re-unite dissidents, and to enlighten infidels.[254]

The Sacred Congregation had taken steps from the outset to insure the success of its program for the Catholics of the Oriental Rite and their separated brethren. As early as April 15, 1622,[255] it constituted a special commission to examine along with the other Colleges in Rome the affairs of the Greek, Maronite and Armenian Colleges. The reason? To discover whether these institutions were fulfilling the end for which they had been founded, because the Sacred Congregation intended to intervene wherever it was found necessary to do so.

---

[253] "(1) Bulgaria: In Sophia: two Catholic families, one chapel. Scattered Catholics everywhere. 'Infinità de Bulgari scismatici, incapaci di conversione.' (2) Serbia: Hostility of the numerous schismatics towards the Pope. 'Come la Servia, Bulgaria e Grecia è piena di schismatici, così la maggior parte dell' Albania è piena di cattolici.'" Pastor, *op. cit.,* XXVII, 140–141 footnote. Cf. also the other reports given here on the Catholics and the dissidents of the Oriental Rite.

[254] Pastor, *The History of the Popes,* XXVII, 139–140, footnote 5.

[255] Pastor, *ibid.,* p. 139. The English edition has April 15, 1652, which is obviously a misprint—cf. the German edition, XIII, 107.

CHAPTER II

FROM POPE URBAN VIII TO THE PROMULGATION OF THE *CODEX IURIS CANONICI*

ARTICLE I. INNOVATIONS AND THEIR DEVELOPMENT WITHIN THE SACRED CONGREGATION OF THE PROPAGATION OF THE FAITH

During Pope Urban VIII's pontificate (1623–1644) problems of the Oriental Church were handled by the Sacred Congregation of the Propagation of the Faith. This Congregation issued answers to various kinds of questions concerning the Ruthenians in the year 1624.[1] The first major change within this Sacred Congregation respecting the solution of Oriental matters came in 1627.[2] At that time Pope Urban VIII appointed some cardinals of the Sacred Congregation of the Propagation of the Faith to treat the more important or more serious business (*graviora negotia*) [3] of the Orientals, i. e., affairs which demanded greater examination and study.[4] This select group, called the *Congregatio super*

[1] Cf. *Codificatione Canonica Orientale, Fonti* (Typografia Poliglotta Vaticana, 1930–), Vol. XI (*Ius Particulare Ruthenorum*), p. 45, n. 40; pp. 48–49, n. 42; p. 217, n. 179; p. 771, n. 584.

[2] *Statistica,* p. 12; Staffa, "De Sacrae Congregationis pro Ecclesia Orientali competentia"—*Apollinaris,* XI (1938), 361.

Others who do not give the date of formation seem by their manner of presentation to give the wrong impression that both the *Congregatio super dubiis Orientalium* and the *Congregatio super correctione Euchologii Graecorum* were formed at the same time. Petrani, "De Sacra Congregatione pro Ecclesia Orientali eiusque facultatibus"—*Apollinaris,* X (1937), 29; Monin, *De Curia Romana,* p. 70. In fact, some mention the *Congregatio super correctione Euchologii Graecorum* before the *Congregatio super dubiis Orientalium* in speaking of the erection of these two Congregations. Cf. Petrani, *loc. cit.;* V. Martin, *Les Congrégations Romaines,* p. 191.

[3] Pius IX, Constitution "*Romani Pontifices,*" of January 6, 1862—*Fontes,* II, n. 531, p. 948; Monin, *loc. cit.;* Staffa, *ibid.,* pp. 360–361.

[4] Pius IX, *loc. cit.;* Monin, *loc. cit.*

dubiis orientalium,[5] continued to form a part of the Sacred Congregation of the Propagation of the Faith: it was not a separate, independent Sacred Congregation of the Roman Curia; it simply discharged one of the many functions of the general Congregation.[6] Whether the members of the *Congregatio super dubiis orientalium* were limited to the *graviora Orientalium negotia* without a share in the other work of the Sacred Congregation *de Propaganda Fide* is not definitely clarified. It should be noted, moreover, that the Acts of the Sacred Congregation of the Propagation of the Faith revealed that when an Oriental question of the greatest importance ("*summi momenti*") demanded attention, its care and examination were entrusted to special commisions of the Sacred Congregation *de Propaganda Fide,* as was the case with matters which concerned Melchite Greeks, Armenians, Copts, Maronites, Ruthenians, and other Oriental nations.[7]

However, it must be noted that not all the writers report the division indicated here, though they agree on the general procedure. Victor Martin speaks of the formation of the *Congregatio super dubiis Orientalium* within the bosom of the Sacred Congregation *de Propaganda Fide* for the disciplinary affairs of the Orientals, with no further limitations or qualifications. Then he mentions that it lost its proper fixed form to become merged with the rest of the Sacred Congregation; and that the latter named a commission of cardinals, chosen from among those of its members who knew the country in question, to handle the affairs of a non-Latin Church whenever they were proposed.

---

[5] Pius IX, *loc. cit.;* Monin, *loc. cit.;* Staffa, *ibid.,* p. 361.

[6] Since the Sacred Congregation of the Propagation of the Faith had other Congregational units within it, the Sacred Congregation of the Propagation of the Faith when considered as a whole is referred to as the general Sacred Congregation; a meeting of the general Sacred Congregation meant the assembly of all the cardinals of the S. C. *de Propaganda Fide,* according to Baart (*The Roman Court,* pp. 222–223, and esp. p. 227).

For the explanation of the expression *Congregatio Generalis de Prop. Fide,* see *infra,* p. 56, footnote 32. Therefore the expression "general Sacred Congregation of the *Propaganda Fide*" might refer to the *S. Congregatio de Propaganda Fide pro Negotiis Ritus Latini,* as Monin mentions.

[7] Pius IX, *loc. cit.*

This process was repeated every time such a situation arose.[8] Petrani's version adds little, and differs but slightly. He declares that during the first ten years of its existence the *Congregatio super dubiis Orientalium* (which he refers to as a section of the Sacred Congregation of the Propagation of the Faith) was kept quite occupied, since the greater part of the business concerned the Orient. But little by little this preoccupation dwindled and languished and in the end the whole *section* was occupied with the missions of the Latin Church. Every single time that a non-Latin case was presented, a new special commission composed of cardinals who were acquainted with that region or that particular Church of the Orient was named by the pope.[9]

Finally, another explanation,[10] after pointing to the establishment of the Sacred Congregation of the Propagation of the Faith, affirms that the need of stabilizing some Congregations, or rather Commissions, within the bosom of the general Sacred Congregation was soon seen to be imperative. Wherefore Pope Urban VIII instituted two of them, one of which was called *super dubiis Orientalium* (1627). Nevertheless, so the account continues, when matters of greater importance were to be treated, the pope still had to constitute particular Commissions or Congregations for the Orientals as well as for the Occidentals.

One of the innovations within the Sacred Congregation of the Propagation of the Faith on the part of Pope Urban VIII occurred between 1636–1644,[11] when he constituted the *Congregatio super correctione Euchologii Graecorum* to correct the liturgical books written in the Greek language.[12] The pope was led to take such a step upon receiving information from messengers sent by

[8] V. Martin, *Les Congrégations Romaines*, pp. 191–192.

[9] Petrani, "De Sacra Congregatione pro Ecclesia Orientali eiusque facultatibus"—*Apollinaris*, X (1937), 29.

[10] *Statistica*, pp. 11–12.

[11] *Statistica, loc. cit.;* Staffa, "De Sacrae Congregationis pro Ecclesia Orientali competentia"—*Apollinaris*, XI (1938), 361; both of these explanations place the time between 1636–1645, but Urban VIII died on July 29, 1644, and therefore the dates must range from 1636–1644.

[12] *Statistica, loc. cit.;* Staffa, *loc. cit.;* V. Martin, *Les Congrégations Romaines*, p. 191. Petrani, *loc. cit.;* Pius IX, Constitution "*Romani Pontifices*"—*Fontes*, II, n. 531, p. 948; Monin, *De Curia Romana*, p. 70.

the King of Spain, Philip IV (1621–1665), which uncovered the fact that the Italo-Greeks of Calabria and of Sicily were still using Missals of schismatic production, which therefore contained the latter's dogmatic errors.[13] This Congregation like the *Congregatio super dubiis Orientalium* remained a part of the general Sacred Congregation *de Propaganda Fide,* and it continued as such until Pope Clement XI (1700–1721) changed its status. The latter, wishing that the Sacred Congregation should complete its work with the Greek books and also extend its scope to all the liturgical books of the Oriental Church, transformed it into a new stable Sacred Congregation, separate and distinct from the Sacred Congregation of the Propagation of the Faith. This new *Congregatio super correctione librorum Orientalium* (1717)[14] had its own Prefect and Secretary, five cardinals, and several theologians and other scholars who had expert knowledge of the Oriental rites and languages as consultors.[15]

In his encyclical letter "*Ex quo,*" of March 1, 1756,[16] Pope Benedict XIV (1740–1758) announced the completion of the Greek Manual or Ritual, upon which the *Congregatio super correctione Euchologii Graecorum* had commenced to labor a century earlier under Pope Urban VIII. Throughout this letter, in his solving of questions pertaining to rites, the pope made several references to the previous discussions and decrees on these points issued by the above Congregation under Pope Urban VIII, and likewise by the *Congregatio super correctione librorum Orientalium* within his own pontificate.[17] In this letter no mention is made of any decrees of this Congregation during the reigns of the intermediate popes. Monin covers this period of time by asserting that the activity of the Congregation gradually dimin-

[13] Petrani, *loc. cit.;* V. Martin, *Les Congrégations Romaines,* pp. 191–192.

[14] *Statistica,* p. 12.

[15] Pius IX, *loc. cit.;* Pius XI, motu proprio "De iurisdictione Sacrae Congregationis pro Ecclesia Orientali"—*Apollinaris,* XI (1938), 339; Staffa, *loc. cit.;* Petrani, *loc. cit.;* Monin, *De Curia Romana,* p. 71; V. Martin, *Les Congrégations Romaines,* p. 192.

[16] To the Archbishops, Bishops, and other Ecclesiastics both Secular and Regular of the Greek Rite in communion with the Apostolic See—*Fontes,* n. 438.

[17] *Fontes,* n. 438, § 9, § 34, § 38, § 43, § 46, § 58.

ished, but that Pope Benedict XIV renewed it and set it in order.[18] It was indeed active during his tenure of the supreme pontifical office.

Article II. The Contribution of Pope Pius IX [19]

There was no doubt about the loving, paternal solicitude of Pope Pius IX for the Orientals. In his intent to provide in a greater degree for their spiritual good he commissioned a number of cardinals of the Sacred Congregation *de Propaganda Fide* and some prelates of the Roman Curia to study their problems, and then to propose what should be undertaken for the promotion of their spiritual welfare. These cardinals and prelates realized how multiple and grave were the needs of the Orientals, and how necessary it was that in view of the variety of their languages, rites, and disciplines their affairs should receive special and more immediate and constant attention. On the other hand, they were cognizant of how great were the cares and occupations of the Sacred Congregation of the Propagation of the Faith as a result both of the admirable progress of the Faith, especially at the beginning of that century in North America, India, China, Oceania, and in places of Europe subject to the particular care of this same Sacred Congregation, and of the increase in the number of episcopal sees, Apostolic Vicariates, and Missions.

In the light of their deliberations they were convinced that the Sacred Congregation of the Propagation of the Faith needed added adaptations in order to be able without mounting difficulties to provide specifically for the affairs of the Orientals. Wherefore, reflecting on the procedure of the Sacred Congregation of forming special Congregations or Commissions for the handling of grave matters, they concluded that it would be wholly opportune for the end in view to institute a special, fixed Sacred Congregation which would administer solely and exclusively all the business—both of discipline and of rite (including the correction of liturgical books)—of the Oriental Church. They formulated a

[18] Monin, *De Curia Romana*, p. 71.

[19] This article is based on his Const. "*Romani Pontifices*," of January 16, 1862—*Fontes*, II, n. 531, pp. 946–953, except for the places which are clearly specified.

plan of drawing upon the Sacred Congregation *de Propaganda Fide* itself for the personnel of this new Sacred Congregation: the prefect of the general Sacred Congregation of the Propagation of the Faith would also be its prefect; cardinals likewise would be selected from the latter Sacred Congregation; the newly formed Sacred Congregation would have its own Secretary, Consultors, and Officials. The pope whole-heartedly approved this projected plan.

Hence, Pope Pius IX by means of the Constitution "*Romani Pontifices*," of January 6, 1862, instituted this Sacred Congregation, whose full title was *Sacra Congregatio de Propaganda Fide pro negotiis ritus orientalis,* as one section of the general Sacred Congregation of the Propagation of the Faith, and he decreed that thenceforth all the affairs which up to that time pertained to the *Congregatio de Propaganda Fide* were to be divided into two completely distinct classes: the affairs (*negotia*) of the Latin Rite, and the affairs of the Oriental rite. The latter would be expedited exclusively by this newly created section. Among these affairs were included also matters pertaining to the correction of the Oriental books, as Pope Pius IX expressly stated in this Constitution in suppressing and abolishing the former *Congregatio super correctione librorum Orientalium.* The so-called mixed business (*negotia mixta*)—matters which either by reason of object or person involved both the Oriental and the Latin Church—likewise was allocated to the jurisdiction of the Sacred Congregation *pro negotiis ritus orientalis,* unless the latter decided that it should be transmitted to a meeting of the general Sacred Congregation of the Propagation of the Faith.

What power did the newly formed Sacred Congregation possess over these matters? Its power was the same in extent as that of the vast competence bestowed previously upon the *Propaganda Fide* by Pope Gregory XV, and thereafter recognized and approved by his successors. Pope Pius IX expressly confirmed this. He stated that, since this new Sacred Congregation was a part of the *Congregatio de Propaganda Fide,* all the faculties and privileges attributed to the officials of the older Sacred Congregation by the preceding popes were conceded and imparted to the officials of the new Sacred Congregation. Therefore, at least in regard to matters of the external forum, it was only in the questions touching the *graviora negotia* that there was need of a specific recourse to the Holy Father on the part of this Sacred Congregation *pro negotiis ritus orientalis.*

Monin in referring to this matter contends that the word *omnia Orientalium negotia* in the Constitution "*Romani Pontifices*"[20] should not be accepted without any limitations, but rather that they refer only to those matters which concerned the rites or the discipline of the Orientals: for, in these alone the Orientals differed from the Latins. Wherefore, he continues, it seems that whatever pertained to doctrine was completely reserved to the Holy Office, although perhaps the supervision of the discipline to be used among the Orientals for protecting doctrine might be conceded to the Sacred Congregation for affairs of the Oriental Rite. Likewise, according to him, whatever concerned the internal forum seems to have belonged entirely to the Sacred Penitentiaria. In short, he maintains that all matters of the Orientals, even though they were mixed matters, with the exception of doctrinal questions and affairs of the internal forum, pertained to the Sacred Congregation *pro negotiis ritus orientalis.*[21]

In regard to doctrinal questions the powers of the Sacred Congregation *pro negotiis ritus orientalis* are analogous to the powers of the Sacred Congregation *de Propaganda Fide,* as previously stated.[22] When the Orientals sought a clarification of some doctrine, or presented a question which demanded such a clarification or an instruction or even a decree, such a matter was presented to the Holy See through the Sacred Congregation established for those very communications—at the beginning the *Congregatio de Propaganda Fide* was this Sacred Congregation; after January 6, 1862, it was the *Congregatio de Propaganda Fide pro negotiis ritus orientalis.* Once the matter reached the latter

---

[20] "Nova Congregatio a Nobis instituta omnia Orientalium negotia, etiamsi mixta, quae scilicet sive rei, sive personarum ratione Latinos attingant, tractare debebit, nisi eadem Congregatio negotia ipsa ad generalem Propagandae Fidei Congregationem deferenda esse interdum existimaverit."—*Fontes,* II, n. 531, pp. 949–950.

[21] Monin, *De Curia Romana,* p. 285.

[22] Cf. *supra,* pp. 36–38.

Sacred Congregation, there was only one limitation to its competency, namely, that the *graviora* had to be referred to the pope. The writer could find no source which placed doctrinal questions in this group. However, it is easily conceivable that some doctrinal questions might have been considered under the *graviora* classification. In that case when the matter was submitted to the pope, he could transfer it to the Holy Office, if he so willed. But if the question or matter under consideration was not such as to be classed *graviora*, the Sacred Congregation for affairs of the Oriental Rite could handle it, or else transfer it to the general Sacred Congregation of the Propagation of the Faith, or even to transfer it to another Sacred Congregation. Whether it had to obtain papal permission to transfer business to a Sacred Congregation other than the general Sacred Congregation of the Propagation of the Faith could not be determined, but it seems as though no such permission was necessary. Therefore, the Holy Office obtained such doctrinal questions of the Oriental Rite either from the pope or from the Sacred Congregation for affairs of the Oriental Rite. No written law obliged the latter Sacred Congregation to transfer its doctrinal questions to the Holy Office. But it was a prudent practise which the Sacred Congregation for affairs of the Oriental Rite did use at times.

The organization of the *Congregatio de Propaganda Fide pro negotiis ritus orientalis* was of a detailed character in its every aspect. The Cardinal Prefect of the Sacred Congregation of the Propagation of the Faith was always to hold that same position in the *Congregatio pro negotiis ritus orientalis.* Consequently Alessandro Cardinal Barnabo was the first to become the prefect of this Sacred Congregation.[23] The cardinals of the Sacred Congregation of the Propagation of the Faith chosen to serve in this newly established Sacred Congregation were: Constantino Patrizi,[24] Ludovico Altieri,[25] Camillo di Pietro,[26] Karl Reisach,[27]

[23] In the College of the Cardinals the new prefect was a cardinal-priest.

[24] "Episcopus Portuensis et S. Rufinae;" therefore, a cardinal-bishop.

[25] "Episcopus Albanensis;" a cardinal-bishop.

[26] "S. Ioannis ante Portam Latinam;" a cardinal-priest.

[27] "S. Cæciliæ;" a cardinal-priest.

Antonio M. Panebianco,[28] Pietro Marini,[29] Giacomo Antonelli,[30] Prospero Caterini.[31] The Cardinal *ponens* named by the pope was Karl Cardinal Reisach—this office was a remnant of the abolished *Congregatio super correctione librorum Orientalium:* the reigning pope was always to appoint a Cardinal *ponens* in this Sacred Congregation, who was to promote the studies which were necessary for collecting the canons of the Oriental Church and for examining, when there was need of it, Oriental books of every kind, whether these dealt with the versions of the Holy Bible, or the catechism, or matters of discipline. Thus the work of the former Sacred Congregation in these matters was neither discarded nor neglected nor minimized in any way whatsoever, but carefully directed by the Cardinal *ponens.*

The Sacred Congregation, moreover, had its own secretary, a secretariate of its own officials, and also its own consultors. The secretary, who was Giovanni Simeoni (an Apostolic Prothonotary), was to exercise his duties in exactly the same way as the secretary for the Latin Rite.[32] Both in the conduct of the business of the Oriental Rite and in the holding of meetings in the new Sacred Congregation he was to follow the same method as that which was used by the Sacred Congregation of the Propagation of the Faith. In order that the secretary of each Sacred Congregation might properly know all the business both of the Latin and of the Oriental Rites, both secretaries were to be present at the meetings of each other's Sacred Congregation; however, the secretary of the general Sacred Congregation of the Propagation of the Faith by reason of his office had precedence over the secretary of the Sacred Congregation *pro negotiis ritus orientalis.* Likewise, since a mutual correlation sometimes obtained between the business of the Sacred Congregation of the Latin Rite and that

28 "SS. XII Apostolorum;" a cardinal-priest.

29 "S. Nicolai in Carcere Tulliano;" a cardinal-deacon.

30 "S. Agathae ad Suburram;" a cardinal-deacon.

31 "S. Mariae de Scala;" a cardinal-deacon.

32 The secretary for the Latin Rite was also known as the secretary of the general Sacred Congregation of the Propagation of the Faith; for, according to Monin: "Haec S. Congregatio de Propaganda Fide pro Negotiis Ritus Latini saepius dicitur S. C. de Propaganda Fide sine addito; vel etiam Congregatio Generalis de Prop. Fide." *De Curia Romana,* p. 275, footnote 1.

of the Oriental Rite, the secretary of each Sacred Congregation was a Consultor of the other Sacred Congregation. In addition to its own secretary, the Sacred Congregation *pro negotiis ritus orientalis* had its own officials in the secretariate; they were to be in sufficient numbers to carry out their assignments.

Just as every Sacred Roman Congregation retained consultors, who carefully studied the graver and more difficult matters, and then submitted an exposition of them with counsel and judgment to the prudent and wise examination of the cardinals, so also this Sacred Congregation employed them in study of the idioms in the Oriental languages and especially of the variety of the rites. Knowledge regarding these factors was decidedly important for the rendering of an accurate judgment and opportune counsel. The consultors employed by the Sacred Congregation were to be versed not only in theology, but also in other Oriental matters concerning which knowledge would prove useful and helpful to the cardinals. In the beginning, in order that such men might serve within the membership of the Sacred Congregation, Pope Pius IX brought to Rome a number of ecclesiastics known for their proficiency in the knowledge of Oriental rites, laws and customs. But, in order to make circumspect provision for the future, two proposals were offered: (a) Alessandro Cardinal Barnabo suggested that a certain number of ecclesiastics, chosen from those who had attended the Urban College or from the members of various Religious Institutes (*Familiis*), should come to Rome and designedly direct all their studies towards this end; and (b) it was the wish of Pope Pius IX that some of the junior Roman Clergy, who had completed *cum laude* their course of studies, and likewise gave good promise for the future, should apply themselves assiduously to the studies of ecclesiastical Oriental matters under the guidance of some consultor, so that in time they themselves could assume the duties of consultors. In the meantime in the first group of consultors were named: Most Rev. Alessandro Franchi, Archbishop of Thessalonica and secretary of the Sacred Congregation for Extraordinary Ecclesiastical Affairs; Bishop Giuseppe Cardoni; Luigi Ferrari, prefect of pontifical ceremonies; Dominico Bartolini, secretary of the Sacred Congregation of Sacred Rites; Joseph Fessler, professor of Canon

Law at the University of Vienna in Austria; Bonifacius Haneberg, O.S.B., abbot of the monastery of St. Boniface and professor of Sacred Scripture at the University of Munich; Luigi Vincenzi, professor of the Hebrew language at the Roman University; Paolo Scapaticci, professor of the Syro-Chaldaic language at the Roman University; Filippo De Angelis, professor of Canon Law at the Roman University; Carlo Vercellone, General Procurator of the Congregation CC. RR. of Clerks Regular of Saints Paul and Barnabas, Apostles; Johannes B. Franzelin, S.J., professor of Sacred Theology in the Roman College; Augustin Theiner, priest of the Oratory of St. Philip Neri; and three members of the Benedictine Order: Jean Baptiste Pitra, Pius Zingerle, Bernard Smith.

Finally, the Sacred Congregation *pro negotiis ritus orientalis* was to use the same seal, the same archives and the same printing press as the *Congregatio de Propaganda Fide.*

A new arrangement for the cardinals was to be employed by the Sacred Congregation *pro negotiis ritus orientalis.* The cardinals were to divide among themselves the proper business of each nation of the Orientals. This division was to be so effected that each cardinal would have under his control in a fixed manner the affairs of one or of several Oriental nations according as allotted in the partition. His position naturally included the work of a Cardinal *relator,* whose duty it was to inform the Sacred Congregation accurately about the affairs placed in his charge when such information was desired. Possible eventualities were foreseen, for in case a cardinal could perform his task no longer, the cardinals who were present at the meeting of the Sacred Congregation were to enjoy the right of option (*optionis iure*). Thus, every Oriental nation had a cardinal *relator* at the Sacred Congregation.

The jurisdiction of this Sacred Congregation, as previously stated, regarded the affairs of the Oriental rites, i. e., the affairs of the Greek, Armenian, Syrian, and Coptic rites.[33] These prin-

[33] This division is based upon Pope Benedict XIV's Constitution "*Allatae sunt,*" of July 26, 1755—*Fontes,* n. 434, § 3: "Orientalem autem Ecclesiam omnibus notum est quatuor ritibus constare, graeco videlicet, armeno, syriaco et coptico, qui sane ritus universi sub uno nomine Ecclesiae Graecae aut

cipal Oriental rites at that time were subdivided as follows according to the data furnished by the *Annuario Pontificio* of 1864: [34] (a) Greek rite: Greek Ruthenian, Greek Slavonic-Ruthenian, Greek Melkite, Greek Bulgarian; (b) the Armenian rite had no subdivisions; (c) Syrian rite: Syrian (pure), Syro-Chaldean, Syro-Maronite; (d) Coptic rite: Copto-Egyptian, and Copto-Ethiopian or Abyssinian. The *Annuario Pontificio* of 1864 also contains the following interesting facts concerning these rites:

Ecclesiastical Provinces of the Oriental Rite [35]

Europe

Armenian Rite

Ecclesiastical Province	Archi-episcopal See	Suffragan Episcopal Sees
Lwów or Lemberg (Galicia, Poland)	Lwów or Lemberg	

Orientalis intelliguntur, non secus ac sub Ecclesiae Latinae Romanae nomine, ritus Romanus, Ambrosianus, Mozarabicus, et varii peculiares ritus Ordinum Regularium comprehenduntur." Cicognani (*Canon Law* [2. ed., authorized English version by J. O'Hara and F. Brennan, Philadelphia: Dolphin Press, 1935], p. 446) states: "There are five original rites used by the Oriental Churches: the Alexandrian, Antiochene or Syrian, Armenian, Byzantine or Greek, and the Chaldean or Syro-Chaldean. The Copti or Egyptian, and the Ethiopian or Abyssinian rites (celebrated in the Geez language) are derived from the Alexandrine rite. . . . The subdivisions of the Chaldean rite are, the Chaldean (pure) or simple Chaldean and Malabar Rites." Cf. also *Statistica*, p. 29. This Chaldean rite is listed under the Syrian rite in the above four-fold division, so that all the rites are accounted for in both divisions, though in different ways.

[34] The *Annuario Pontificio* (Roma: Typografia Poliglotta Vaticana, 1912–) was entitled *Notizie* from 1716(?)–1858; *Annuario Pontificio* from 1860–1871; *La Gerarchia Cattolica* from 1872–1911; and again *Annuario Pontificio* from 1912 on. None was published for 1813–14, 1848–1850, 1859(?).

[35] The cities as here listed are associated with cities of the name given in accordance with the geographical boundaries as they existed in 1936. The geographical location of these cities under their Latin names can be found in Streit, *Atlas Hierarchicus* (Paderbonae in Guestfalia: Sumptibus Typographiae Bonifacianae, 1913), No. 34. Those who wish to associate these cities with their proper countries in 1864, cf. *Annuario Pontificio* for the year 1864, pp. 53–55, and pp. 111–226.

Greek Ruthenian Rite

Fogaras or "Alba Giulia" (Transylvania, Hungary)	Fogaras or "Alba Giulia"	Szamos—Ujvar, (Transylvania, Hungary), Nagy Várad or Grosswardein (Rumania), Lugos (Rumania)

Greek Slavonic Ruthenian Rite

Lwów or Lemberg	Lwów or Lemberg (Galicia, Poland), Halicz, Kiev, and Kamenets (all in Russia)	Przemysl, Sanechia, Samboria—all in Galicia, Poland; Nagy-Körös or Krizevac (Hungary), Eperies (Czechoslovakia), Munkacs (Czechoslovakia), the suffragan sees of Esztergom (Hungary)

Oriental Patriarchates

Distinguished according to the National rites

Armenian Rite

Patriarchate — Cilicia.
Archi-episcopates — Adana or Seyhan (Turkey), Alep or Aleppo (Syria), Alexandria (Egypt), Cæsarea (Cappadocia), Diarbekir (Turkey), Jerusalem (Palestine), Marash (Turkey), Mardin (Turkey), Melitene (Turkey), Tokat (Turkey), Sebaste (Turkey).
Primatial Archi-episcopate—Constantinople.
Episcopates — Ankara (Turkey), Artvin (Turkey), Brusa or Bursa (Turkey), Erzerum or Erzurum (Turkey) Trebizond or Trabson (Turkey), Ispahan or Isfahan (Iran)—provisionally a suffragan see.

Copto-Egyptian Rite

The Catholics of this rite did not have an established hierarchy, and were dependent upon the Vicar Apostolic of Egypt of this same rite.

Copto-Ethiopian or Abyssinian Rite

There was not an established hierarchy among these Catholics; they were under the jurisdiction of a Latin Vicar Apostolic who resided in Abyssinia, and of another Latin Vicar Apostolic residing among the Gallas.

Greek Rite

Greek Melchite (Melkite)

Patriarchate — Antioch
Archi-episcopates—Damascus (Syria), Homs and Hama (Syria), Tyre (Phœnicia).
Episcopates — Aleppo (Syria), Beirut (Syria), Bosra (Phœnicia), Baalbek (Syria), Zahle (Syria), Jerusalem (Palestine), Hauran (Syria), Sidon (Syria).

Greek Bulgarian Rite

The Catholics of this rite did not have a constituted hierarchy, and were confided to the care of the Latin Vicars Apostolic of the places where these Catholics were found.

Syrian Rite

Syrian

Patriarchate — Antioch
Archi-episcopates—Baghdad (Iraq), Damascus or Damas (Syria), Diabekr or Diyarbekir (Turkey).
Episcopates — Aleppo (Syria), Alexandria (Egypt), Beirut or Beyrouth (Syria), Homs and Hama (Syria), Keriatim (Syria), Madiat or Midyat (Turkey), Mardin (Turkey), Mosul (Iraq).

Syro-Chaldean

Patriarchate — Baghdad (Iraq)

Archi-episcopates—Amadia (Iraq), Diarbekir or Diyarbekir (Turkey).

Episcopates — Gezira (Iraq), Kerkuk or Kirkuk (Iraq), Mardin (Turkey), Mosul (Iraq), Salmas or Chosrawa (Iran), Sert or Siirt (Turkey).

Syro-Maronites

Patriarchate — Antioch

Archi-episcopates—Damascus or Damas (Syria).

Episcopates — Alep or Aleppo (Syria), Beirut (Syria), Cyprus (island), Baalbek (Syria), Gebail and Batrum or Batroun (Syria), Tripoli (Syria).

Article III. A New Commission

The Sacred Congregation for affairs of the Oriental Rite maintained its constitution during the reign of Pope Leo XIII (1878–1903). However, the latter, in addition to his legislation for Catholics of the Oriental Rite, provided a new group for a more far-reaching consideration of ways and means to promote the reunion of the separated brethren of the Orthodox Church when he instituted on March 19, 1895, a pontifical Commission for fostering the reconciliation of dissidents with the Church. The purpose of this Commission was the reconciliation of those nations which had fallen away from the Church through schism or heresy. Thus, the "dissidents" in the title do not refer exclusively to Oriental schismatics and heretics. But, as it happened, the dissidents of the Oriental Church were their first care. The pope himself presided over the meetings which were held on set days. The cardinals who composed this Commission were: Mieczyslaw Ledochowski, who was at that time prefect of the Sacred Congregation *de Propaganda Fide pro negotiis ritus orientalis;* Benoît M. Langénieux; Mariano Rampolla del Tindaro, who was secretary for the Sacred Congregation *pro negotiis ritus orientalis* from 1877–1880; Vincenzo Vannutelli; Luigi Galimberti; Herbert Vaughan; Giuseppe M. Granniello; Camillo Mazzella. There were also a convenient number of consultors, who employed their knowledge and prudence to draw up the cases which were submitted to the deliberation of the pontiff and the cardinals. The Catholic Oriental Patriarchs' legates at Rome also were regarded as consultors of this Commission. The pope designated the consultor in each case, and the selected one was present *ex officio* at the pontifical congresses.[36]

Article IV. The Constitution "Sapienti consilio"

When Pope Pius X (1903–1914) reformed the Roman Curia in 1908,[37] the *S. C. de Propaganda Fide pro negotiis ritus orientalis*[38] remained united[39] with the *Congregatio de Propaganda Fide.* But, whereas the latter was limited somewhat in its powers by the provisions of the Constitution "*Sapienti consilio,*" I, 6°, 4–5,[40]

[36] *Leonis XIII Pontificis Maximi Acta* (23 vols., Romae: Ex Typographia Vaticana, 1881–1905), XV, 80–82.

[37] Constitution "*Sapienti consilio,*" of June 29, 1908—*Fontes,* n. 682.

[38] Referred to as the Sacred Congregation "*pro Negotiis rituum orientalium*"—*Fontes,* n. 682, I, 6°, 6.

[39] *Loc. cit.*: "[*Congregatio de Propaganda Fide*] Unitam habet Congregationem pro Negotiis rituum orientalium, cui integra manent quae huc usque servata sunt." This latter Sacred Congregation, though it alone administered the affairs of the Oriental rite since 1862, was always united to the Sacred Congregation of the Propagation of the Faith as a part or section of it with specific, distinct work. The Constitution "*Sapienti consilio*" merely confirmed that position for the Sacred Congregation *pro negotiis ritus orientalis.*

[40] "In this Constitution ["*Sapienti consilio*"] it is set forth that the *Congregatio de Propaganda Fide* is not, even within its territory, to transact business which relates to faith, or matrimony, or to the discipline of the sacred rites. Whenever such questions are proposed by any one [anyone] subject to the Propaganda, this Congregation must hand them over for settlement to the proper Congregation."—M. Martin, *The Roman Curia,* p. 71. Cf. also *Fontes,* n. 682. M. Martin continues: "Matters concerning doctrine are to be transmitted to the Holy Office; matters regarding matrimony are to be referred to the Congregation on the Sacraments; and questions relating to the sacred rites are to be answered by the Congregation of Rites according to its competence." That was true as a general rule, but it must be remembered that not all matters of matrimony were to be submitted to the Sacred Congregation of the Discipline of the Sacraments, for those that concerned the Pauline Privilege, the impediments of disparity of cult and mixed religion, and the dogmatic questions on matrimony were to be submitted to the S. C. of the Holy Office according to the Constitution. Also, what related to discipline in Religious Institutes, including studies,

the former was untouched by those provisions. That the circumscriptions applied only to the Sacred Congregation *de Propaganda Fide* in relation to the Latin Rite and not to the Sacred Congregation for affairs of the Oriental Rite is apparent, for immediately following the paragraphs in which the restrictions were imposed upon the *Congregatio de Propaganda Fide,* the Constitution stated that united to the latter was the Sacred Congregation *pro Negotiis rituum orientalium,*[41] *cui integra manent quae huc usque servata sunt;"*[42] and up to that time the latter still possessed the vast powers conferred by Pope Pius IX. Therefore, it was to continue to attend to affairs of the Oriental Rite as it had done hitherto. This was also confirmed in the "*Normae Peculiares*"[43] which, though issued three months later,[44] were given in conjunction with the Constitution "*Sapienti consilio.*" Therein it was reaffirmed that this Sacred Congregation would keep its functions "*ex integro*";[45] but it would adhere to the general and specific norms given in respect to the internal discipline of the Sacred Congregations and the way of treating affairs within their jurisdiction.[46]

---

promotion to Sacred Orders, etc., had to be referred to the Sacred Congregation for Affairs of Religious. Cf. M. Martin, *The Roman Curia,* p. 72; *Fontes,* n. 682.

[41] Let it be noted that the Constitution "*Sapienti consilio*" here uses the plural "rituum orientalium," but the "*Normae Peculiares*" retains the singular form "*ritus orientalis.*" The title according to Pope Pius IX's Constitution "*Romani Pontifices,*" of January 6, 1862, was in the singular form. Cf. *supra,* p. 53.

[42] Italics ours.

[43] Simier, *La Curie Romaine,* pp. 240-264, and esp. p. 258, Art. VI, § 4; *AAS,* I (1909), 59-108, esp. 97-98; Ojetti, *De Romana Curia,* pp. LIX-XCI, and esp. p. LXXXIV.

All references in this work to "*Normal Communes*" and "*Normae Peculiares*" refer to these norms as associated with the Constitution "*Sapienti consilio.*"

[44] Simier, *op. cit.,* p. 264; *AAS,* I (1909), 108; Ojetti, *op. cit.,* p. XCI.

[45] At least "*ratione materiae.*" Cf. Monin, *De Curia Romana,* p. 285, footnote 3.

[46] "Congregatio de Propaganda Fide pro Negotiis ritus orientalis sua munia ex integro servabit. In iis tamen, quae internam Officii disciplinam et modum tractandi negotia spectant, huius legis normis sive communibus

The non-limitation of the powers of the Sacred Congregation for affairs of the Oriental Rite as distinct from the limitation of the powers of the *Congregatio de Propaganda Fide* by the provisions of the Constitution "*Sapienti consilio,*" I, 6°, 4–5, is not expressly indicated by authors in commenting on this Constitution; Monin, however, does make such a distinction.[47] A decree of the *S. C. de Propaganda Fide pro negotiis ritus orientalis* of August 6, 1909, contained the pope's direction that the Constitutions of the Mechitharist Armenian Monks should be submitted after six years to the Sacred Congregation for affairs of the Oriental Rite to obtain their perpetual confirmation. Rightly did Cappello in commenting on this decree conclude that this Sacred Congregation underwent no change in regard to these matters.[48] But if the limitations of the *Propaganda Fide* provided by the Constitution "*Sapienti consilio,*" I, 6°, 4–5, had applied also to the Sacred Congregation *pro negotiis ritus orientalis,* the above mentioned case would have been referred to the Sacred Congregation for Affairs of Religious. Just as the Sacred Congregation for affairs of the Oriental Rite was not limited in this matter, so also it was not limited in affairs of faith and matrimony. It is recalled that this Sacred Congregation as part of the Sacred Congregation *de Propaganda Fide* formerly employed the practice of sending matters of faith to the Sacred Congregation of the Holy Office; however, this was not because its jurisdiction in such problems at that time was restricted, but rather because it chose to proceed in that fashion.[49] If after the

sive peculiaribus inhaerebit."—*AAS,* I (1909), 97–98; Ojetti, *op. cit.,* p. LXXXIV; Simier, *op. cit.,* p. 258, Art. VI, § 4.

[47] Monin, *De Curia Romana,* pp. 285–287. De Smet (*De Sponsalibus et Matrimonio Tractatus Canonicus et Theologicus* [Brugis: Car. Beyaert, 1909], pp. 433, footnote 5, and 435) applies this distinction to matrimonial dispensations.

[48] Cappello, *De Curia Romana* (2 vols., Romae, Ratisbonae, Neo-Eboraci, Cincinnati: Fridericus Pustet, 1911–1912), I, 156. But, on the other hand, Cappello restricted the powers of the Sacred Congregation for affairs of the Oriental Rite in regard to matrimonial cases—cf. *infra,* pp. 66–67.

[49] "When questions of doctrine were proposed to the *Propaganda* for solution, it was the general practice of this Congregation to refer them to the Holy Office. There was not, however, any obligation of this kind im-

Constitution "*Sapienti consilio,*" the Sacred Congregation *pro negotiis ritus orientalis* still continued in that practice in regard to those matters, it likewise was not due to the lack of jurisdiction. Furthermore, had Pope Pius X desired to limit the faculties in this regard, he would have done so in just as explicit a manner as Pope Benedict XV was to do in 1917 in order to denote a change in the jurisdiction of the Sacred Congregation when he established the Sacred Congregation for the Oriental Church.

Hence, the writer takes exception to Cappello's answer to the question as to which Sacred Congregation ought to consider the matrimonial and ecclesiastical cases of the Orientals. Cappello traced the reason for the doubt to Pope Leo XIII's Constitution "*Orientalium dignitas Ecclesiarum,*" in which the pope decreed:

> Matrimoniales et ecclesiasticae, quaecumque sint causae, de quibus ad Apostolicam Sedem appellatio fiat, nequaquam Delegatis Apostolicis definiendae, nisi aperte ea iusserit committantur, sed ad sacrum Consilium christiano nomini propagando omnino deferantur.

Of course, it is understood that the pope meant the *S. C. de Propaganda Fide pro negotiis ritus orientalis,* which at that time was a separate part of the Sacred Congregation *de Propaganda Fide* (the "*Consilium christiano nomini propagando*"). Cappello, however, did not make this distinction, for he based his solution upon the declaration of the Constitution "*Sapienti consilio*" that the cases which regarded faith, matrimony, and the discipline of the rites had to be referred to the proper particular Sacred Congregations by the Sacred Congregation *de Propaganda Fide* whenever it received such matters. Hence, he concluded that the cases which regarded matrimony—with the exception of the dispensation from the impediment of disparity of cult and mixed religion, which could be given by the Sacred Congregation for affairs of the Oriental Rite; and also with the exception of cases which concerned the Pauline Privilege, because this pertained to the Holy Office—were to be remitted to the Sacred Congregation

posed upon the *Propaganda* Congregation, since no prohibition was issued to prevent it from giving a decision on doctrinal matters."—M. Martin, *The Roman Curia,* pp. 70–71.

of the Discipline of the Sacraments for solution in a disciplinary way (*in via disciplinari*), and to the Sacred Rota for judiciary solutions (*in via contentiosa*).[50] Concerning the solutions *in via disciplinari* the writer re-asserts that while this may have been the practice, it was not the law, and therefore there was no obligation to remit such cases to the Sacred Congregation of the Discipline of the Sacraments according to the Constitution "*Sapienti consilio.*"

Monin states, in support of this view, that the *Congregatio pro negotiis ritus orientalis* replaced the Sacred Congregation of the Discipline of the Sacraments in matters pertaining to matrimony which were to be adjudged *in via disciplinari.*[51] In defending his assertion that the restrictions in the Constitution "*Sapienti consilio,*" I, 6°, 4,[52] did not pertain to the Sacred Congregation for affairs of the Oriental Rite, he adds the following arguments. If the text in question (I, 6°, 4) were to be applied to matrimonial cases of the Orientals, *a pari* it would apply to problems which would arise concerning their rites; hence, accordingly, questions about the rites of Orientals would have to be remitted to the Sacred Congregation of Sacred Rites: and such a conclusion is obviously contrary both (a) to the mind of Pope Pius IX in instituting the special Sacred Congregation *pro negotiis ritus orientalis;*[53] and (b) to the express words of this very Constitution of Pope Pius X restricting the jurisdiction of the Sacred Congregation of Sacred Rites to the sacred rites and ceremonies of the Latin Church.[54] Besides, he adds the reason for this restriction in the Sacred Congregation *de Propaganda Fide,*

---

[50] Cappello, *De Curia Romana,* I, p. 247, quaest. VI.

[51] *De Curia Romana*, pp. 285-286, and 287, footnote 1.

[52] *Fontes,* n. 682; Simier, *La Curie Romaine,* p. 208; Ojetti, *De Romana Curia,* p. XV; *AAS,* I (1909), 12: "Nihilominus, ut unitati regiminis consulatur, volumus ut Congregatio de Propaganda Fide ad peculiares alias Congregationes deferat quaecumque aut fidem attingunt, aut matrimonium aut sacrorum rituum disciplinam."

[53] Cf. *supra,* p. 53; Constitution "*Romani Pontifices,*" of January 6, 1862—*Fontes,* n. 531.

[54] Constitution, "*Sapienti consilio,*" I, 8°, 1—*Fontes,* n. 682; Simier, *La Curie Romaine,* p. 208; Ojetti, *De Romana Curia,* p. XVI; *AAS,* I (1909), 13.

namely, "*ut unitati regiminis consulatur,*" is indeed valid if it concerned the marriage of Latins because their marriages both in territories under the common law of the Church and in missionary lands were subject to the same laws; the Orientals, on the other hand, had special matrimonial laws.[55] Therefore, he holds that the matrimonial cases of the Oriental rites which were to be treated in an administrative, disciplinary manner (*causae non contentiosae* in his terminology) belonged to the Sacred Congregation for affairs of the Oriental Rite, and this also in mixed marriages; but, whenever the Pauline Privilege was to be applied, the Holy Office alone was competent.[56] It may also be noted here that according to his view the matrimonial cases of Orientals which were to be judged in a strictly judicial manner (*causae contentiose tractandae*) were to be sent to the Sacred Rota.[57]

The following considerations are helpful to appreciate fully Monin's view on the jurisdiction of the Sacred Congregation for affairs of the Oriental Rite and the Sacred Rota in regard to matters of the Oriental Rite. These considerations are all the more important because they also form a background for the law of the Code of Canon Law. The Constitution "*Sapienti consilio*" makes a distinction between the administrative and judicial or contentious (*contentiosa*) powers of the dicasteries of the Roman Curia, but it does not give a definite, fixed and clear norm on which to base that distinction.[58] For a clearer notion of these two powers in regard to the Sacred Congregations it is useful to review the chief difference between a judge and a public administrator. Both the judge and the public administrator are executors of laws, but with this difference that the former executes the law by judging (*iudicando*) and the latter by doing or acting (*faciendo seu agendo*). The end sought by the judge

[55] Monin, *De Curia Romana*, pp. 286–287.

[56] The fact that the Sacred Congregation for affairs of the Oriental Rite was to refer the application of dispensations for the Pauline Privilege to the Sacred Congregation of the Holy Office was announced in a response of the Sacred Consistorial Congregation on November 1, 1908. Cf. *infra*, p. 77 and footnote 91.

[57] Monin, *De Curia Romana*, p. 287, footnote 1. Cf. also Cappello, *De Curia Romana*, I, p. 247, quaest. VI.

[58] Wernz-Vidal, *Ius Canonicum*, II (1943), n. 487, p. 569.

is the observance of the law; the end sought by the public administrator is the public welfare or utility. The judge settles conflicts which arise between citizens in the exercise of a disputed right; the public administrator removes obstacles which may arise in the observance of laws, that is, either he prevents them from arising through the use of preventive remedies, or he promotes the activity of the citizens in one way or another. In other words, both procure the execution of the laws and the social end: the one by protecting the rights of the people, the other by procuring their welfare or utility.[59]

In ecclesiastical law the pope and the bishops act in both capacities, i. e., as judges and as administrators. But if the organs through which the Supreme Pontiff exercises his jurisdiction are considered, or if the superiors of the bishops are considered, there is a distinction between the judicial and administrative powers according to the Constitution "*Sapienti consilio.*" The Sacred Rota and the Apostolic Signatura, Tribunals of the Roman Curia, exercise the judicial power in the name of the pope, while the Sacred Congregations of the Curia exercise the administrative power with papal authority; the superiors of the bishop as a judge are the Metropolitan and the above named Tribunals of the Curia, but the Sacred Congregations alone are the superiors of a bishop as an administrator.[60]

The norm for judging which cases are to be referred to the Tribunals and which to the Sacred Congregations is resolved into two different opinions. On the one hand according to Ojetti the causes which concern some right (*aliquod ius*) are to be referred to the judge and therefore to the bishop or to the Tribunals; those which touch merely the welfare (*interesse*) pertain to the administrator, and therefore are to be proposed either to the bishop or to the Sacred Congregations.[61] Thus he seems to conclude that the Sacred Congregations are differentiated from the tribunals not only by reason of the different way in which they treat matters, but also and principally by reason of the different nature of the matters involved. In other words, the distinction

[59] Ojetti, *De Romana Curia,* p. 20.

[60] Ojetti, *De Romana Curia,* p. 23; Monin, *De Curia Romana,* p. 179.

[61] Ojetti, *De Romana Curia,* n. 13, pp. 23–24; Monin, *loc. cit.*

between the judicial and administrative orders lies in this that matters which concern some right always ought to be treated in a judicial way (*via iudiciaria*) and by the Tribunals; while matters which pertain to the mere welfare always are to be treated in a disciplinary manner (*in linea disciplinari*) and by the Sacred Congregations.[62]

On the other hand, Cappello proposes an altogether different criterion to distinguish the jurisdiction of the Sacred Congregations from the jurisdiction of the Tribunals, namely, that the quality or kind of procedure, and not the nature of the matters, principally must be attended to so that matters which are considered in a strictly judicial manner (*in via iudiciaria seu contentiosa*)[63] are deferred to the Tribunals, and those which are considered in an administrative disciplinary manner (*in linea disciplinari*)[64] are remitted to the Sacred Congregations.[65] Cappello also notes that the administrative power is closely associated with the power of deciding judicial controversies of the same order (*eiusdem ordinis*), because each is a part of the executive power. Sometimes it is very difficult, in fact impossible, to solve an administrative affair without deciding at the same time the controversies themselves.[66] Whence it follows that it is not

---

[62] Ojetti, *loc. cit.;* Monin, *De Curia Romana,* p. 181; Cappello, *De Curia Romana,* I, 48.

[63] Cappello (*De Curia Romana,* I, 49) defines contentious jurisdiction (*iurisdictio contentiosa*) as follows: "Est illa, ut communiter docent Canonistae, quae exercetur etiam in invitos v. gr. in ius vocando, puniendo, et alia huiusmodi exercendo, quae expediri non possunt nisi iudice pro tribunali sedente, seu quando inter duos pluresque contenditur."

[64] "Causae vero quae *in linea disciplinari* aguntur, sunt quae arcte sese referunt ad exsecutionem alicuius legis disciplinaris, licet ius privatum attingant, quaeque pertractantur *sine contestatione litigiosa et sine iuris solemnitatibus determinatis.*"—Cappello (*De Curia Romana,* I, 50). Cf. also Wernz-Vidal, *Ius Canonicum,* II (1943), n. 487 III, p. 572. The "*Normae Peculiares*" (cap. III, art. II, n. 7) state: "In causis aqud sacras Congregationes administrationis ac disciplinae tramite agitandis, remota litis contestatione, exclusa auditione testium nullisque scriptis patronorum receptis habebitur quaestio; audientur tamen semper partes quorum interest, ab iisque producta documenta excutientur."

[65] Cappello, *De Curia Romana,* I, 48–53; Monin, *De Curia Romana,* p. 181.

[66] Cappello, *De Curia Romana,* I, 49; Monin, *De Curia Romana,* p. 182.

repugnant that one should define even controverted rights through the use of administrative power. It is true that the public administrator does not use the formal procedure of a judgment, but he investigates only the truth of the fact, and terminates the matter "*sine contestatione litigiosa partium et sine iuris solemnitatibus*"; i. e., he defines the controverted right *in linea disciplinari.*[67] Therefore, Cappello contends that the Sacred Congregations could handle all kinds of cases whether they concern a strict right or merely the welfare of the parties, provided they were treated in an administrative, disciplinary manner.[68]

The practical difference between these two opinions is evident. Both Cappello and Ojetti agree that matters which concern only the welfare (*quoddam interesse*) do not admit a strictly judicial process, and thus are to be sent exclusively to the Sacred Congregations. But as to matters regarding some controverted right Cappello thinks that they can be decided sometimes in a disciplinary manner and sometimes in a strictly judicial manner, and accordingly they should be sent respectively to the Sacred Congregations and to the Tribunals; thus he differs from Ojetti who is of the opinion that such matters are to be sent exclusively to the Tribunals. Both admit that all cases regarding a right *can* be sent to the Tribunals since all cases of this kind admit a strictly judicial process. Cappello, however, completely disagrees with Ojetti when the latter contends that all cases concerning a right *must* be proposed to the Tribunals.[69]

Cappello[70] demonstrates that his opinion is in accord with the various texts of the Constitution "*Sapienti consilio,*" "*Lex propria Sacrae Romanae Rotae et Signaturae Apostolicae,*"[71] and the "*Normae Peculiares.*" The writer agrees with Monin on the following two of Cappello's arguments as most convincing:[72] (a) In the "*Normae Peculiares,*" cap. III, art. II, n. 10, it is

[67] Monin, *loc. cit.*

[68] Monin, *loc. cit.;* Cappello, *De Curia Romana,* I, 51, 53.

[69] Monin, *De Curia Romana,* p. 182.

[70] *De Curia Romana,* I, 51–53.

[71] Issued in conjunction with the Constitution "*Sapienti consilio.*" Cf. *AAS,* I (1907), 20-36; Ojetti, *De Romana Curia,* pp. XXIII–XLIII.

[72] Monin, *De Curia Romana,* p. 183–184.

written that when a case has once been introduced in some Sacred Congregation to be treated by way of administration and discipline (*administrationis et disciplinae tramite*), and the latter way of defining the case has been accepted or at least has not been refused by the parties, it is no longer permitted the parties to institute a strictly judicial trial concerning this same case. Yet the Sacred Congregation has the faculty to defer the cause to the ordinary judges at any time during its consideration of the question.[73] Thus this principle is obvious, namely, that at least from the consent or tolerance of the parties a cause which *per se* could be treated *ordine iudiciario* can be treated *in linea disciplinari.*[74] The above clearly has reference to matters which could be deferred to the Tribunals, and therefore refers to matters which concern a right. But, as Cappello rightly states,[75] if the Sacred Congregations are incompetent in regard to causes which concern a right, the parties could not have proposed them before the Sacred Congregations, nor could the Sacred Congregations have accepted them; while on the other hand the "*Normae Peculiares*" clearly state that once the disciplinary manner of proceeding has been accepted or at least not refused by the parties, the strict judicial procedure cannot be exacted by them. Whence judicial competence is based not on the nature of the case, but on a procedural way of treating it.

(b) Towards the end of the Constitution "*Sapienti consilio*" the following rule appears: all sentences, whether of favor or justice, need papal approbation, with the exception of: (1) those for which special faculties have been conceded to the moderators of those Offices, Tribunals, and Sacred Congregations; and (2) the sentences of the Sacred Rota and Apostolic Signatura which

---

[73] "Quaestione semel instituta penes Congregationem aliquam administrationis ac disciplinae tramite, et a partibus admisso aut saltem non recusato hoc agendi modo, his iam non licet eadem de causa actionem stricte iudicialem institutere.

Eoque minus, deliberata re atque ad sententiam deducta, fas erit hoc agere. Est nihilominus Congregationi sacrae facultas, quovis in stadio quaestionis, ad iudices ordinarios causam deferre."—*AAS,* I, 65; Ojetti, *De Romana Curia,* p. LXIII.

[74] Wernz-Vidal, *Ius Canonicum,* II (1943), n. 487, p. 570.

[75] *De Curia Romana,* I, 51.

are given within their jurisdiction.[76] Without doubt these words are decisive. For, as Cappello remarks,[77] it decrees explicitly that all sentences whatsoever either of favor or of justice need pontifical approbation, the sentences of the Sacred Rota and Apostolic Signatura always excepted. These words show that other Offices and Sacred Congregations also are able to give not only sentences of favor, but also sentences of justice; otherwise, this precept of the pope would be useless, not to say absurd. What, then, is said to be a sentence of justice? That which regards not merely the welfare, but directly and immediately touches the right itself. Therefore, not only administrative matters, but also affairs concerning rights can be deferred to the Sacred Congregations in order to be treated in a disciplinary manner, i. e., *ordine iudiciario non servato.*

In truth, it is not to be denied that the nature of the case is considered in determining the way in which it is to be treated, but it is not to be admitted that this consideration is so decisive that as often as the matter pertains to some right (*aliquod ius*), it must necessarily be handled always and in every case in a strictly judicial manner before the Tribunals.[78] The Constitution "*Sapienti consilio*" (II, 2°) in defining the jurisdiction of the Sacred Rota states that contentious cases, both civil and criminal, requiring a judicial trial with a process and proofs, are no longer to be received or treated by the Sacred Congregations, and that all contentious cases which are to be treated in the Roman Curia, provided they are not the so-called major cases, are to be handed over to the Sacred Rota with the exception of the cases which are assigned to the Sacred Congregations by this Constitution.[79] This last exception includes the jurisdiction of the

---

[76] "Praeterea, sententiae quaevis, sive gratiae via, sive justitiae, pontificia approbatione indigent, exceptis iis pro quibus eorumdem Officiorum, Tribunalium et Congregationum moderatoribus speciales facultates tributae sint, exceptisque semper sententiis Sacrae Rotae et Signaturae Apostolicae de ipsarum competentia latis." Cf. *AAS,* I, 18; *Fontes,* III, n. 682, p. 736; Ojetti, *De Romana Curia,* p. XXII.

[77] *De Curia Romana,* I, 53.

[78] Monin, *De Curia Romana,* p. 185.

[79] *AAS,* I, 15; *Fontes,* n. 682, cap. II, 2°; Ojetti, *De Romana Curia,* p. XVIII.

Sacred Congregations in contentious cases to be solved *in linea disciplinari.*

However, it cannot be denied that there are causes which are *in se* contentious requiring the solemnities of law and thus must be handled always in a strictly judicial manner by the Sacred Rota; such from their very nature are: (a) criminal causes; and (b) causes which are sent to the Roman Curia because of appeal from the sentence of Ordinaries.[80]

The preceding comments form a basis for a better understanding of Monin's opinion that the matrimonial cases of the Oriental rites which are treated in an administrative, disciplinary manner ("*causae non contentiosae*" in his terminology) belong to the Congregation for affairs of the Oriental Rite, and that those cases which are to be judged in a strictly judicial manner ("*causae contentiose tractandae*") are to be sent to the Sacred Rota.[81] Moreover, this distinction of the powers of these two dicasteries of the Roman Curia applies to all cases, and not merely to matrimonial cases, of the Oriental Rite. Monin[82] maintains that the two specific references to the Sacred Congregation for affairs of the Oriental Rite, namely, "*cui integra manent quae huc usque servata sunt,*"[83] and "*Congregatio de Propaganda Fide pro Negotiis ritus orientalis sua munia ex integro servabit. In iis tamen, quae internam Officii disciplinam et modum tractandi negotia spectant, huius legis normis sive communibus sive peculiaribus inhaerebit*"[84] are to be understood in such a way that the distinction between contentious and non-contentious business is preserved (i. e., the distinction between matters which are considered *in linea disciplinari* and matters which are considered *in ordine iudiciario seu summo iure*). Wherefore, he proposes, the jurisdiction of this Sacred Congregation remains the same by reason of the matter ("*ratione materiae*"); it is only when this

80 Wernz-Vidal, *Ius Canonicum,* II (1943), n. 487, II, p. 571.

81 Monin, *De Curia Romana,* pp. 285, 287, footnote 1.

82 *De Curia Romana,* p. 285.

83 Constitution "*Sapienti consilio,*" I, 6o, 6—*Fontes,* n. 682; *AAS,* I, 13; Ojetti, *De Romana Curia,* p. XVI.

84 *Normae Peculiares,* cap. VII, art. VI, n. 4—*AAS,* I, 97-98; Ojetti, *De Romana Curia,* p. LXXXIV.

matter is to be judged in a strictly judicial manner that it is to be deferred to the competent Tribunal. This interpretation, he continues,[85] fits in better with the whole economy of the new discipline, and does not seem to contradict the above references to the Sacred Congregation; moreover, it seems to be confirmed from the practise of the Curia in the case of the Patriarch of the Greek Rite in Egypt.[86]

It seems, however, that the qualification "*cui integra manent quae huc usque servata sunt*" especially places in bold relief the fact that the Sacred Congregation for affairs of the Oriental Rite was not subject to the restrictions of the Sacred Congregation *de Propaganda Fide* mentioned in the two paragraphs of the Constitution "*Sapienti consilio*" (I, 6°, 4–5) preceding it, and at the same time positively re-affirms the *status quo* of the Sacred Congregation for affairs of the Oriental Rite as to the matter of its jurisdiction. This same idea is retained in the second reference to the Sacred Congregation for affairs of the Oriental Rite with the only additional notation that it observe the rules governing: (a) the internal discipline of the Sacred Congregations; and (b) the way of treating affairs prescribed for the Sacred Congregations. These rules are mentioned expressly as being the general and special norms of this law (therefore the "*Normae Communes*" and the "*Normae Peculiares*"). Both these norms contain rules on the way to handle affairs, and the "*Normae Peculiares*" has a distinct heading under the title of the way of treating affairs which are not strictly judicial. But neither the "*Normae Communes*" nor the "*Normae Peculiares*" provides a heading under the title of the way of treating affairs which are strictly judicial since such matters are thoroughly provided for in the "*Lex propria Sacrae Romanae Rotae et Signaturae Apostolicae.*" So, it seems from the wording of the law that it might be defended that the Sacred Congregation for affairs of the Oriental Rite was not obliged by law to remit to

[85] Monin, *De Curia Romana,* p. 285, footnote 3.

[86] Cf. *AAS,* III (1911), 438–450. But, the fact that the Sacred Roman Rota decided this case is no proof that the Sacred Congregation for affairs of the Oriental Rite lacked jurisdiction over such cases, for this case may have been directed to the Sacred Rota by the Sacred Congregation.

the Sacred Rota matters which were to be judged in a strictly judicial manner, and that this Sacred Congregation could continue to solve such matters as it had done before the appearance of the Constitution "*Sapienti consilio.*" Of course, it could avail itself of the use of the Sacred Rota.

It is interesting to note that Monin's interpretation is set forth in Canon 257 § 3 of the Code of Canon Law. However, whether or not it really was already law under the Constitution "*Sapienti consilio*" cannot be said to be definitely determined.

In regard to matters pertaining to the jurisdiction of the Holy Office, Monin maintains his distinction between the doctrinal and disciplinary aspects in such matters. According to him the doctrinal function (*munus*) of the Holy Office was entirely reserved to it, even towards the Oriental faithful; and hence he explains that the application of the Pauline Privilege was reserved exclusively to the Holy Office: for, this application not rarely involved a doctrinal question, namely, the declaration of the divine law. On the other hand, the disciplinary function of the Holy Office was exercised by the Sacred Congregation for affairs of the Oriental Rite towards its subjects of the Oriental Rite; and thus he accounts for the fact that the faculty of dispensing from the impediments of mixed religion and disparity of cult was acknowledged to the *Congregatio pro negotiis ritus orientalis.* Besides, he adds, this distinction between the doctrinal and disciplinary functions seems to be wholly congruous with the principle received in law, namely, that Orientals were bound by dogmatic decrees, but not at all by the disciplinary decrees of the Latin Church unless these decrees were expressly extended also to the Orientals.[87]

The Constitution "*Sapienti consilio*" stated that the Sacred Congregation for affairs of the Oriental Rite retained its functions "*ex integro;*" and thus this Constitution did not change the jurisdiction of the Sacred Congregation for affairs of the Oriental Rite in regard to matters which for the Latin Rite pertained to the Holy Office.[88] In reference to the Pauline

---

[87] Monin, *De Curia Romana,* p. 287 and footnote 2.

[88] Cf. *supra,* pp. 36–38, 54–55.

Privilege it may be here remarked that the Sacred Congregation of the Propagation of the Faith up to the time of the Constitution "*Sapienti consilio*" answered questions and issued instructions concerning the Pauline Privilege;[89] in fact, it is also recorded that Pope Gregory XVI (1831–1846) granted a dispensation of interpellations for a Pauline Privilege case which was presented to him by the Sacred Congregation *de Propaganda Fide.*[90] The fact that the Sacred Congregation for affairs of the Oriental Rite was to refer the application of dispensations for the Pauline Privilege to the Holy Office was made definite in the response of the Sacred Consistorial Congregation on November 1, 1908, to the doubt: Whether the Sacred Congregation for affairs of the Oriental Rite can continue to concede the matrimonial dispensations of mixed religion and disparity of cult. The reply was: In the affirmative, with the exception of the Pauline Privilege alone, which is of the competency of the Holy Office.[91] That doubt was directly concerned with the faculty of granting matrimonial dispensations of mixed religion and disparity of cult; nothing was mentioned about other matters concerning these impediments—such as instructions, answering of questions and problems—and in the material available to the writer there wasn't anything that revealed the practice of the Sacred Congregation for affairs of the Oriental Rite in this respect. Like-

[89] Cf. *Collectanea,* I (1907), nn. 517, 589, 634, 665, 690, 704, 743, 845, 1088, 2245, 2265.

[90] Cf. *Collectanea,* I (1907), n. 845.

[91] "Se la Congregazione per gli Affari di rito orientale possa continuare a concedere dispense matrimoniali di mista religione e di disparità di culto." —*AAS,* I (1909), 149 ad. VI. "Affermativamente, fatta eccezione del solo privilegio Paolino, il quale è di competenza del S. Officio."—*AAS,* I, 151 ad VI. Cf. also *Sylloge praecipuorum documentorum recentium Summorum Pontificum et S. Congregationis de Propaganda Fide necnon aliarum SS. Congregationum Romanorum ad usum missionariorum* (Typis Polyglottis Vaticanis, 1939), pp. 20–21.

Wernz-Vidal (*Ius Canonicum,* II [1943], n. 495, footnote 86) in referring to this response say: "Ex eadem decis. constat S. C. de P. F. . . . posse concedere subditis dispensationes ab impedimento mixtae religionis et disparitatis cultus, non autem in Privilegio Paulino (ad VI), . . ." Let it be noticed that this reply referred expressly to the Sacred Congregation for affairs of the Oriental Rite and not to the Sacred Congregation *de Propaganda Fide.*

wise it is not clear whether the second part of the response pertaining to the Pauline Privilege referred only to granting dispensations or to all matters concerned with that Privilege.

Finally, even though Catholics of the Oriental Rite were bound by the doctrinal decrees of the Latin Church, this in itself in no way prevented the Sacred Congregation for affairs of the Oriental Rite from handling doctrinal matters. However, there was a new law in the Constitution "*Sapienti consilio*" which did prevent this Sacred Congregation from considering directly and immediately grave doctrinal matters, namely, in all Sacred Congregations, Tribunals, and Offices anything grave and extraordinary should not be considered unless it previously had been made known to the pope by the moderators.[92] At this time of notification the Supreme Pontiff could take the matter into his own hands, remit it to the same Sacred Congregation which presented it, or transfer it to the Holy Office, if he so desired. In fact, as was mentioned previously in this consideration, it was the practise of the Sacred Congregation to refer such grave doctrinal matters to the Holy Office.

With the exception of but two of the rest of the Sacred Congregations existing at that time, there is no doubt that the Sacred Congregation for affairs of the Oriental Rite supplied the functions of these Sacred Congregations whenever the affairs of their jurisdiction in the Latin Church, in addition to the so-called *negotia mixta,* concerned or involved Catholics of the Oriental Rite. Monin avers that the functions of the Sacred Ceremonial Congregation and the Sacred Congregation for Extraordinary Ecclesiastical Affairs were not supplied by the Sacred Congregation for affairs of the Oriental Rite, as, he claims, is evident from the very nature of these Sacred Congregations.[93] The Sacred Ceremonial Congregation was charged with the regulation (*moderatio*) of the

[92] "In omnibus autem et singulis superius recensitis Congregationibus, Tribunalibus, Officiis hoc in primis solemne sit, ut nil grave et extraordinarium agatur, nisi a Moderatoribus eorumdem Nobis Nostrisque pro tempore Successoribus fuerit ante significatum."—*Fontes,* n. 682, III, 5º.

[93] Monin, *De Curia Romana,* p. 286. Cf. *infra,* pp. 107–110 for comments on the jurisdiction of the Sacred Congregation for the Oriental Church under the Code.

ceremonies performed in the papal chapel and the papal court, and also of the sacred functions which the cardinals performed outside the papal chapel; it likewise considered questions about the precedence both of the cardinals and of legates sent by the various nations to the Holy See.[94] The Sacred Congregation for Extraordinary Ecclesiastical Affairs handled those matters which the Supreme Pontiff through the Cardinal Secretary of State submitted to its examination, especially affairs connected with the Civil Laws and the agreements of the Holy See with the various nations;[95] thus in the case of the Sacred Congregation for Extraordinary Ecclesiastical Affairs, it is also evident that no other Sacred Congregation can claim jurisdiction in those particular circumstances.

It is recalled that the decrees of the Sacred Congregation *de Propaganda Fide*[96] and of the Sacred Congregation *pro negotiis ritus orientalis*[97] formerly had the value and force of an Apostolic Constitution. It is clear from the Constitution "*Sapienti consilio*" that henceforth in all Sacred Congregations, Tribunals and Offices all sentences, whether of favor or of justice, needed the approbation of the pope unless the Supreme Pontiff had given *special* faculties to the moderator,[98] and so the papal approbation was required also for authentic interpretations of the law by the Sacred Congregations;[99] moreover, grave and extraordinary matters were not to be treated unless they were previously made known to the pope by the moderator.[100] So, as Cappello points out, the former faculty no longer existed, and under the new law the approbation

---

[94] Constitution "*Sapienti consilio*," I, 9o—*Fontes*, n. 682; *AAS*, I, 14; Ojetti, *De Romana Curia*, p. XVII.

[95] Constitution "*Sapienti consilio*," I, 10o—*Fontes*, n. 682; *AAS*, *loc. cit.*; Ojetti, *loc. cit.*

Compare with *infra*, pp. 108–110.

[96] *Supra*, pp. 43–44.

[97] *Supra*, pp. 53–54.

[98] *Fontes*, n. 682, III, 5o; *AAS*, I, 18; Ojetti, *De Romana Curia*, p. XXII.

[99] Cf. the response of the Sacred Consistorial Congregation, of February 11, 1911, to doubts 1o and 2o—*AAS*, III (1911), 99–100; Monin, *De Curia Romana*, p. 199.

[100] *Fontes*, *loc. cit.*; *AAS*, I, 18; Ojetti, *loc. cit.*

of the Roman Pontiff given *in forma specifica* [101] was necessary in order that a decree of the Sacred Congregation have the value of an Apostolic Constitution.[102] Of course, this decree had its force only after having been legitimately promulgated.[103]

Mention also is made in the Constitution "*Sapienti consilio*" that the pontifical Commission *pro unione Ecclesiarum dissidentium* [104] was annexed to the *Congregatio de Propaganda Fide.*[105] This Commission, it is remembered, was instituted for the purpose of reconciling nations which had fallen away from the

---

[101] When a decree is approved *in forma communi*, it remains in its intrinsic nature an act of the Sacred Congregation; but when it is approved *in forma specifica*, it becomes really and properly a pontifical decree and must be considered as given by the pope himself. Cf. Cappello, *De Curia Romana*, I, 54.

From a practical viewpoint, the formula which the Roman Pontiff uses in granting his approbation indicates the type of *forma;* v. g., the following formulae indicate an approbation conceded *in forma communi: Facto verbo cum Sanctissimo,* or *SS. mus D. N. resolutionem Eñorum Patrum approbavit et confirmavit,* or *SS. mus D. N. Pius Papa X, audita relatione R. P. D. Secretarii eiusdem S. Congregationis, supra relatam Eñorum Patrum declarationem ratam habere et confirmare dignatus est.* Whereas the following formulae signify an approbation granted *in forma specifica: Ex motu proprio,* or *Ex scientia certa,* or *De Apostolicae auctoritatis plenitudine declaramus, statuimus . . . ,* or *Non obstante quacumque lege seu consuetudine in contrarium . . . ,* or *Supplentes omnes iuris et facti defectus,* or *In audientia SS. mus D. N. benigne dispensare dignaturs est.* Cf. Cappello, *De Curia Romana,* I, 54–55; Beste, *Introductio in Codicem* (Collegeville, Minn.: St. John's Abbey Press, 1938), p. 241. Cf. also Reiffenstuel, *Ius Canonicum Universum* (5 vols. in 7, Parisiis, 1864–1870), lib. II, tit. XXX, n. 8; Pirhing, *Jus Canonicum in V Libros Decretalium Distributum Nova Methodo Explicatum* (4 vols., Dilingae, 1674–1677), lib. II, tit. XXX, n. VIII.

[102] Cappello, *De Curia Romana,* I, 242; Monin, *De Curia Romana,* p. 216.

[103] Monin, *loc. cit.* Pope Pius X in the Constitution "*Promulgandi,*" of September 29, 1908, decreed that with the beginning of the year 1909 all acts of the Roman Pontiff and of the Sacred Congregations and Offices, whenever there was need of promulgation, would be had as legitimately promulgated by their insertion in the "*Commentarium officiale de Apostolicae Sedis actis,*" unless it was otherwise provided by the Holy See.—*Fontes,* n. 684; *AAS,* I, 6; Cappello, *De Curia Romana,* I, 56.

[104] *Supra,* p. 62.

[105] *Fontes,* n. 682 (I, 6o, 8); *AAS,* I, 13; Ojetti, *De Romana Curia,* p. XVI.

Church through schism or heresy; it was by no means limited merely to dissidents of the Oriental Rite. M. Martin, after having remarked that its labors extended to all—whether in the Eastern or Western hemisphere—who had fallen away from the Catholic Church through heresy or schism, states that under the new law of Pope Pius X the scope of its labors and the general personnel remained the same.[106] It seems to Ojetti, however, that the pope no longer retained the prefecture of the Commission, and that this position was assumed by the Cardinal Prefect of the Sacred Congregation *de Propaganda Fide.* Yet, Ojetti insists that he makes the above assumption with doubt, for although express mention of this Commission was made in the Constitution "*Sapienti consilio,*" there was no mention of it or its officials in the official publications of the Holy See for the year 1909.[107] Thus the uncertainty of whether or not the pope remained at the head of this group. However, the *Annuario Pontificio* for the years 1912–1917 in a brief summary of the Constitution "*Sapienti consilio*" (I, 6°) which preceded the enumeration of the personnel of the *Congregatio de Propaganda Fide* did mention this Commission as being annexed to the Sacred Congregation *de Propaganda Fide.*[108] Unfortunately there is no mention of its prefect, or other officials so that a definite conclusion cannot be made.

The personnel of the *S. Congregatio de Propaganda Fide pro negotiis ritus orientalis* in 1909 consisted of the following members:[109]

---

[106] M. Martin, *The Roman Curia,* p. 75.

[107] Ojetti, *De Romana Curia,* pp. 126–127.

[108] In the *Annuario Pontificio* of 1912 on p. 32, it is reported as follows: "Ipsi [*Congregatio de Propaganda Fide*] commissa est administratio omnium bonorum, etiam Rev. Camerae Spoliorum, et coniunctus fuit coetus pro unione Ecclesiarum dissidentium." In the *Annuario Pontificio* of 1915, p. 330, it is written: "—Unitam habet Congregationem pro Negotiis Rituum Orientalium, cui adiunctus est coetus pro unione ecclesiarum dissidentium." The latter version appeared until 1917 inclusively, then it no longer was mentioned—let it be noticed, however, that the "*cui*" referred to the Sacred Congregation *de Propaganda Fide* and not to the Sacred Congregation *pro negotiis ritus orientalis,* as one would be inclined to think from the above version.

[109] *AAS,* I (1909), 120–121.

Cardinals

Gotti, Girolamo Maria, *Prefect.*
Oreglia di Santo Stefano, Luigi, Bishop of Ostia and Velletri.
Vannutelli, Serafino, Bishop of Porto and S. Rufina.
Agliardi, Antonio, Bishop of Albano.
Vannutelli, Vincenzo, Bishop of Palestrina.
Satolli, Francesco di Paolo, Bishop of Frascati.
Cassetta, Francesco di Paolo, Bishop of Sabina.
Rampolla Del Tindaro, Mariano.
Cretoni, Serafino.
Martinelli, Sebastiano.
Gennari, Casimiro.
Cavicchioni, Beniamino.
Cavallari, Aristide.
Lualdi, Alessandro.
Segna, Francesco.
Della Volpe, Francesco Salesio.
Vives y Tuto, Giuseppe Calasanzio.
Msgr. Rolleri, Girolamo, *Secretary.*

Consultors

Msgr. Lancia di Brolo, Domenico Gaspare, Archbishop of Monreale.
" Zaleski, Ladislao, Titular Archbishop of Thebes.
" Van den Branden de Reeth, Vittore, Titular Archbishop of Tyre.
" Steyaert, Dionisio Alfonso, Titular Archbishop of Damascus.
" Baccini, Luigi, Bishop of S. Angelo in Vado and Urbania.
" Veccia, Luigi.
" Laemmer, Ugo.
" Spezza, Cesare.
" Sebastinelli, Guglielmo.
" Battandier, Alberto.
Very Rev. Pellegrini, Arsenio, Abbot of the Basilian Monks of Grottaferrata.
" " Bedjian, Paolo, of the Congregation of the Missions.
" " Eschbach, Alfonso, Procurator General of the Congregation of the Holy Ghost.
" " de Hemptinne, Ildebrando, Abbot Primate of the Order of Saint Benedict.
" " Malfatti, Luigi, of the Carmelite Fathers.
" " Serafini, Mauro, Abbot General of the Cassinesi of the Primitive Observance.

" " Valenzuela, Pietro A., Master General of the Mercedarian Fathers.
" " Buonpensiere, Enrico, of the Order of Preachers.
" " Kauffmann, Giuseppe, of the Friars Minor.
" " Sleutjes, Michele, of the Friars Minor.
" " Ojetti, Benedetto, of the Society of Jesus.
" " Benedetti, Claudio, of the Congregation of the Most Holy Redeemer.
" " Coperé, Luigi, Procurator General of the Marist Fathers.
" " Biederlak, Giuseppe, of the Society of Jesus.
" " Arndt, Agostino, of the Society of Jesus.

OFFICIALS

Msgr. Chiesa, Luigi.
Rev. Lucchetti, Giovanni.
" Benedetti, Enrico.
" Pazzini, Pietro.
" Gionfra, Domenico (scrittore)
" Rossignani, Pio "
" Ferrari, Alfredo "

INTERPRETERS

Msgr. Bugarini, Vincenzo.
" Ugolini, Mariano.
" Sandalgian, Giuseppe.

ARTICLE V. THE SACRED CONGREGATION FOR THE ORIENTAL CHURCH

It was Pope Benedict XV (1914–1922) who determined the final stage of development towards which the Sacred Congregation for affairs of the Oriental Rite had been progressing, namely, the establishment of a distinct Sacred Congregation for the Oriental Church. In his Motu proprio "*Dei providentis,*" of May 1, 1917,[110] he stated that he was well aware that there were some who were displeased with the arrangement whereby the Sacred Congregation for affairs of the Oriental Rite remained annexed to the Sacred Congregation of the Propagation of the Faith—a mere supplement, as they thought, subordinate to the latter. The ones who thus felt aggrieved were plagued with the unjustified notion that the Roman Pontiffs considered the Cath-

[110] *AAS,* IX (1917), 529–531; *Fontes,* n. 710*.

olics of the Oriental Rite to be of secondary or only of little importance, that they (the popes) wished the Orientals to be subject to the Latins, and that they placed the Orientals on the same level with the heretics of the Occident and the infidels in keeping them under the *Sacra Congregatio de Propaganda Fide.* These contumelious suspicions were very effectively dispelled by the enactment of Pope Benedict XV. In his Motu proprio *"Dei providentis"* he decreed that the *Sacra Congregatio de Propaganda Fide pro negotiis ritus orientalis* would cease to exist on November 30 of that year, and its work would be assumed on the following day, December 1, by a new Sacred Congregation of the Roman Curia, completely separated from and totally independent of the Sacred Congregation of the Propagation of the Faith. Its title would be the *Sacra Congregatio pro Ecclesia Orientali;* its prefect, none other than the Holy Pontiff himself. The rest of its constitution called for a certain number of cardinals, one of whom would be secretary; an assessor, and several consultors selected from notable clergy of both Latin and Oriental Rites; in addition, a suitable number of officials chosen from clerics who were well versed in Oriental matters. Pope Benedict XV expressly stated that this new Sacred Congregation was instituted for the so-called United or Uniate Orientals,[111] i.e., Catholics of the Oriental Rite.[112]

To this Sacred Congregation was reserved all business of every kind which pertained to persons or discipline or the rites of the

[111] "Itaque deliberatum Nobis est pro unitis, qui dicuntur, orientalibus propriam Sacram Congregationem instituere, cuius Nosmet ipsi geramus, Nostrique deinceps successores, praefecturam."—Motu proprio *"Dei providentis"—AAS,* IX (1917), 530; *Fontes,* n. 710*. A Uniate can be defined as a member of any Eastern Church who is in communion with the Holy See, or else as a Catholic of any Eastern rite. For a lucid explanation of the meaning of the word "Uniate" and its application, see Fortescue, *The Uniate Eastern Churches* (edited by George D. Smith, New York, Cincinnati, Chicago: Benziger Brothers, 1923), pp. 1-7.

[112] Cicognani (*Canon Law,* p. 445) says: "These Orientals are known as 'Catholics of the Oriental Rite' and form the 'Uniate Eastern Churches,' while those who remained in schism chose to call themselves 'Orthodox,' though improperly, as they are better styled 'the separated or dissidents.'" Cf. also Cicognani-Staffa, *Commentarium ad Librum Primum Codicis Iuris Canonici* (Romae: Ex Officinia Typographica Romana "Buona Stampa,"

Oriental Church, even if it were of a mixed nature (i. e., it also affected Latins by reason of thing or person), with the sole exception of matters falling under the jurisdiction of the Holy Office. Thus, the Sacred Congregation for the Oriental Church possessed in regard to Catholics of the Oriental Rite all the faculties which the Sacred Congregations for Catholics of the Latin Rite possessed together, with the exception of matters which appertained to the jurisdiction of the Sacred Congregation of the Holy Office. But its faculties extended only to settling matters in a disciplinary manner (*modo disciplinari*); all questions which were to be settled in a strictly judicial manner (*modo iudiciario*) had to be referred to the tribunal which the Sacred Congregation for the Oriental Church would designate.[113] Since the above noted positions have been entirely incorporated into the Code of Canon Law, its meaning is explained in the next chapter.

Let it be remarked that the Motu proprio "*Dei providentis,*" which announced the forthcoming institution of the new Sacred Congregation, was dated May 1, 1917, and thus preceded the promulgation of the Code by the Constitution "*Providentissima Mater Ecclesia,*" of May 27, 1917.[114] The provisions about the jurisdiction of the Sacred Congregation for the Oriental Church in the Motu proprio "*Dei providentis*" are identical with Canon 257 of the Code. Thus, although the Code was to go into effect and have the force of law on May 19, 1918, the provisions of Canon 257 really went into effect with the establishment of the Sacred Congregation for the Oriental Church on December 1, 1917.

In his concern for promoting the welfare of the Orientals Pope

---

1939), Vol. I, pp. 8–9; Michiels, *Principia Generalia de Personis in Ecclesia* (Lublin, Polonia: Universitas Catholica, 1932), 263–264.

For a thorough work in English on the history and facts concerning the various dissident sects, consult the following two books of Adrian Fortescue: *The Orthodox Eastern Church* (3. ed., London: Catholic Truth Society, 1929) and *The Lesser Eastern Churches* (London: Catholic Truth Society, 1913).

[113] *AAS,* IX (1917), 531; *Fontes,* n. 710*.

[114] *AAS,* IX (1917), 8; *Codex Iuris Canonici Pii X Pontificis Maximi iussu digestus Benedicti XV auctoritate promulgatus* (Westminster, Maryland: The Newman Book Shop, 1942), pp. XLV–XLIX.

Benedict XV in another Motu proprio, namely, the "*Orientis Catholici,*" of October 15, 1917, decreed the founding of a pontifical institute for the study of Oriental matters (*Institutum studiis rerum orientalium provehendis*), whose site was near the Vatican in those buildings at that time known as the *Hospitium de Convertendis.* This institute was subject directly to the Sacred Congregation for the Oriental Church. Its courses of study were offered to priests of the Latin Rite who were destined to exercise their ministry among the Orientals. However, both the clerics of the Catholic Oriental rites and those Orthodox (those who remained in schism after separating from the Catholic Church) desiring further knowledge of the truth were welcomed to attend this institute: the former could complete the ordinary course of doctrinal instruction, and the latter would have an opportunity to discard their prejudices and penetrate deeper into the truth. Wherefore in the lectures both the Catholic and the Orthodox doctrines were presented and the origin and source of both doctrines were clearly established so that it was evident which flowed from the preaching of the Apostles continued through the permanent magisterium of the Church, and which had its beginning elsewhere. The courses of study, which were completed in two years, were listed as follows:

(a) Theology with the various doctrines of the Oriental Christians on divine things (*de rebus divinis*), with courses of Oriental Patrology, historical Theology and Patristics.

(b) Canon Law of all the Christian nations of the Orient.

(c) The various Liturgies of the Orientals.

(d) Both the sacred and civil history of Byzantium and the rest of the Orient, in addition to lectures on the ethnographic geography, the sacred archeology, the civil and political constitution of these nations.

(e) The literatures and languages of the Orientals.

This pontifical institute was well supplied with books and periodicals on these subjects.[115]

---

[115] *AAS,* IX (1917), 531-533. Cf. Villien, "L'Institut Pontifical pour l'Etude des Questions Orientales"—*Le Canoniste Contemporain* (45 vols., Paris: P. Lethielleux, 1878-1922; from 1924-1926 entitled *Le Canoniste*), XL (1917), 502-505.

PART II

THE SACRED CONGREGATION FOR THE ORIENTAL CHURCH SINCE THE PROMULGATION OF THE *CODEX IURIS CANONICI*

CHAPTER III

THE SACRED CONGREGATION FOR THE ORIENTAL CHURCH ACCORDING TO THE CODE

ARTICLE I. THE SACRED ROMAN CONGREGATIONS IN GENERAL

A. GENERAL CHARACTERISTICS

The Roman Pontiff usually transacts the affairs of the universal Church through the Roman Curia, which consists of the Sacred Congregations, Tribunals and Offices.[1] The Sacred Congregations can be described as stable bodies of cardinals instituted by the Roman Pontiffs to expedite and decide ecclesiastical affairs of the external forum.[2] They may decide cases and receive appeals

[1] Canons 7 and 242.

There are eleven Sacred Congregations, three Tribunals, six Offices listed in the Code. The Sacred Congregations in the order found in the Code (Canons 247–257) are: Congregation of the Holy Office, Consistorial Congregation, Congregation of the Discipline of the Sacraments, Congregation of the Council, Congregation of Religious, Congregation of the Propagation of the Faith, Congregation of Sacred Rites, Ceremonial Congregation, Congregation for Extraordinary Ecclesiastical Affairs, Congregation of Studies for Seminaries and Universities, Congregation for the Oriental Church. The Tribunals (canons 258–259) are: Sacred Penitentiaria, Sacred Roman Rota, Apostolic Signatura. The Offices (canons 260–264) are: Apostolic Chancery, Apostolic Dataria, Apostolic Camera, Secretariate of State, Secretariate of Briefs to Princes, Secretariate of Latin Letters. The Sacred Congregations, Tribunals and Offices also are commonly referred to as dicasteries of the Roman Curia.

The Congregation of the Fabric of St. Peter's is not mentioned among the Sacred Congregations in the Code, though it is indicated in the official "*Annuario Pontificio.*" Prümmer gives as the reason for this that it is concerned now only with the care and temporal administration of the Vatican Basilica, and does not handle any matter pertaining to the Church at large; hence, it does not pertain to the common law of the Church. Cf. Prümmer, *Manuale Iuris Canonici in Usum Scholarum* (5. ed., Friburgi Brisgoviae: Herder & Co., 1907), quest. 102.

[2] Cance, *Le Code de Droit Canonique* (3 vols., Paris: J. Gabalda et Fils, 1927–1929), I (6. ed., 1930), 247.

in an extrajudicial, disciplinary manner (*in linea disciplinari*),[3] but they lack the power of judging in a strictly judicial form (*ordine iudiciario*), save for a few exceptions in certain cases,[4] whether in the first instance or in appeals.[5] Each Sacred Congregation has its own exactly circumscribed jurisdiction.[6] In general the personnel of the Sacred Congregations is as follows:[7]

(a) A Prefect,[8] who is designated by the pope,[9] and who is always a cardinal except when the Roman Pontiff occupies that position, as he does in the case of the Sacred Congregation of the Holy Office, the Sacred Consistorial Congregation and the Sacred Congregation for the Oriental Church.[10]

(b) A Secretary who is a prelate and who is customarily a Titular Archbishop.[11] However, in the three Sacred Congregations of which the Roman Pontiff is Prefect, the Secretary is a cardinal who directs or in general does the work that is done by the Cardinal Prefect in the other Sacred Congregations,[12] while

---

[3] Wernz-Vidal (*Ius Canonicum,* II [1943], n. 484, III) remarks: "His demptis exceptionibus, SS. CC. vi Const. '*Sapienti consilio*' potestate iudicandi tum in *prima instantia* tum in *appellatione* carent, nec causas decidunt aut appellationes recipiunt nisi in linea disciplinari."

[4] Cf. Wernz-Vidal (*Ius Canonicum,* II [1943], n. 483 III) in reference to the Sacred Congregations of the Holy Office (Canon 247, § 2) and of Sacred Rites (canon 253, § 3).

[5] Wernz-Vidal (*Ius Canonicum,* II [1943], n. 482) defines the Sacred Congregations as follows: "Collegia minora Cardinalium per Romanos Pontifices instituta ad certa negotia ecclesiastica discutienda et per vota maiora, ordinarie etiam decisiva, non tantum consultiva, definienda."

[6] Sägmüller, *Lehrbuch des katholischen Kirchenrechts* (4. ed., Freiburg im Breisgau: Herdersche Verlagshandlung, 1925–1934), 330.

[7] Canon 246.

[8] Maroto notes that the Cardinal who presides over a Sacred Congregation is accustomed to be called Prefect, while the Cardinal who presides over a Commission is called President—Maroto, *Institutiones Iuris Canonici ad Normam Novi Codicis* (2 vols., Matriti: Typis "Imprenta Ibérica" Stanislai Maestre, 1919), II, 238. Hereafter referred to as *Institutiones.*

[9] Maroto, *Institutiones,* II, 238, 242.

[10] Beste, *Introductio in Codicem,* p. 242; De Meester, *Juris Canonici et Juris Canonico-civilis Compendium,* II (1923), n. 581; Maroto, *Institutiones,* II, 238; Wernz-Vidal, *Ius Canonicum,* II (1943), n. 483.

[11] Wernz-Vidal, *loc. cit.*

[12] Maroto, *Institutiones,* II, 238.

his duties of a Secretary are assumed by an Assessor, who is a prelate.[13] Moreover, in several Sacred Congregations besides the Secretary and Assessor there are Subsecretaries [14] or Substitutes,[15] and they are likewise prelates.

(c) A number of cardinals designated by the pope.[16] The Roman Pontiff likewise determines how many cardinals shall be assigned to the various Sacred Congregations, since there is no number fixed by law.[17] The cardinals, including those who do not reside in Rome, are assigned to several different dicasteries.[18] Some of the cardinals by virtue of their office in one Sacred Congregation belong *ex officio* to another Sacred Congregation, as for instance, the Cardinal Secretary of the Holy Office and the Cardinal Prefect of the Sacred Congregation of Studies for Seminaries and Universities in regard to the Sacred Consistorial Congregation,[19] and the Cardinal Secretary of the Sacred Con-

---

[13] Vermeersch-Creusen, *Epitome Iuris Canonici* (Mechlinae-Romae: H. Dessain, 1921–1923) 3 vols. (Vol. I, 6. ed., 1937; Vols. II–III, 5. ed., 1934–1936), I, n. 359; Choupin, *Valeur des Décisions Doctrinales et Disciplinaires du Saint-Siège* (3. ed., Paris: Gabriel Beauchesne, 1928), p. 437; De Meester, *Juris Canonici et Juris Canonico-civilis Compendium,* II, 70, footnote 2.

[14] The Sacred Congregation of the Discipline of the Sacraments has three Subsecretaries. For the other Sacred Congregations, see Maroto, *Institutiones,* II, 239, or an *Annuario Pontificio.*

[15] There are two Substitutes in the Sacred Consistorial Congregation and the Sacred Congregation for Extraordinary Ecclesiastical Affairs. As to Substitutes in other Sacred Congregations, consult Maroto, *loc. cit.,* or an *Annuario Pontificio.*

[16] Canon 246; Maroto, *Institutiones,* II, 242.

[17] Cf. Wernz-Vidal, *Ius Canonicum,* II, n. 483, where it is also stated that Pope Sixtus V in his organization of the Roman Curia in 1588 had assigned five cardinals to each Sacred Congregation with the exception of the Sacred Congregation of the Inquisition, which had seven.

[18] Maroto, *Institutiones,* II, 238, footnote 1.

Dennis Cardinal Dougherty, Archbishop of Philadelphia, has been a titular member of the following Sacred Congregations since the day of his reception of the red hat, March 10, 1921: the Sacred Congregation for the Oriental Church, the Sacred Congregation of the Discipline of the Sacraments, the Sacred Congregation of the Propagation of the Faith, the Sacred Congregation of Sacred Rites.—*AAS,* XIII (1921). Cf. also *infra,* p. 100, footnote 52.

[19] Canon 248, § 1.

sistorial Congregation in regard to the Sacred Congregation for Extraordinary Ecclesiastical Affairs,[20] etc.

(d) The major and minor Officials (*maiores et minores Administri seu Officiales*). The major Officials (*maiores Administri*),[21] namely, the Secretary (who is not a cardinal), the Assessor, the Substitutes, the Subsecretaries—all prelates—are elected freely by the pope.[22] On the other hand, the minor Officials (*minores Administri* or simply *Officiales*), such as "*minutanti*" (who are also known as *studii adiutores seu informatores*),[23] writers (*scriptores*), archivists (*archivistae*), protocollists (*protocollistae*), distributors (*distributores*), after having passed a concursus, are chosen by secret ballots of the *Congressus* and the approval of the pope.[24] Usually mentioned along with this group are the apparitors (*apparitores seu ianitores*) who are known as the "*deservientes*," and they are appointed by the Cardinal Prefect or Secretary on the proposal of the major Officials.[25]

(e) The Consultors. They are usually appointed by the pope

---

[20] Canon 256, § 2.

[21] Also called Prelates because of their rank. Maroto, *Institutiones,* II, 238.

[22] Maroto, *Institutiones,* II, 242; Wernz-Vidal, *Ius Canonicum,* II, n. 483.

[23] They are called "*minutanti*" in the Sacred Congregation of the Propagation of the Faith and the Sacred Congregation for the Oriental Church, as well as in the Secretariate of State. Cf. Maroto, *Institutiones,* II, 240, footnote 1. "*Minutanti*" is an Italian expression for the Latin "*minutantes.*"

Their functions are described in the "*Normae Peculiares,*" cap. VI, nn. 3-5—*AAS,* I (1909), 71-73.

The "*minutanti*" are found in almost all the Sacred Congregations (the Holy Office and Sacred Ceremonial Congregations excepted).

[24] "*Normae Communes,*" cap. II, nn. 2-11—*AAS,* I (1909), 37-40; Ojetti, *De Romana Curia,* pp. XLV-XLVI. Cf. also Wernz-Vidal, *Ius Canonicum,* II (1943), n. 483.

Maroto (*Institutiones,* II, 242, footnote 5) mentions that *de facto* they are often elected freely, especially the "*minutanti.*" The functions of these minor Officials are described in the "*Normae Peculiares,*" cap. VI, nn. 6-15—*AAS,* I, 73-77.

[25] Maroto, *Institutiones,* II, 241; Wernz-Vidal, *Ius Canonicum,* n. 483; "*Normae Communes,*" cap. II, n. 12—*AAS,* I, 40; "*Normae Peculiares,*" cap. VI, n. 16—*AAS,* I, 77.

upon the suggestion of the moderator of the Sacred Congregation;[26] however, there are some persons who by their office in one Sacred Congregation automatically become Consultors of another Sacred Congregation, v. g., the Assessor of the Holy Office, the Secretary of the Sacred Congregation for Extraordinary Ecclesiastical Affairs and the Secretary of the Sacred Congregation of Studies for Seminaries and Universities are *ex officio* Consultors of the Sacred Consistorial Congregation.[27]

The authoritative members of the Sacred Congregations are the cardinals.[28] This fact becomes clear from a consideration of the handling of business within the Sacred Congregations. The more serious affairs (*negotia graviora*) are proposed to the so-called full Sacred Congregation (*plena Congregatio*), i. e., to the deliberation and judgment of the cardinals of the Sacred Congregation. Some examples of such more serious business are as follows: the application of the law to particular questions and cases, the examination of grave controversies of the administrative, disciplinary order, of concessions and faculties of greater importance, of all acts of the public and general order, and the like.[29] The cardinals in the more difficult questions make use of the consultative vote of one or more Consultors.[30]

The Prefect with the Secretary and major Officials (*maiores*

---

[26] Maroto, *Institutiones,* II, 243. As to their functions, consult Maroto, *Institutiones,* II, 241; "*Normae Peculiares,*" cap. VI, n. 1—*AAS,* I, 70.

[27] Canon 248, § 1.

[28] Coronata (*Institutiones Iuris Canonici,* I [1928], n. 338) expresses himself thus: "Constituuntur autem SS. Congregationes ex solis Cardinalibus: ipsi enim soli suffragium ferunt deliberativum. Sunt tamen et alii administri et officiales inferiores." Similarly, Wernz-Vidal, *Ius Canonicum,* II (1943), n. 483.

[29] "*Normae Peculiares,*" cap. II, n. 1—*AAS,* I (1909), 61; Ojetti, *De Romana Curia,* p. LX; De Meester, *Juris Canonici et Juris Canonico-civilis Compendium,* II (1923), n. 581; Maroto, *Institutiones,* II, 246–247.

[30] "*Normae Peculiares,*" cap. IV, n. 2—*AAS,* I (1909), 66; De Meester, *op. cit.,* II, 71, footnote 1. For a description of the *modus procedendi plenarum Congregationum,* see the "*Normae Peculiares,*" cap. IV—*AAS,* I (1909), 65–69.

Administri) constitute what is known as the *Congressus.*[31] The functions of this particular group are: [32]

(a) to prepare according to regulations matters which are to be treated by the cardinals;

(b) to consider the nature of the requests and questions presented to the Sacred Congregation in order to determine whether it is to be treated in a disciplinary manner (*in linea disciplinari*) or in a strictly judicial manner (*ordine iudiciario*), and to dispatch this matter accordingly to the proper section of the Sacred Congregation or to the proper tribunal; [33]

(c) to execute the deliberations and decisions of the cardinals after the approval of the Supreme Pontiff has been given, in cases where such approbation is needed; [34]

(d) to grant according to the powers given by the pope faculties, concessions and indults which are customary; to expedite *de stylo Curiae* minor matters of some importance which are evident, obvious and ordinary. Such matters have the signature of the Secretary or of the Prefect and the seal of the Sacred Congregation, and so are ascribed to the authority of the Sacred Congregation. However, the authentic rescript of a *Congressus* does not enjoy the same authority as a rescript which comes from a full Sacred Congregation (i. e., from the deliberation of the cardinals)., since a recourse to the full Sacred Congregation can always be made from a decision of a *Congressus.*[35]

(e) to see to it that all things are performed according to the general and particular norms for the Sacred Congregations. The

---

[31] "*Normae Communes,*" cap. I, n. 3—*AAS,* I, 37; Ojetti, *De Romana Curia,* p. XLIV. At times the "*minutanti*" (*studii adiutores seu informatores*) are present at the *Congressus.* Cf. "*Normae Peculiares,*" cap. VI, n. 3 b—*AAS,* I, 72; Ojetti, *De Romana Curia,* p. LXVII; Maroto, *Institutiones,* II, 240, footnote 2.

[32] "*Normae Peculiares,*" cap. II, n. 2—*AAS,* I, 62.

[33] "*Normae Peculiares,*" cap. I, n. 3—*AAS,* I, 61; Ojetti, *De Romana Curia,* p. LX.

[34] De Meester, *Juris Canonici et Juris Canonico-civilis Compendium,* II, n. 581, 2ºb.

[35] De Meester, *ibid.,* p. 70, footnote 8.

Congressus which convenes once or twice a week, is therefore a consultive and executive body.[36]

Provisions are also made to expedite business of minor importance without the use of the *Congressus*.[37]

Thus, the Sacred Congregations center about the cardinals; for while others share in the ordinary, routine matters which present no serious difficulty, it is for the cardinals to handle the more serious and difficult affairs, and they alone of all in the Sacred Congregations can exercise a deliberative vote.

B. GENERAL NORMS GOVERNING THE SACRED CONGREGATIONS

In each of the Sacred Congregations, Tribunals and Offices discipline is preserved and affairs are transacted according to the general and particular norms which the Roman Pontiff has prescribed.[38] In great part the general and particular norms accompanying the Constitution "*Sapienti consilio*" of Pope Pius X have been retained by the succeeding popes.[39] The Code lists some general norms for the dicasteries of the Roman Curia in canons 243–245. Canon 243, § 2 states that all who belong to the Sacred Congregations, Tribunals or Offices of the Roman Curia are bound to secrecy within the limits and according to the laws laid down for each. Canon 244, § 1 requires that any matter of importance or of any extraordinary character is not to be treated by the Sacred Congregations, Tribunals and Offices unless the Roman Pontiff has first been notified by the Moderator. The second paragraph of this same canon states that all concessions (*gratiae*) and resolutions need papal approval, except those for which special faculties have been given to the Moderators of the Offices, Tribunals and Sacred Congregations, and except also for the sentences of the Tribunals of the Roman Rota

---

[36] De Meester, *ibid.*, p. 70, footnote 6.

[37] De Meester, *Juris Canonici et Juris Canonico-civilis Compendium,* II, n. 581, 2oa; Maroto, *Institutiones,* n. 830; "*Normae Peculiares,*" cap. VII, art. 3, n. 17 a—*AAS,* I, 90.

[38] Canon 243, § 1.

[39] Woywod, *A Practical Commentary on the Code of Canon Law* (6. ed., 2 vols., New York: Joseph F. Wagner, 1941), I, n. 188.

and the Apostolic Signatura.[40] The Code in canon 245 enacts a new law for settling controversies among the Sacred Congregations concerning jurisdiction. For, whereas formerly according to the Constitution "*Sapienti consilio*" the Sacred Consistorial Congregation solved these problems,[41] now a committee of cardinals, which the Roman Pontiff shall appoint in each individual case, decides that controversy, if such a one should arise among the dicasteries of the Roman Curia. It seems fitting to mention here the law of Canon 43, namely, if any Sacred Congregation or Office has refused a favor (*gratia*) asked of it, the same favor cannot be *validly* obtained from another Second Congregation or Office or from the local Ordinary, even though they have that power, unless the Sacred Congregation or Office from which the favor was first asked gives its consent—this canon, however, makes an exception for the Sacred Penitentiaria, which has a right to grant favors in the internal forum independently of any previous application in the same matter to one of the Sacred Congregations.[42]

Article II. Introduction to Canon 257

It is recalled that the Sacred Congregation for the Oriental

[40] The substance of Canon 244, § 1 and § 2, is found towards the end of the Constitution "*Sapienti consilio*"—*AAS*, I, 18; Ojetti, *De Romana Curia*, pp. XXI-XXII.

[41] "*Sapienti consilio*," I, 2°, 4, states: "Huius Congregationis [Consistorialis] erit, in conflictatione iurium, dubia solvere circa *competentiam* Sacrorum Congregationum."—*AAS*, I, 10; Ojetti, *De Romana Curia*, p. XI. Wherefore the writer takes exception to Augustine's general statement: "Formerly the Signatura Apostolica had power to settle all controversies about competency, which were quite frequent when the '*Sapienti consilio*' first went into effect."—Augustine, *A Commentary on the New Code of Canon Law* (8 vols., St. Louis: B. Herder, 1921–1938 [Vol. I, 6. ed., 1931; Vol. II, 6. ed., 1936; Vol. III, 5. ed., 1938; Vol. IV, 3. ed., 1925; Vol. V, 5. ed., 1935; Vol. VI, 3. ed., 1931; Vol. VII, 3. ed., 1930; Vol. VIII, 3. ed., 1931], II, 6. ed., 1936), 249. As to the time when the *Signatura Justitiae* and *Signatura Gratiae* were active and as to their respective jurisdictions in settling controversies of Tribunals and Sacred Congregations, see Maroto, *Institutiones*, II, 260.

[42] Woywod, *A Practical Commentary on the Code of Canon Law*, I, n. 32. Cf. also "*Normae Peculiares*," cap. I, n. 2—*AAS*, I, 60–61; Ojetti, *De Romana Curia*, p. LX.

Church was instituted by Pope Benedict XV for the Catholics of the Oriental Rite.[43] Today the Catholics of the Oriental Rite are grouped into five major branches or families or *disciplinae,*[44] namely, the Alexandrian, the Antiochene (or Syrian), the Armenian, the Byzantine (or Greek), and the Chaldean (or Syro-Chaldean). Of these, the Armenian *disciplina* alone has only one rite—the Armenian rite. As to the others, the Coptic (or Egyptian) rite and the Ethiopian (or Abyssinian) rite belong to the Alexandrian *disciplina.* The Maronite rite, the pure Syrian (or simply Syrian) rite, and the Malankar rite[45] belong to the An-

[43] *Supra,* p. 84.

[44] One should notice the special meaning of the word *disciplina* when used to denote one of the major groups of the Oriental Church. From the viewpoint of canonists of the Oriental Church there are six *disciplinae* in the whole Church: five *disciplinae* of the Oriental Church, and one *disciplina* of the Latin Church; and just as various rites are grouped in a *disciplina* of the Oriental Church (except for the Armenian), so also it is in the Latin Church—for, in the latter there are the Roman rite, the Ambrosian rite (used in Milan, Italy), the Lyonese or Gallican rite (in France), the Mozarabic rite (used in Toledo, Spain), and also the rites of certain religious orders, i. e., Dominicans, Carthusians, Carmelites.

Some authors refer to the major groups or families of the Oriental Church as the Alexandrian Rite, the Antiochene Rite, the Armenian Rite, the Byzantine Rite, and the Chaldean Rite; others refer to them as the Alexandrian Church, the Antiochene Church, etc. In order to avoid possible confusion and for the sake of greater clarity, the writer in this work henceforth refers to the above major groups as *disciplinae,* and to the various rites in each group as rites, e.g., the Coptic rite and the Ethiopian rite belong to the Alexandrian *disciplina.*

For a definition of a rite according to its full juridical concept with reference to the Oriental Church, consult Cicognani-Staffa, *Commentarium ad Librum Primum Codicis Iuris Canonici,* pp. 11–12. Cf. also Herman, "De 'Ritu' in Iure Canonico"—*Orientalia Christiana* (Roma: Pont. Institutum Orientalium Studiorum, 1923-), XXXII (1933), 105; Michiels, *Principia Generalia de Personis in Ecclesia,* pp. 260–261; Wernz-Vidal, *Ius Canonicum,* II (1943), n. 21; Duskie, *Canonical Status of the Orientals in the United States,* The Catholic University of America Canon Law Studies, n. 48 (Washington, D. C.: The Catholic University of America, 1928), p. 18.

[45] The Malankars are the most recent group to be re-united to the Roman Catholic Church. They were Jacobites from a region in southern India which used to be called Malankar, whence they derive their name—the former Malankar region is now called Malabar. The reunion commenced in 1930 with the return of the Jacobite Patriarch Mar Ivanios, his suffragan

tiochene *disciplina.* The Byzantine (or Greek) *disciplina* includes the following rites: Albanian, Bulgarian, Georgian (which has no hierarchy),[46] pure Greek (or simply Greek), Italo-Albanian, Oriental Jugoslavonic, Melkite, Rumanian, Russian, Ruthenian, Oriental Hungarian. The pure Chaldean (or simply Chaldean) rite and the Malabar rite[47] belong to the Chaldean *disciplina.* It was for all these rites that the Sacred Congregation for the Oriental Church was instituted; it is to these that Canon 257 is directed.

Was the Sacred Congregation, therefore, to have nothing to do with the dissidents of the Orthodox Church? As has been noticed in the various stages of the historical development of the Sacred Congregation for the Oriental Church, the Sacred Congregations dealing with the Orientals always have been solicitous and concerned with the reunion of the separated brethren of the Orthodox Church. In addition, Pope Leo XIII had established in 1895 a special Commission for fostering the reconciliation of nations which had fallen away from the Church through heresy or schism. This Commission under the title *coetus pro unione Ecclesiarum dissidentium* was attached to the *Congregatio de Propaganda Fide* under the Constitution "*Sapienti consilio*" of 1908, and mention of its existence was reported yearly from 1912–1917 inclusively under the Sacred Congregation of the Propagation of the Faith in the official publications of *La Gerarchia Cattolica* and *Annuario Pontificio.* However, neither in the *Annuario Pontificio* for 1918 nor in any of its volumes published since that time, has any mention of this *coetus* been made. Wherefore, Wernz-Vidal concluded that this group seems to have ceased to exist, and its assignment (*negotium*)

Bishop Mar Theopolis, and the monastic Congregation of the Imitation of Christ. In 1932 a new Catholic hierarchy was established by Pope Pius XI with Mar Ivanios as Archbishop of Trivandrum and Mar Theopolis as Bishop of Tinnevelly.

[46] "Since there is no hierarchy, this rite, it would seem, is no longer distinguishable from the Armenian Rite followed by the Catholic Georgians within the dominion of the Turkish Empire, and the Latin Rite adopted by the remainder."—Cicognani, *Canon Law,* p. 446, footnote 5.

[47] The counterpart of the Nestorians in India.

has fallen to the lot of the Sacred Congregation for the Oriental Church.[48] There seems to be no doubt that the group has ceased to exist; but it is recalled that the functions of this group pertained not only to the dissidents of the Orthodox Church, but also to the separated brethren of the Latin Church.[49] Accordingly, it seems logical to conclude that only the care for the reunion of the separated brethren of the Orthodox Eastern Churches is assumed by the Sacred Congregation for the Oriental Church. An example of the care exercised by the Sacred Congregation for the Oriental Church for the reunion of separated Oriental brethren is found in the numerous works dedicated to that cause under the jurisdiction of this Sacred Congregation.

Petrani states that the Sacred Congregation for the Oriental Church has first of all the function (*munus*) of governing the Catholics of the Uniate Eastern Churches, and secondly, of recalling to Catholic unity their brethren formerly one with them and now separated by schism or heresy.[50]

Article III. Canon 257, § 1

The first part of § 1 of canon 257 states that the Roman Pontiff is the prefect of the Sacred Congregation for the Oriental Church:

> **Canon 257, § 1: *Congregationi pro Ecclesia Orientali praeest ipse Romanus Pontifex . . .***

Only two other Sacred Congregations have been similarly honored, namely, the Sacred Congregation of the Holy Office and the Sacred Consistorial Congregation. Wherefore, even though it was the last of the permanent Sacred Congregations to have been instituted, nevertheless it is proper for the Sacred

---

[48] Wernz-Vidal, *Ius Canonicum,* II (1943), 603, footnote 99.

[49] *Supra,* pp. 62, 80–81.

[50] " S. Congregationi pro Ecclesia Orientali munus ergo demandatur imprimis regendi catholicos ecclesiarum orientalium unitarum sive in regionibus, in quibus schisma et haeresis adhuc grassatur sive in partibus praecipue a catholicis latinis incultis viventes, atque deinde etiam revocandi ad catholicam unitatem omnes christianos orientales schismate vel haeresi dissidentes." —Petrani, " De Sacra Congregatione pro Ecclesia Orientali eiusque facultatibus "—*Apollinaris,* X (1937), 31.

Congregation for the Oriental Church to occupy the third place in the listing of the Sacred Congregations of the Roman Curia. Whatever may have been the reason for its position as last of the Sacred Congregations in the Code, its rightful rank behind the two above mentioned Sacred Congregations has been recognized in the official publications of the Holy See since 1928.[51]

Since the Roman Pontiff is the Prefect, the immediate director or moderator of this Sacred Congregation is the Cardinal Secretary. As to the personnel of this Sacred Congregation for the year 1945, there are 17 Cardinals,[52] 1 Assessor, 1 Substitute, 53 Consultors, 14 Officials, and 1 Interpreter.

The second part of § 1 of canon 257 speaks in general terms of the jurisdiction of this Sacred Congregation, and the extent of this jurisdiction is determined specifically by paragraphs 2 and 3 of this same canon, as well as by later pontifical decrees.

> ***Canon* 257, § 1: . . . *Huic Congregationi reservantur omnia cuiusque generis negotia quae sive ad personas, sive ad disciplinam, sive ad ritus Ecclesiarum orientalium referuntur, etiamsi sint mixta, quae scilicet sive rei sive personarum ratione latinos quoque attingant.***

Thus, to this Sacred Congregation are reserved all affairs of every kind relating either to persons or to discipline or to rites

[51] "Beginning with the March, 1928, issue of the *Acta Apostolicae Sedis,* it is to be observed that the documents pertaining to this Sacred Congregation are given place immediately following those of the Sacred Consistorial Congregation. The Sacred Oriental Congregation thus precedes all the other Sacred Congregations except the Holy Office and the S. C. Consist. The probable reason for this arrangement is the fact that the Holy Father in person is the President [Prefect] of these three Congregations." Bouscaren, *The Canon Law Digest,* I, 172. Cf. also *Periodica de Re Canonica, Morali, Liturgica,* XVII (1928), 131. Hereafter cited as *Periodica.*

[52] Among these is Dennis Cardinal Dougherty, Archbishop of Philadelphia, who has been associated with this Sacred Congregation as a Cardinal ever since the day on which he received his red hat, March 10, 1921. However, due to the fact that he lives outside of Rome, he has been only a titular member of this Sacred Congregation. "Cardinales extra Curiam degentes adscribi possunt S. Congregationibus, non ut membra effectiva, sed ut membra titularia." Coronata, *Institutiones Iuris Canonici,* I (1928), 394, footnote 3.

of the Oriental Church, even if such affairs are of a mixed nature—that is to say, even if such affairs either by reason of the object (*res*) or by reason of the persons concern also Catholics of the Latin Rite (examples of affairs of a mixed nature are: (a) marriages between a Catholic of the Latin Rite and a Catholic of an Oriental Rite; (b) the celebration of mass by priests of the Oriental Rite in a church of the Latin Rite and vice versa).[53] So, the law clearly provides for the jurisdiction of this Sacred Congregation in matters concerning Catholics, i. e., when the parties involved are both of the Oriental Rite, or when one party is of the Oriental Rite and the other party is of the Latin Rite, or when a case of *negotia mixta* within the Catholic Church is had. But canon 257, § 1, also provides implicitly and in a general way for the jurisdiction of the Sacred Congregation for the Oriental Church in matters where one of the parties or objects pertains to the Catholic Oriental Rite and the other party or object is of the Orthodox or of any other non-Catholic sect—this follows also from canon 257, § 2, which states as a guiding principle that the Sacred Congregation for the Oriental Church has jurisdiction in those cases in which the other Sacred Congregations, whose place it supplants, have jurisdiction in similar cases where the Catholic party or object is of the Latin Rite.

Article IV. Canon 257, § 2

Canon 257, 2: *Quare pro Ecclesiis ritus orientalis haec Congregatio omnibus facultatibus potitur, quas aliae Congregationes pro Ecclesiis ritus latini obtinent, incolumine tamen iure Congregationis S. Officii ad normam can. 247.*

According to this canon the Sacred Congregation for the Oriental Church in its jurisdiction for the Oriental Rite has all the powers which the other Sacred Congregations have for the Latin Rite, except for matters which belong to the jurisdiction of the Sacred Congregation of the Holy Office as enumerated in canon 247. This law does not mean that the Sacred Congregation for the Oriental Church *de facto* in practice exercises all

[53] Woywod, *A Practical Commentary on the Code of Canon Law,* I, n. 201.

the powers of the other Sacred Congregations with the exception of the Holy Office, since there are certain affairs which it always transfers to the other Sacred Congregations which are adept at handling such matters in the Latin Rite; and besides, there are certain functions of the Sacred Congregation for Extraordinary Ecclesiastical Affairs which pertain to it alone, regardless of the Rite. Moreover, the law of canon 257, § 2, has been slightly modified by a subsequent decree of the Holy See. All these considerations must be incorporated in a complete explanation of this canon.

A. The Sacred Congregation of the Holy Office

First of all, it is expressly stated in canon 257, § 2, that the Sacred Congregation for the Oriental Church has no jurisdiction in matters which appertain to the jurisdiction of the Sacred Congregation of the Holy Office as prescribed in canon 247. The jurisdiction of the Holy Office as determined in canon 247, supplemented with comments, is as follows:

§ 1. The Sacred Congregation of the Holy Office guards the doctrine of faith and morals. Wherefore, it handles business pertaining to the truths of faith and revelation as well as the doctrinal and dogmatic aspects of the sacraments (the minister, matter and form),[54] of indulgences, of new prayers and of devotions, and the like.[55]

§ 2. It judges those delicts which according to its own proper law are reserved to it, and it has the power to judge these criminal cases not only in an appeal from the court of a local Ordinary, but even in the first instance if the case has been brought directly before this Sacred Congregation.[56]

---

[54] Cappello, *De Curia Romana,* I, 65–66, 99–100.

[55] Beste, *Introductio in Codicem,* p. 243; Choupin, *Valeur des Décisions Doctrinales et Disciplinaires du Saint-Siège,* p. 434; De Meester, *Juris Canonici et Juris Canonico-civilis Compendium,* n. 585, 2o; Vermeersch-Creusen, *Epitome Iuris Canonici,* I (1937), n. 362, 2; Wernz-Vidal, *Ius Canonicum,* II (1943), n. 488 III.

[56] Toso (*Ad Codicem Iuris Canonici Benedicti XV Pont. Max. Auctoritate Promulgatum Commentaria Minora* [5 vols. in 2, Tiferni Tiberini: Ex Offic. Typogr. Vinciana, 1921–1927], III, 53 [hereafter cited *Commentaria Minora*]) lists the following as some of the delicts: "Quapropter eius est

§ 3. It alone takes cognizance of cases which either directly or indirectly, in law or in fact, involve the Pauline Privilege, and the matrimonial impediments of disparity of cult and mixed religion; to it likewise pertains the faculty of dispensing from these impediments. Wherefore every question of this kind must be submitted to this Sacred Congregation, which may, if it so judges and *si casus ferat,* refer the question to another Sacred Congregation or to the Tribunal of the Sacred Roman Rota. Hence, by this law the Sacred Congregation for the Oriental Church does not enjoy the faculty of dispensing from impediments of disparity of cult and mixed religion which the *Congregatio de Propaganda Fide pro Negotiis ritus orientalis* enjoyed.[57]

§ 4. To this Sacred Congregation pertains not only the careful examination of books denounced to the Holy See and their prohibition, if necessary, but also the granting of dispensations from this prohibition to read books forbidden by it. It is likewise to investigate *ex officio* in the most suitable way available the published writings of any kind which it conceives should be prohibited, and to remind the Ordinaries of their duty to proceed

---

in primis, videre de delictis contra fidem, veluti apostasiae, haeresis, schismatis, magiae, sortilegii, etc.; aut de delictis, quae haeresis suspicionem secum ferant, veluti est cum haereticis cooperatio aut *in divinis* communicatio (can. 2316); pactio ante matrimonium de prole extra Ecclesiam educanda (can. 2319, § 1, n. 2); liberorum baptizandorum oblatio ministris acatholicis (*ibid.,* n. 3) eorumve traditio, uti acatholice educentur (*ibid.,* n. 4); specierum consecratarum abiectio, ad malum finem abductio aut retentio (can. 2332); per annum, obdurato animo, in censura excommunicationis permansio (can. 2340, § 1); simoniaca sacramentorum ministratio vel receptio (can. 2371); aut de delictis, quae gravitatem prae se ferant, veluti ad turpia sollicitatio ad normam can. 904 (can. 2368) vel legis ieiunii eucharistici, de quo infra, ad normam can. 2322 [rather 2321] transgressio." Beste, *Introductio in Codicem,* p. 243 specifies a few more, namely: ". . . spiritismus, superstitio . . . absolutio complicis, violatio sigilli, simonia, matrimonium clerici, adhaesio sectae massonicae vel alii societati prohibitae." Cf. also Blat, *Commentarium Textus Codicis Iuris Canonici* (6 vols., Romae: Collegio "Angelico," 1920–1927), II (2. ed., 1921), n. 237; De Meester, *Juris Canonici et Juris Canonico-civilis Compendium,* II (1923), 77; Sipos, *Enchiridion Iuris Canonici,* p. 207; Vermeersch-Creusen, *Epitome Iuris Canonici,* I (1937), 295; III (1936), 7–8.

[57] Cf. *supra,* p. 77.

conscientiously against pernicious writings and to denounce them to the Holy See in accordance with canon 1397.

It is proper to mention here that the Sacred Congregation for the Oriental Church was asked whether Orientals are bound by the decrees of the Sacred Congregation of the Holy Office condemning books and papers. The Sacred Congregation for the Oriental Church declared on May 26, 1928, that the aforesaid decrees apply to the faithful of all rites and bind them all in the same way since these decrees directly concern the doctrine of the Church rather than the discipline. The Church [the declaration continues] wishes by such decrees to preserve and safeguard faith and morals; and for this purpose the Code in canon 1396 [58] clearly provides that all books condemned by the Holy See are considered as prohibited in all places and in whatever language they are translated.[59]

§ 5. It alone is competent in all matters relating to the eucharistic fast for priests celebrating the Holy Sacrifice of the Mass.

In connection with canon 247, § 3, it is fitting to note the response of the Sacred Congregation of the Holy Office on January 18, 1928, to the following doubt: Whether the Supreme Sacred Congregation of the Holy Office has exclusive jurisdiction in all matrimonial causes which are in any way brought before the Holy See between a Catholic party and a non-Catholic party, whether baptized or unbaptized. The reply was: In the affirmative, especially in consideration of Canon 247, § 3, and without prejudice to the prescription of canon 1557, § 1, 1°.[60] Aguirre

[58] "Libri ab Apostolica Sede damnati ubique locorum et in quodcunque vertantur idioma prohibiti censeantur."

[59] Bouscaren, *The Canon Law Digest,* I, 685; *AAS,* XX (1928), 195; *Periodica,* XVII (1928), 131; *Jus Pontificium* (Romae, 1921–), VIII (1928), 60.

[60] [Suprema S. C. S. Officii, die 18 Ianuarii 1928 ad *Dubium*] . . . II. "Utrum in quibuslibet causis matrimonialibus inter partem catholicam et partem acatholicam, sive baptizatam sive non baptizatam, quocumque modo ad Sanctam Sedem delätis, Suprema Sacra Congregatio Sancti Officii exclusivam habeat competentiam . . . " [respondendum decrevit] : "*Affirmative,* habita praesertim ratione can. 247, § 3, et salvo praescripto can. 1557, § 1, 1°."—*AAS,* XX (1928), 75; *Periodica,* XVII (1928), 54; *Jus Pontificium,*

rightly says that this response of the Holy Office seems to interpret in a wide sense those words of canon 247, § 3, by which it is decreed that the Holy Office has exclusive jurisdiction over matters which are concerned either directly or *indirectly* with the matrimonial impediments of disparity of cult and mixed religion.[61] At any rate, since this response of the Holy Office, the Sacred Congregation for the Oriental Church has absolutely no jurisdiction over any matrimonial case brought in any way before the Holy See in which a Catholic of the Oriental Rite and a non-Catholic party, either baptized or unbaptized, are concerned. However, let it be noted as of historical interest that before this response of January 27, 1928, the jurisdiction for cases

---

VIII (1928), 9; *Theologisch-praktische Quartalschrift* (Linz, 1832–), LXXX (1928), 388; *The Irish Ecclesiastical Record* (Dublin, 1864–), XXXI (1928), 455; Bouscaren, *The Canon Law Digest,* I, 763.

Canon 1557, § 1, 1o, refers to the fact that the Roman Pontiff has the exclusive right to judge: (a) those who hold the highest governmental rank in a nation; (b) their sons and daughters; (c) those who have the immediate right of succession.

[61] Together with this statement Aguirre avers that causes of this kind can be treated in the first and second instances in diocesan tribunals, since the declaration of the Holy Office expressly refers to cases brought in any way before the Holy See. Cf. Wernz-Vidal, *Ius Canonicum,* II (1943), 576, footnote 39*. Beste, *Introductio in Codicem,* pp. 832–833 clearly states his conclusions: "Omnibus perpensis, sequentem interpretationem pro certo amplectimur et proponimus, donec contrarium authentice declaretur. Omnes actiones iudiciales inter litigantes quorum altera pars est catholica altera acatholica exagitatae, etiamsi impedimentum cultus disparis aut mixtae religionis directe tangant, nulla praehabita venia a Sancta Sede, regulariter institui et pertractari valent penes ordinaria tribunalia primae et secundae instantiae, dummodo coniux catholicus partem actoris agat; quodsi deinde ad S. Sedem qualibet ex causa devolverint, sive iudiciali appelatione sive extraiudiciali recursu aut expostulatione, praedicta S. C. S. O. privative erit forum competens. Eodem modo ad hanc S. Cong. vi can. 247, § 3, recurrendum erit, quotiescumque dubium occurrat quod circa hoc duplex impedimentum mixtae religionis et disparitatis cultus in via disciplinari extraiudicialiter (sine processu iudiciali) resolvi nequeat ab ordinario loci."

Cf. also Hilling, "Die Entscheidung des Hl. Offiziums vom 18. Januar 1928 über seine Kompetenz in Ehesachen"—*Archiv für katholisches Kirchenrecht,* CVIII (1928), 536–548, as against Arendt, "De Exclusiva S. Officii Competentia circa Matrimonium Mixtum (Can. 247)"—*Jus Pontificium,* VII (1927), 120–137.

of ratified and non-consummated marriage between a Catholic and non-Catholic seemed to have been interpreted otherwise. For, according to canon 249, § 3, of the Code[62] and chapter II, n. 9, § 2,[63] of the Rules to be observed in drawing up the process in cases of ratified and non-consummated marriages—these rules were given by the Sacred Congregation of the Discipline of the Sacraments,—it would seem as though the Sacred Congregation of the Discipline of the Sacraments was considered competent to handle cases of ratified and non-consummated marriage between a Catholic and non-Catholic. Since the Sacred Congregation for the Oriental Church in regard to its subjects of the Oriental Rite always has enjoyed the same faculties as the Sacred Congregation of the Discipline of the Sacraments in regard to subjects of the Latin Rite, *a pari* by the law of canon 257, § 2, it likewise must have been considered competent (in theory at least, if not in practice to handle cases of ratified and non-consummated marriage between a Catholic of the Oriental Rite and a non-Catholic up to the time of the above response of the Sacred Congregation of the Holy Office in 1928. Since that response, however, all matrimonial cases between a Catholic party (either of the Latin Rite or of the Oriental Rite) and a non-Catholic party (either baptized or unbaptized), which are brought in any way before the Holy See, belong to the jurisdiction of the Sacred Congregation of the Holy Office.

B. Other Sacred Congregations and Canon 257, § 2

Only matters belonging to the jurisdiction of the Sacred Congregation of the Holy Office as prescribed in canon 247 are ex-

[62] "Ipsa [Congregatio de disciplina Sacramentorum] cognoscit quoque et exclusive de facto inconsummationis matrimonii et de exsistentia causarum ad dispensationem concedendam, nec non de iis omnibus quae cum his sunt connexa." Cf. also canon 1962.

[63] "Si contingat dispensationem peti a parte acatholica, Ordinarius petitionem ad hanc Sacram Congregationem aeque remittat; additis tamen necessariis et opportunis explicationibus de petitionis fundamento, de oratoris qualitatibus personalibus, aliisque adiunctis ad rem facientibus."—*Regulae Servandae in Processibus Super Matrimonio Rato et Non Consummato,* 7 Maii, 1923—*AAS,* XV (1923), 389. Cf. also Bouscaren, *The Canon Law Digest,* I, 767.

pressly stated in canon 257, § 2, as being excluded from the jurisdiction of the Sacred Congregation for the Oriental Church. However, due to the legislation of Pope Pius XI after the promulgation of the Code, certain other affairs have been withdrawn from the jurisdiction of the Sacred Congregation for the Oriental Church and placed under the jurisdiction of the Sacred Congregation of Studies for Seminaries and Universities. Besides, there are some functions of other Sacred Congregations which the Sacred Congregation for the Oriental Church does not perform, and there are other functions which are excluded from the jurisdiction of the Sacred Congregation for the Oriental Church by virtue of § 3 of canon 257. A summary of the relation of the Sacred Congregation for the Oriental Church to the functions of these other Sacred Congregations follows.

1. THE SACRED CEREMONIAL CONGREGATION

The Sacred Ceremonial Congregation retains in canon 254 the very same jurisdiction it possessed under the Constitution "*Sapienti consilio,*" i. e., the regulation (*moderatio*) of the ceremonies performed in the papal chapel and the papal court, and of the sacred functions which the cardinals perform outside the papal chapel;[64] it likewise decides questions of precedence among cardinals as well as among the legates whom the various nations send to the Holy See.[65]

It is evident that the ceremonies in the papal chapel have been thus far the care of the Sacred Ceremonial Congregation alone, since the popes have been of the Latin Rite. Similarly up to the time of the creation of the first cardinal of the Oriental Rite, since the promulgation of the *Codex Iuris Canonici,* namely, Ignatius Cardinal Tappouni (Syrian Patriarch of Antioch), on December 16, 1935,[66] the Sacred Ceremonial Congregation alone handled all questions of precedence among cardinals. But as to the ceremonies at the papal court as well as the questions of precedence among the legates sent by the various nations to the

[64] Cf. Ojetti, *De Romana Curia,* p. 145.
[65] Cf. *supra,* p. 79.
[66] *AAS,* XXVII (1935), 459.

Holy See there has always been present the possibility of *negotia mixta;* and since the creation of Cardinal Tappouni, all questions of precedence in which he is involved have the character of *negotia mixta.* But, in view of the fact that the Sacred Ceremonial Congregation has fixed regulations for most of the above noted matters, it has been the practise of the Sacred Congregation for the Oriental Church to entrust (remit) these matters to the Sacred Ceremonial Congregation.[67] However, it is to be observed that the law of canon 257, § 1 and § 2, does not exclude the functions attributed to the Sacred Ceremonial Congregation from the jurisdiction of the Sacred Congregation for the Oriental Church whenever Catholics of the Oriental Rite are concerned.

2. SACRED CONGREGATION FOR EXTRAORDINARY ECCLESIASTICAL AFFAIRS

The functions assigned to the Sacred Congregation for Extraordinary Ecclesiastical Affairs can be classed under a twofold division:

(a) It is within its jurisdiction to erect and divide dioceses and to promote suitable ecclesiastics to vacant dioceses in countries where the civil governments have to be dealt with in doing these things.

(b) It has charge of affairs submitted to it for examination by the Supreme Pontiff through the Cardinal Secretary of State—these are chiefly affairs connected with the civil laws and the agreements of the Holy See with the various nations.[68]

Even though the affairs mentioned in (b) concern the Oriental Rite, the Sacred Congregation for the Oriental Church has no claim on those particular matters since they are assigned by the pope to the other Sacred Congregation. But in reference to the functions described in (a), it is to be observed that ordinarily with regard to the Oriental Rite the Sacred Congregation for the Oriental Church establishes and divides dioceses, and proposes

[67] Staffa, "De Sacrae Congregationis pro Ecclesia Orientali competentia" —*Apollinaris,* XI (1938), 372, 375.

[68] Canon 255. Cf. Woywod, *A Practical Commentary on the Code of Canon Law,* I (1941), 100.

Compare with *supra,* p. 79.

to the Supreme Pontiff for election or confirmation—according to the laws proper to each Oriental Rite—suitable ecclesiastics for vacant sees.[69] However, when the Church has to deal with the civil governments in these matters,[70] Petrani states that these affairs are entrusted to the Sacred Congregation for Extraordinary Ecclesiastical Affairs.[71] It is not clear whether he means that the jurisdiction of the Sacred Congregation for the Oriental Church is limited in these cases or that the practice of the latter Sacred Congregation is to remit them to the Sacred Congregation for Extraordinary Ecclesiastical Affairs. Petrani in the very next paragraph following the above assertion states that the Sacred Congregation for the Oriental Church gives orders for the canonical investigation or process concerning the clerics who are to be appointed to the aforesaid positions, and carefully examines these acts of the process, and, if there is need, remits them to the Sacred Congregation for Extraordinary Ecclesiastical Affairs[72]—which in any case definitely indicates that by no means all aspects of these cases are even then withdrawn from the Sacred Congregation for the Oriental Church.

Unless a concession has been made orally (*vivae vocis oraculo*) to the Sacred Congregation for Extraordinary Ecclesiastical Affairs for these acts (the erection and division of dioceses, and the promotion to vacant sees), it seems that the force of canon

---

69 Canons 257, § 2, and 248, § 2.

70 Bouscaren (*The Canon Law Digest,* I, 168–169): "His Holiness, Pope Pius XI, in a Letter of 5 July, 1925, to the Cardinal Secretary of State, declared and decreed:

1. Canon 255 providing for the appointment by the Sacred Congregation for Extraordinary Ecclesiastical Affairs of fit men to vacant sees whenever any negotiations with civil governments are required, is to be understood in the sense that it pertains to that Sacred Congregation to appoint Bishops even in cases where governments are to be consulted regarding possible difficulties of a political nature against persons who have been chosen for that office." Cf. also *AAS,* XVIII (1926), 89; *Periodica,* XV (1926), 31; *Jus Pontificium,* VI (1926), 14.

71 Si verum contingat ut circa ea . . . cum civilibus guberniis agendum sit, tunc res demandatur S. Congregationi pro negotiis ecclesiasticis extraordinariis."—Petrani, "De Sacra Congregatione pro Ecclesia Orientali eiusque facultatibus"—*Apollinaris,* X (1937), p. 32, n. 3.

72 Petrani, *ibid.,* n. 4.

257, § 2, controls the case so that jurisdiction in these affairs remains intact in the Sacred Congregation for the Oriental Church, even though its practice or procedure is to defer them to the other Sacred Congregation. Of course, as particular cases present themselves, the pope obviously can assign them to the Sacred Congregation for Extraordinary Ecclesiastical Affairs, if he so wills.

3. THE SACRED CONGREGATION OF SACRED RITES

Petrani states that affairs which in any way refer to the beatification and canonization of the Servants of God or to sacred relics, even if it concerns Orientals, pertain to the Sacred Congregation of Sacred Rites. He gives no explanation for this assertion beyond his reference to canon 253, § 3, which reads as follows:

> ***Denique* [*Congregatio Sacrorum Rituum*] *ea omnia agit quae ad beatificationem et canonizationem Servorum Dei vel ad sacras reliquias quoquo modo referuntur.***

Wherefore it seems as though Petrani holds that the Sacred Congregation of Sacred Rites has universal jurisdiction in such matters.

On the other hand, Staffa[73] indicates that it is within the jurisdiction of the Sacred Congregation for the Oriental Church to handle matters which refer to sacred relics, but it can send them to the Sacred Congregation of Sacred Rites if it so decides. Similarly, he states, matters which pertain to beatification and canonization of its subjects are not explicitly excluded from the jurisdiction of the Sacred Congregation for the Oriental Church; however, because of the special process involved and other preparations required for such affairs,[74] these matters always are entrusted to the Sacred Congregation of Sacred Rites.

The solution of this question must be in accord with the prescription of § 3 of canon 257. Wherefore matters concerning

---

[73] " De Sacrae Congregationis pro Ecclesia Orientali competentia "—*Apollinaris,* XI (1938), 372, 374, 375.

[74] Cf. Blat, *Commentarium Textus Codicis Iuris Canonici,* II (2. ed., 1921), 270; Wernz-Vidal, *Ius Canonicum,* II (1943), 598, footnotes 89*, 90.

sacred relics are within the jurisdiction of the Sacred Congregation for the Oriental Church, for (a) they are definitely not excluded from its jurisdiction in canon 257, § 2; and (b) they can be treated *in linea disciplinari* in accordance with the norm of canon 257, § 3—in cases which demand greater investigation, however, they can be referred to the Sacred Congregation of Sacred Rites. But whatever pertains to the beatification and canonization of the Servants of God, even though it is not explicitly excluded from the jurisdiction of the Sacred Congregation for the Oriental Church in § 2 of canon 257, is not to be treated by the latter Sacred Congregation according to the norm of § 3 of this same canon, since such matters are decided *ordine iudiciario.* The explanation of this last assertion is given in the present chapter under article V.[75]

4. SACRED CONGREGATION OF STUDIES FOR SEMINARIES AND UNIVERSITIES

There is no doubt that the Sacred Congregation for the Oriental Church has jurisdiction for the government, discipline, temporal administration, and studies of the seminaries and ecclesiastical colleges of the Oriental Rite wherever they exist, even when these institutes are directed by religious Congregations or Orders of the Latin Rite;[76] it likewise has jurisdiction over the societies of ecclesiastics and the seminaries which have been founded exclusively in order to train missionaries for missions of the Oriental Church.[77] But with respect to its jurisdiction in regard to the erection and direction of universities and faculties of ecclesiastical studies[78] (i. e., those which by the authority of the Holy See have been established for teaching and cultivating the sacred sciences or sciences connected with them, with the right

---

[75] Cf. *infra,* pp. 118 sq.

[76] Canons 257, § 2, and 256, § 1; Petrani, "De Sacra Congregatione pro Ecclesia Orientali eiusque facultatibus"—*Apollinaris,* X (1937), p. 33, n. 17; Staffa, "De Sacrae Congregationis pro Ecclesia Orientali competentia" —*Apollinaris,* XI (1938), 375.

[77] Canons 252, § 3, and 257, § 2; Staffa, *loc. cit.*

[78] It possessed these powers up to the time of the Constitution *"Deus scientiarum Dominus."* Canons 257, § 2, and 256, § 1.

of conferring academic degrees),[79] it is definitely declared in the Constitution "*Deus scientiarum Dominus,*" of May 24, 1931,[80] that the canonical erection and supreme control (*suprema moderatio*) of every university and faculty of ecclesiastical studies, even in those places and institutes which are subject to the Sacred Congregation for the Oriental Church[81] and the Sacred Congregation of the Propagation of the Faith, and the canonical erection and supreme control of faculties of ecclesiastical studies which are destined for any of the religious houses (*Familiis*) are reserved to the Sacred Congregation of Studies for Seminaries and

---

[79] Constitution "*Deus scientiarum Dominus*"—*AAS,* XXIII (1931), 247:

TITULUS I

ART. 1

Universitates et Facultates studiorum ecclesiasticorum eae sunt, quae auctoritate Sanctae Sedis ad disciplinas sacras vel cum sacris conexas tradendas et excolendas instituuntur, cum iure conferendi gradus academicos.

ART. 2

Universitatum et Facultatum studiorum ecclesiasticorum finis est: auditores disciplinis, quae sacrae vel cum sacris conexae sunt, secundum doctrinam catholicam altius instituere; eos ad fontium cognitionem, ad investigationis laborisque scientifici usum atque ad magisterium exercendum instruere; denique iisdem disciplinis excolendis provehendisque quam maxime consulere.

ART. 3

§ 1.—Facultates studiorum ecclesiasticorum censentur: Theologicae, Iuridicae, Philosophicae, aliae denique omnes, quae ad finem, de quo in art. 2, a Sancta Sede instituantur.

§ 2.—Nomine Universitatum vel Facultatum comprehenduntur etiam haec Instituta a Sancta Sede in Urbe erecta:

Pontificium Institutum Biblicum, Pontificium Institutum Studiorum Orientalium, Pontificium Institutum Utriusque Iuris, Pontificium Institutum Archaeologiae Christianae, Pontificium Institutum Musicae Sacrae.

[80] *AAS,* XXIII (1931), 241–262.

[81] By this Constitution the *Pontificium Institutum Studiorum Orientalium* [cf. *supra,* p. 86], which had been attached to the Gregorian University in 1928, henceforth was no longer subject to the Sacred Congregation for the Oriental Church as heretofore. Dausend, *Das interrituelle Recht im Codex Iuris Canonici—Görres-Gesellschaft* (Köln: J. P. Bachem, 1908; Paderborn: Ferdinand Schoningh, 1909–), LXXIX (1939), 174.

Universities.[82] Thus, the jurisdiction of the latter Sacred Congregation according to the norms of the Constitution "*Deus scientiarum Dominus*" is exclusive and universal.

5. THE SACRED PENITENTIARIA

a. *Canon 258, § 1*

Canon 258, § 1: ***Sacrae Poenitentiariae praeficitur Cardinalis Poenitentiarius Maior. Huius tribunalis iurisdictio coarctatur ad ea quae forum internum, etiam non sacramentale, respiciunt; quare hoc tribunal pro solo foro interno gratias largitur, absolutiones, dispensationes, commutationes, sanationes, condonationes; excutit praeterea questiones conscientiae easque dirimit.***

According to canon 258, § 1, of the Code the jurisdiction of the Sacred Penitentiaria is limited to affairs of the internal forum, both sacramental and non-sacramental; and hence solely for the internal forum it grants favors, absolutions, dispensations, commutations, sanations, condonations. Moreover, it considers and decides questions of conscience. This tribunal previously possessed these very same faculties under the Constitution "*Sapienti consilio*" of 1908,[83] and in reference to its faculties under that Constitution Cappello claimed that its jurisdiction was universal in regard to persons.[84] Under the Code the doubt as to whether or not the jurisdiction of the Sacred Penitentiaria over the internal forum also extended to those who were subject to the Sacred Congregation for the Oriental Church was solved ultimately by a reply of the latter Sacred Congregation. The reply dated July 26, 1930, was in the affirmative to the question: Whether in regard to those things which pertain to the internal

---

[82] Constitution "Deus scientiarum Dominus," title I, art. 4—*AAS*, XXIII (1931), 248; Bouscaren, *The Canon Law Digest*, I, 172; *Periodica*, XX (1931), 298; Staffa, "De Sacrae Congregationis pro Ecclesia Orientali competentia"—*Apollinaris*, XI (1938), 373.

[83] *AAS*, I (1909), 15; Ojetti, *De Romana Curia*, p. XVIII.

[84] "Hinc relate ad Sacrae Poenitentiariae competentiam dicimus: (a) eam esse pro foro interno *universalem* sive quoad personas sive quoad materias aliquo sensu saltem; sive quoad loca; . . . ."—Cappello, *De Curia Romana*, I, 357.

forum, even non-sacramental, mentioned in canon 258, the faithful who belong to Churches of the Oriental rites must have recourse to the Sacred Penitentiaria.[85]

The above doubt did not arise because of canon 257, § 2 (which is concerned only with Sacred Congregations), since the Sacred Penitentiaria is a Tribunal and not a Sacred Congregation. But the doubt was based on the general statement of canon 257, § 1, concerning the jurisdiction of the Sacred Congregation for the Oriental Church,[86] namely, that all affairs of every kind relating either to persons, or to the discipline, or to the rites of the Oriental Church, even if such affairs are of a mixed nature, are reserved to this Sacred Congregation.[87] Wherefore it now seems evident that the meaning of canon 257, § 1, is not as general as it may first appear to be, and that its real meaning is to be had only when it is applied to or taken in conjunction with the jurisdiction given to the Sacred Congregation by § 2 and § 3 of that canon.

b. *Canon 258, § 2*

> Canon 258, § 2: ***Eiusdem insuper est de iis omnibus iudicare quae spectant ad usum et concessionem indulgentiarum, salvo iure S. Officii videndi ea quae doctrinam dogmaticam circa easdem indulgentias vel circa novas orationes et devotiones respiciunt.***

According to canon 258, § 2, the Sacred Penitentiaria is to consider all things that pertain to the use and concession of indulgences, the right of the Holy Office with regard to the dogmatic doctrine about these same indulgences or about new prayers and devotions remaining intact.

Under the Constitution "*Sapienti consilio*" (I, 1°, 3), of June 29, 1908, indulgences both as to doctrine and as to use were

---

[85] *AAS,* XXII (1930), 394; Bouscaren, *The Canon Law Digest,* I, 174; *Periodica,* XIX (1930), 339; *Jus Pontificium,* X (1930), 243.

[86] Toso, "De competentia S. Poenitentiariae Ap. circa negotia fori interni Orientalium"—*Jus Pontificium,* X (1930), 243.

[87] Canon 257, § 2: ". . . Huic Congregationi reservantur omnia cuiusque generis negotia quae sive ad personas, sive ad disciplinam, sive ad ritus Ecclesiarum orientalium referuntur, eiamsi sunt mixta, quae scilicet sive rei sive personarum ratione latinos quoque attingant."

under the jurisdiction of the Sacred Congregation of the Holy Office,[88] that is, for the faithful of the Latin Rite under its jurisdiction; the *Congregatio de Propaganda Fide pro negotiis ritus orientalis* had competence in these matters for the faithful of the Oriental Rite.[89] But by the Motu proprio "*Alloquentes,*" of March 25, 1907, Pope Benedict XV transferred this charge over indulgences from the Holy Office to the Sacred Penitentiaria in stating that whatever concerned indulgences now pertained to the Sacred Penitentiaria; then, he related the very words of canon 258, § 2. This Motu proprio terminated with the words: "*Haec statuimus et praecipimus, contrariis quibuslibet, etiam speciali mentione dignis, non obstantibus.*" [90] It is not clear whether this clause was meant for the Oriental Rite as well as of the Latin Rite. But not long after the Motu proprio "*Alloquentes,*" the Sacred Penitentiaria gave an affirmative response on July 7, 1917, to the doubt proposed by a bishop of the Oriental Rite as to whether the faithful of the Oriental Rite could gain all the indulgences granted by the Roman Pontiff in a general decree.[91] It is to be noted that this doubt was submitted to the Sacred Penitentiaria and not to the Sacred Congregation for the Oriental Church.

Villien [92] in commenting on the transfer of the section for indulgences from the Sacred Congregation of the Holy Office to the Sacred Penitentiaria remarked that indulgences operate in the internal forum alone, and that they do not produce any juridic effect of the external forum, and thus the Sacred Penitentiaria remained a Tribunal for the internal forum in accordance with the Constitution "*Sapienti consilio*" (II, 1°): "Huius sacri iudicii seu tribunalis iurisdictio coarctatur ad ea dumtaxat quae forum internum, etiam non sacramentale, respiciunt." [93]

---

[88] *AAS,* I (1909), 9; Ojetti, *De Romana Curia,* p. XI.

[89] Cf. *supra,* pp. 64–67.

[90] *Le Canoniste Contemporain,* XL (1917), 154–155. Cf. also the allocution of Pope Benedict XV in the secret consistory of March 22, 1917—*Le Canoniste Contemporain,* XL (1917), 153–154.

[91] *AAS,* IX (1917), 399; *Le Canoniste Contemporain,* XL (1917), 373.

[92] Villien, "Le Saint-Office et la Suppression de la Congrégation de l'Index"—*Le Canoniste Contemporain,* XL, 111.

[93] *AAS,* I (1909), 15; Ojetti, *De Romana Curia,* p. XVIII.

Finally, a notification, dated July 21, 1935, of the Sacred Congregation for the Oriental Church stated that in audiences granted on June 1 and 22, 1935, to the Cardinal Secretary of the Sacred Congregation for the Oriental Church and to the Cardinal Major Penitentiary respectively, Pope Pius XI decreed that the faithful of every Oriental Rite also are to have recourse to the Sacred Penitentiaria in everything that concerns indulgences.[94] In other words, the powers conceded to the Sacred Penitentiaria in canon 258, § 2, are universal.[95]

6. THE REMAINING SACRED CONGREGATIONS

As to the other Sacred Congregations mentioned in the Code, namely, the Sacred Consistorial Congregation, the Sacred Congregation of the Discipline of the Sacraments, the Sacred Congregation of the Council, the Sacred Congregation of Religious, the Sacred Congregation of the Propagation of the Faith, their functions are assumed by the Sacred Congregation for the Oriental Church whenever persons or things of the Oriental Rite are concerned. Thus by way of a practical example, cases of ratified and non-consummated marriage between Catholics of the Latin Rite pertain to the Sacred Congregation of the Discipline of the Sacraments; while cases of ratified and non-consummated marriage between Catholics of the Oriental Rite or between a Catholic of the Oriental Rite and a Catholic of the Latin Rite pertain to the Sacred Congregation for the Oriental Church.[96] Another practical application to be remembered is as follows: whatever is decreed about Orientals and their rites in provincial councils (either regional or national) of the Latin Rite, regardless of whether or not bishops of the Oriental Rite were present, must be submitted to the examination and acknowledgment of the Sacred Congregation for the Oriental Church.[97] Petrani,[98]

---

[94] *AAS,* XXVII (1935), 379; Beste, *Introductio in Codicem,* p. 247.

[95] For more recent examples of the Sacred Penitentiaria handling these matters for the Orientals, consult *AAS,* XXXVI (1944), 47, 245.

[96] Canons 257, § 2, and 249, § 3.

[97] Canons 250, § 4, and 257, § 2; Petrani, "De Sacra Congregatione pro Ecclesia Orientali eiusque facultatibus"—*Appollinaris,* X (1937), p. 33, n. 18.

[98] *Loc. cit.*

moreover, asserts that the same applies to diocesan synods and to meetings or conferences of bishops of the Latin Rite.

It is fitting to treat here the proper authority for the authentic interpretation of the canons of the Code which refer to or include Orientals. First of all by way of introduction it is to be noted that though the Sacred Congregations for the Latin Church now apply the laws of the Code to particular, concrete cases pertaining to their jurisdiction, they do not have the faculty of interpreting authentically the canons of the Code.[99] Previously under the Constitution "*Sapienti consilio*" the Sacred Congregations did possess the power of authentic interpretation both as to the decrees of the Council of Trent as well as to other ecclesiastical laws according to the respective competence of each of the Sacred Congregations with regard to ecclesiastical matters committed to its jurisdiction; this interpretation, however, needed the approbation of the pope.[100] But by the Motu proprio "*Cum iuris canonici*" Pope Benedict XV instituted a Commission for the authentic interpretation of the canons of the Code, and to it alone this function has been entrusted.[101] Hence, there is a clear distinction between the work of this Commission and that of the Sacred Congregations of the Latin Rite: the first pronounces authentically the meaning of a law in the Code in a general and abstract manner—it decrees in what sense a canon

[99] Boudinhon, "La Commission pour l'Interpretation Officielle du Code"—*Le Canoniste Contemporain,* XL (1917), 397; Brems, "De Interpretatione Authentica Codicis I. C. per Pont. Commissionem"—*Jus Pontificium,* XVI (1936), 92-93; Hilling, "Die gesetzgeberische Tätigkeit Benedikts XV seit der Promulgation des Codex iuris canonici"—*Archiv für katholisches Kirchenrecht,* CIII (1923), 9; Schmidt, *The Principles of Authentic Interpretation in Canon 17 of the Code of Canon Law,* The Catholic University of America Canon Law Studies, n. 141; (Washington, D. C.: The Catholic University of America Press, 1941), p. 61.

[100] ". . . An facultas authentice interpretandi Concilii Tridentini decreta aliasque leges ecclesiasticas vi Constitutionis *Sapienti consilio* sit singulis Sacris Congregationibus commissa secundum propriam cuiusque competentiam, salva Romani Pontificis approbatione; . . ." [Resp.] Affirmative.—*Fontes,* n. 2079; Schmidt, *op. cit.,* pp. 56–57, footnote 17.

[101] The Motu proprio under section I reads: ". . . Consilium seu *Commissionem,* uti vocant, constituimus, cui uni ius erit Codicis authentice interpretandi . . ."—*AAS,* IX (1917), 483.

or part of the canon must be understood; the second applies the law to concrete cases.[102] Moreover, it is important to note that the Commission is restricted to interpreting only the canons of the Code so that the liturgical laws of the Latin Church which are not contained in the Code, are not subject to this Commission for their authentic interpretation, but rather to the Sacred Congregation of Sacred Rites, with the approbation of the pope.[103] Wherefore in regard to Orientals it is clear that the Commission interprets authentically only those canons of the Code which from the very nature of the matter concern also the Oriental Church,[104] while other general laws of the Oriental Church and the particular Pontifical laws issued by the Sacred Congregation for the Oriental Church apparently are interpreted authentically by the latter Sacred Congregation,[105] accompanied by the approbation of the pope.

Article V. Canon 257, § 3

Can. 257, § 3:—*Haec Congregatio controversias dirimit via disciplinari; quas vero ordine iudiciario dirimendas iudicaverit, ad tribunal remittet quod ipsa Congregatio designaverit.*

According to canon 257, § 3, the Sacred Congregation for the Oriental Church decides controversies in a disciplinary manner; but those which, as it will have judged, need to be decided in a judicial manner (*ordine iudiciario*), it shall refer to a tribunal which the Sacred Congregation itself shall have designated. This

---

[102] Boudinhon, "La Commission pour l'Interpretation Officielle du Code"—*Le Canoniste Contemporain*, XL (1917), 397–398; Schmidt, *The Principles of Authentic Interpretation in Canon 17 of the Code of Canon Law*, p. 61.

[103] Cf. Toso, *Commentaria Minora*, III, 51; Schmidt, *op. cit.*, p. 62—consult also pp. 104–106 for Schmidt's comments concerning the Sacred Congregations of the Latin Rite in regard to particular laws and their authentic interpretation.

[104] Canon 1.

[105] Toso (*Commentaria Minora*) III, 70) says: ". . . haec Congregatio [pro Ecclesia Orientali] . . . leges a se latas authentice interpretari posse." Cicognani-Staffa (*Commentarium ad Librum Primum Codicis Iuris Canonici*, p. 264, footnote 3) state: "Sacra Congregatio pro Ecclesia Orientali authentice interpretari potest leges orientalium quae sunt extra codicem."

paragraph makes a distinction between matters which are to be treated by the Sacred Congregation and matters which are not to be treated by it. It is definitely stated that the Sacred Congregation settles matters in a disciplinary, i. e., administrative [106] this law.

manner. Therefore whatever can be treated in a disciplinary, administrative way and is in accordance with the powers given in § 1 and § 2 of canon 257 is within the jurisdiction of this Sacred Congregation. Thus those matrimonial and other processes which are handled in an administrative manner [107] come within

---

[106] Cf. Cappello, *Praxis Processualis* (Taurini-Romae: Domus Editorialis Marietti, 1940), pp. 1-2; Meier, *Penal Administrative Procedure Against Negligent Pastors,* The Catholic University of America Canon Law Studies, n. 140 (Washington, D. C.: The Catholic University of America Press, 1940), pp. 85-86; Noval, *Commentarium Codicis Iuris Canonici,* lib. IV, *De Processibus* (2 vols., Pars I, *De Iudiciis,* 1920; Pars II, *De Causis Beatificationis Servorum Dei et Canonizationis Beatorum,* 1932; Pars IV, *De Modo Procedendi in Nonnullis Expediendis Negotiis vel Sanctionibus Poenalibus Applicandis,* 1932; Augustae Taurinorum-Romae: Marietti), II, n. 459; Rice, *Proof of Death in Pre-Nuptial Investigation,* The Catholic University of America Canon Law Studies, n. 123 (Washington, D. C.: The Catholic University of America Press, 1940), p. 45.

Other names used for a process conducted *via disciplinari* (for instance, the processes described in canons 2142-2194) are "summary," "economic." Cf. Rice, *loc. cit.;* Meier, *loc. cit.;* Roberti, *De Processibus* [2 vols., Romae: Aqud Aedes Facultatis Iuridicae ad S. Apollinaris, 1926], I 26) states that such processes are improperly called "summary."

[107] The following are administrative processes: (a) the processes in canons 2142-2194; (b) the process *super matrimonio rato et non consummato* (cf. the decree "*Catholica doctrina*" issued by the Sacred Congregation of the Discipline of the Sacraments on May 7, 1923—*AAS,* XV [1923], 390); (c) the procedure in declaring a marriage null due to lack of form (cf. the declaration given by the Pontifical Commission for the authentic interpretation of the canons of the Code on October 16, 1919—*AAS,* XI [1919], 479). The process to establish the presumed death of a spouse can be handled in either an administrative or a judicial procedure. Cf. Rice, *Proof of Death in Pre-Nuptial Investigation,* pp. 43, 44, 50, 51—on p. 43 he states: "Although there is apparently nothing to prevent the Ordinary from settling the question through a judicial process if he so desires, it may be said that this process is essentially an administrative one. In the first place it partakes of the nature of a *status liber* case which is further strengthened by the fact that since 1908 such cases have been handled exclusively by the Sacred Congregation of the Sacraments [that

The second part of the canon indicates matters that are not to be treated by this Sacred Congregation, namely, those controversies which are to be decided in a judicial manner (*ordine iudiciario*) —the term *ordo iudiciarius* refers to those formal or strictly judicial procedures similar to those which for Catholics of the Latin Rite[108] are conducted according to the rules of the First Part of the Fourth Book of the Code,[109] and, in the opinion of the writer, also to the very special procedure used in processes for the beatification and canonization of Servants of God. Whenever the Sacred Congregation judges that a controversy is to be decided in a judicial manner,[110] the Sacred Congregation itself designates the tribunal to which it shall commit the matter. The law says that the Sacred Congregation is to designate (in the sense of indicate) the tribunal to handle this matter; it does not say or imply that the Sacred Congregation is free to set up a tribunal within the Sacred Congregation in order to judge the affair.[111] The context points to the fact that the Sacred Con-

is, in regard to Catholics of the Latin Rite], which is competent to handle administrative matters only." Cf. also Doheny, *Canonical Procedure in Matrimonial Cases* (2 vols., Milwaukee: The Bruce Publishing Company, 1938–1944), II (1944), 9, footnote 7; Kay, *Competence in Matrimonial Procedure,* The Catholic University of America Canon Law Studies, n. 53 (Washington, D. C.: The Catholic University of America, 1929), pp. 123–126.

[108] Duskie (*The Canonical Status of the Orientals in the United States,* p. 65) says: "The Legislation of the Western Church may supply deficiencies of the Oriental Codex only in so far as such legislation is not prejudicial to the Eastern rite. . . . Although the norms of judicial procedure given in the Code are strictly proper to the Latin Church, generally speaking, they are not opposed to the rites and customs of Orientals. In times past the Holy See has provided the Orientals with norms of judicial procedure for certain cases which were similar to those of the Latin Church [Cf. *Collectanea,* II (1907), nn. 1587 and 1588]."

[109] Cf. Coronata, *Institutiones Iuris Canonici,* I (1928), 324; Maroto, *Institutiones,* I, n. 724; Rice, *Proof of Death in Pre-Nuptial Investigation,* p. 43.

[110] Cappello (*Praxis Processualis,* p. 2) states: "Utrum controversia dirimenda sit ordine iudiciario an via administrativa, pendet ex ipsa rei natura, vel ex legis praescripto, vel demum ex voluntate litigantium."

[111] Cf. Blat, *Commentarium Textus Codicis Iuris Canonici,* II (1921), n. 257.

gregation for the Oriental Church is not a tribunal for strictly judicial processes, but that it handles affairs only in a disciplinary, administrative way. In support of this one can refer to canons 250, § 5, and 251, § 2, dealing with Sacred Congregations for the Latin Church. These canons state expressly that the latter Sacred Congregations are to handle matters in a disciplinary way, and such matters as need to be treated in a strictly judicial manner are to be referred to a tribunal.[112] There is no doubt that the Sacred Congregations for the Latin Church with the exception of the Sacred Congregation of the Holy Office and the Sacred Congregation of Sacred Rites as stated in canon 259 are not to act as tribunals for causes requiring a formal process of the external forum.[113] That likewise seems to be the proper way to interpret canon 257, § 3, which complements and supplements § 2 of the same canon so that the Sacred Congregation for the Oriental Church has all the faculties of the other Sacred Congregations, except the Holy Office, in regard to Catholics of the Oriental Rite (canon 257, § 2) whenever affairs are to be treated in a disciplinary, administrative manner; but whenever affairs are to be treated in a strictly judicial manner, then they are not to be treated by the Sacred Congregation for the Oriental Church, but are to be sent to a tribunal for strictly judicial processes.[114] This means that it is not within the jurisdiction of the Sacred

It also seems that the Sacred Congregation for the Oriental Church cannot constitute a tribunal outside the Sacred Congregation, but that it is free to select an already existing tribunal to which the matter is to be remitted. This is contrary to Duskie (*The Canonical Status of Orientals in the United States,* p. 69) and Ayrinhac (*Constitution of the Church in the New Code of Canon Law* [London, New York, Toronto: Longmans, Green and Co., 1930], n. 55).

[112] Cf. Chelodi, *Ius de Personis iuxta Codicem Iuris Canonici* (ed. altera a Sac. Ernesto Bertagnolli recognita et aucta, Tridenti: Libr. Edit. Tridentum, 1927), p. 275 (hereafter cited *Ius de Personis*); Dausend, *Das interrituelle Recht im Codex Iuris Canonici,*—Görres-Gesellschaft, LXXIX (1939), 176; Noval, *Commentarium Codicis Iuris Canonici,* lib. IV, *De Processibus,* Vol. II, pp. 390, 392; Choupin, *Valeur des Décisions Doctrinales et Disciplinaires du Saint-Siège,* p. 426.

[113] Canon 259.

[114] Cf. Blat, *Commentarium Textus Codicis Iuris Canonici,* II (1921), 275–276.

Congregation for the Oriental Church to handle causes concerning the beatification and canonization of Servants of God, as is presently explained.

Although authors differ in their views about the nature and classification of causes of beatification and canonization of Servants of God,[115] there is no doubt that such causes have a singular and very rigid process which is altogether special for these affairs, and which may be classed as "sui generis."[116] In the writer's opinion these special processes for causes of beatification and canonization of Servants of God are included under the expression *ordo iudiciarius* as used in canon 257, § 3, for canon 259 which uses this very same expression (*ordo iudiciarius*) states that all causes requiring a strictly judicial procedure (an *ordo iudiciarius*) are handled by the Sacred Roman Rota and the Supreme Tribunal of the Apostolic Signatura within the limits and according to the norms given in canons 1598–1605, except causes proper to the Sacred Congregation of the Holy Office and the Sacred Congregation of Sacred Rites.[117] It is obvious that the causes requiring a strictly judicial procedure (*ordo iudiciarius*) which are referred to in this canon as being proper to the Sacred Congregation of Sacred Rites are causes of beatification and canonization of Servants of God. Blat,[118] Chelodi,[119]

---

[115] Cf. Blat, *Commentarium Textus Codicis Iuris Canonici*, IV (1927), 2–3, 536; Chelodi, *Ius de Personis*, p. 283; Coronata, *Institutiones Iuris Canonici*, III (1933), n. 1573; Kennedy, *The Special Matrimonial Process in Cases of Evident Nullity*, The Catholic University of America Canon Law Studies, n. 93 (Washington, D. C.: The Catholic University of America, 1935), p. 52, footnote 4; Lega, *Praelectiones in Textum Iuris Canonici de Iudiciis Ecclesiasticis*, II (1898), 209, 213; Maroto, *Institutiones*, I (1921), 863, footnote 2; Noval, *Commentarium Codicis Iuris Canonici*, lib. IV, *De Processibus*, Vol. I (1920), pp. 2–3; Vol. II (1932), pp. 1–2, 383–384; Roberti, *De Processibus*, I (1926), 25, 38, 67.

[116] Cf. canons 1999–2141.

[117] Canon 259 reads as follows: "Causae ordinem iudiciarium requirentes aguntur apud Sacram Romanam Rotam et apud Supremum Tribunal Signaturae Apostolicae intra fines et secundum normas traditas in can. 1598–1605, salvo iure Congregationis S. Officii et Congregationis Sacrorum Rituum in causas sibi proprias."

[118] *Commentarium Textus Codicis Iuris Canonici*, II (1921), n. 261.

[119] *Ius de Personis*, p. 286.

De Meester,[120] Oesterle,[121] Wernz-Vidal[122] definitely state that these causes proper to the Sacred Congregation of Sacred Rites in canon 259 refer to the beatification and canonization of Servants of God. Therefore, since the causes of beatification and canonization are to be included under the *ordo iudiciarius*,[123] and since the Sacred Congregation for the Oriental Church cannot handle affairs which are to be conducted in that manner, this Sacred Congregation does not have jurisdiction over such affairs. The causes of beatification and canonization of Servants of God which concern Orientals are under the jurisdiction of the special tribunal in the Sacred Congregation of Sacred Rites.[124]

---

[120] *Juris Canonici et Juris Canonico-civilis Compendium,* II (1923), nn. 591 and 600.

[121] *Praelectiones Iuris Canonici* (Romae: In Collegio S. Anselmi, 1931), p. 142.

[122] *Ius Canonicum,* II (1943), n. 503.

[123] Blat (*Commentarium Textus Codicis Iuris Canonici,* II [1921], 275–276; IV [1927], 2–3, 536) evidently considers it so. Among others whose opinions seem favorable to this interpretation are: Chelodi, *Ius de Personis,* p. 283; Maroto, *Institutiones,* I (1921), 863, footnote 2; Noval, *Commentarium Codicis Iuris Canonici,* lib. IV, *De Processibus,* Vol. I (1920), pp. 2–3; Vol. II (1932), pp. 1–2, 383–384.

[124] Blat, *op. cit.,* II (1921), 275–276.

CHAPTER IV

MOTU PROPRIO "*Sancta Dei Ecclesia*"

Article I. Background

Although the Sacred Congregation for the Oriental Church was completely independent of the Sacred Congregation of the Propagation of the Faith, nevertheless at times both operated in the same territories. For in regions of the Orient where the jurisdiction of the Sacred Congregation for the Oriental Church was predominantly exercised, there were, besides Catholics of the Oriental Rite and dissidents thereof, faithful of the Latin Rite (even though they were of a smaller number) and works committed to religious men and prelates of the Latin Rite. The institutes of the Latin Rite existing in those regions can be distinguished into two classes: (a) works, missions, and Latin dioceses established directly for the faithful of the Latin Rite: such as the Jerusalem Patriarchate for the faithful of the Latin Rite, the Apostolic Vicariate of Egypt, and the like; (b) works or missions founded for the help and support of Orientals, which directly and principally aided the Oriental hierarchy either in the care of the Catholics of the Oriental Rite or in the conversion of dissidents: such as, the missions of the Congregation of the Lazarists in Persia and Ethiopia, the mission of the Friars Preachers in Mesopotamia, the mission of the Franciscans in Egypt, the Carmelite mission in Mesopotamia, the mission of the Capuchins in the colony of Eritrea. These works and missions founded for the aid and support of the Orientals were subject without doubt to the Sacred Congregation for the Oriental Church.[1] On the other hand, the dioceses and works which had

[1] Canon 257. It was so also according to the Constitution "*Romani Pontifices*" and the Motu proprio "*Dei providentis.*" Cf. Staffa, "De Sacrae Congregationis pro Ecclesia Orientali competentia"—*Apollinaris,* XI (1938), 361-363.

Article I of this chapter is based on the above cited article of Staffa.

been established directly and principally for the faithful of the Latin Rite were subject to the Sacred Congregation of the Propagation of the Faith.[2]

According to Canon 252 of the Code the jurisdiction of the Sacred Congregation *de Propaganda Fide* is restricted to those regions where either the hierarchy as yet has not been established, and thus these territories are still in a missionary state, or if the hierarchy has been established, its organization is in some respects incomplete.[3] But in some regions of the Christian Orient the faithful of the Latin Rite had their own hierarchy for a long period of time so that if it were not decreed in 1938 that they were henceforth subject to the Sacred Congregation for the Oriental Church on account of the reasons which shall be stated presently, one might say that they were ready to be placed under the jurisdiction of the other Sacred Congregations of the Latin Church. In other words, they might have been withdrawn from the jurisdiction of the Sacred Congregation of the Propagation of the Faith and placed under the jurisdiction of the other Sacred Congregations for the Latin Rite.

But, in any case, from the multiplicity of jurisdictions of two or more Sacred Congregations, which is useful, in fact necessary, in regions where the Church is firmly and orderly established, serious inconveniences and difficulties arise in mission lands, where all the forces must be united either in order to preach the gospel to the infidels or to open the way for the return of dissidents into the bosom of the Church.[4] This division of jurisdiction makes it very difficult to obtain unity of government whereby all the means for obtaining the end in view can be rightly and more effectively utilized, and to provide that all the future missionaries may be properly prepared for the particular region of their apostolate among the faithful of the Oriental Rite. In regard to this latter point the knowledge which is sufficient for preaching to infidels has been found to be insufficient for a ministry among the Orientals, which, as experience has taught,

[2] Canon 252.

[3] Cf. Smith, *Elements of Ecclesiastical Law,* I (9. ed.), nn. 507 and 508.

[4] Staffa, "De Sacrae Congregationis pro Ecclesia Orientali competentia"—*Apollinaris,* XI (1938), 363, footnote 12.

requires that the history, rites, and discipline of the Oriental Church be known.

It is not difficult to perceive the advantage of having one Sacred Congregation to solve uniformly as well as to enact effective, guiding norms and instructions for the complexities and dissensions which easily arise among faithful of dissimilar rites and different disciplines. Moreover, the dangers threatening the faith in these mission regions demanded that all Catholics should be thoroughly united, and this naturally would be better accomplished under the jurisdiction of one Sacred Congregation.[5]

Wherefore Pope Pius XI (1922–1939) in the Motu proprio "*Sancta Dei Ecclesia,*" of March 25, 1938, conferred full and exclusive jurisdiction[6] on the Sacred Congregation for the Oriental Church in those regions where by far the greater number of Christians were Catholics of the Oriental Rite or dissidents thereof, and the Latins were comparatively small in number. This may be best illustrated by an example: northern Albania was not affected by this Motu proprio, since the greater part of the Christians in this area were Catholics of the Latin Rite (99,217)—there were very few Catholics of the Oriental Rite and the number of dissidents was comparatively small (13,582); hence, both the Sacred Congregation of the Propagation of the Faith and the Sacred Congregation for the Oriental Church retained their jurisdictions here.[7] On the other hand, southern

[5] The Motu proprio "*Sancta Dei Ecclesia,*" of March 25, 1938, succinctly summarizes the disadvantages of the division of jurisdiction in these regions: "Qua posita iurisdictionis duplicitate, perdifficile prorsus erat validam eam assequi regiminis unitatem expeditamque negotiorum administrationem, quae omnino requiruntur, ut et quantocius diversitates dissensionesque dilabantur, quae inter fideles dissimilium rituum absimilisque disciplinae facile oriuntur, et apostolatus caritatisque opera, quae praesertim ad Actionem Catholicam attinent, efficientius usque ordinentur ac promoveantur, et catholicorum denique vires omnes in unum coëant ac coalescant, quemadmodum praesentium rerum adiuncta procul dubio postulant, nedum consulant."—*AAS,* XXX (1938), 157.

[6] The meaning of this expression is to be understood in the sense explained in Article II of this chapter.

[7] One might wonder why the Holy See didn't assign northern Albania to the full and exclusive jurisdiction of the Sacred Congregation of the Propagation of the Faith, and in support of such a thought one might resort to

Albania was assigned to the full and exclusive jurisdiction of the Sacred Congregation for the Oriental Church. Although the Catholics of the Oriental Rite were by no means many in number, there were 187,138 dissidents of the Oriental Rite, while Catholics of the Latin Rite numbered about 1000 and the greater number of them had lived there for only a short time. Hence, the Sacred Congregation of the Propagation of the Faith had no longer any jurisdiction over these faithful of the Latin Rite. It is noticed that in the case of southern Albania jurisdiction was assigned to the Sacred Congregation for the Oriental Church on account of the care necessary for the conversion of the separated brethren of the Oriental Rite.

Let it be noted that both Eritrea and Northern Ethiopia (both of which are mentioned in the Motu proprio "*Sancta Dei Ecclesia*") had already been subject to the exclusive jurisdiction of the Sacred Congregation for the Oriental Church before the issuance of the Motu proprio.[8] Likewise, as Staffa [9] remarked,

---

the arguments used above against division of jurisdiction. The direct answer to this difficulty is that the Holy See did not consider it either advisable or necessary. However, for one who seeks to understand wherein lies the difference between the assignment of Latins to the jurisdiction of the Sacred Congregation for the Oriental Church and the assignment of Orientals to the jurisdiction of the Sacred Congregation of the Propagation of the Faith, the following may be considered: the Sacred Congregation for the Oriental Church knows the laws and customs of the Latin Church and treats the *negotia mixta,* whereas the Sacred Congregation of the Propagation of the Faith does not have jurisdiction over the *negotia mixta,* and there is no reason why it should endeavor to learn thoroughly the differing laws of the different rites since another Sacred Congregation is already acquainted and busied with such matters. Thus, for the Sacred Congregation of the Propagation of the Faith to take upon itself the care of Orientals with their various special laws would be a far too overburdening, and at the same time unnecessary, task; whereas the Sacred Congregation for the Oriental Church can take charge of the Latins with little added difficulty.

[8] Staffa ("*De Sacrae Congregationis pro Ecclesia Orientali competentia*" —*Apollinaris,* XI [1938], 364–365, footnotes 13 and 14) relates: "In quibusdam peculiaribus locis iam antea S. C. pro Ecclesia Orientali iurisdictio super latinis attributa fuerat: semper eidem fuerunt obnoxii Vicariatus Apostolici Erythreae et Abissinae quorum territoria simul sumpta circiter correspondebant praesentibus territoriis Vicariatus Apostolici Erythreae, Praefecturae Apostolicae de Dessiè, Praefecturae Apostolicae de Gondar, Praefec-

not all the regions of the Christian Orient in which the greater number were Catholics of the Oriental Rite or dissidents thereof were assigned to the full and exclusive jurisdiction of the Sacred Congregation for the Oriental Church by the Motu proprio "*Sancta Dei Ecclesia;*" he mentioned the following territories as not having been so assigned: Russia,[10] Rumania,[11] the terri-

turae Apostolicae de Tigrai, et Vicariatus Addis Abebae; item a d. 1 augusti a. 1921 duae paroeciae latinae dioecesis Lungrensis; a d. 21 aprilis a. 1937 tres paroeciae latinae novae eparchiae Planensis Graecorum; tandem d. 8 aprilis a. 1937 Summus Pontifex Erythream et partem septemtrionalem Aethiopiae iurisdictioni exclusivae S. C. pro Ecclesia Orientali relinqui decrevit . . ."

"Praefectura Apostolica Erythreae, quae a d. 13 septembris a. 1894 existebat, d. 7 februarii a. 1911 ad Vicariatum Apostolicum est evecta. Tum antecedens Praefectura tum subsequens Vicariatus S. C. pro negotiis ritus orientalis et postea S. C. pro Ecclesia Orientali erat obnoxius."

The writer has not at his disposal the sources which would enable him to check the meaning of the expression ". . . Summus Pontifex Erythream et partem septemtrionalem Aethiopiae iurisdictioni exclusivae S. C. pro Ecclesia Orientali relinqui decrevit . . ." in order to determine whether these territories previous to the Motu proprio "*Sancta Dei Ecclesia*" had been placed under the jurisdiction of the Sacred Congregation for the Oriental Church in exactly the same manner as Catholics of the Oriental Rite or whether there were reservations to the Sacred Congregation of the Discipline of the Sacraments and the Sacred Congregation of Sacred Rites. On the determination of this fact is the decision to be made whether or not Eritrea and Northern Ethiopia after the Motu proprio "*Sancta Dei Ecclesia*" are governed, as the rest of the territories named in the same Motu proprio are, by the reservations to the Sacred Congregation of the Discipline of the Sacraments and the Sacred Congregation of Sacred Rites. Staffa's use of the expression "*iurisdictio exclusiva*" and his application of the handling of *ratum non consummatum* marriages between Catholics of the Latin Rite in these two regions by the Sacred Congregation for the Oriental Church and not by the Sacred Congregation of the Discipline of the Sacraments point toward the exclusion of any reservations in his opinion.

Another question associated with that noted above likewise might be investigated by those to whom the necessary sources are available, namely, what was the extent of the jurisdiction of the Sacred Congregation for the Oriental Church over Eritrea and Northern Ethiopia (which on March 25, 1937 was divided into the three Apostolic Prefectures of Dessié, Gondar, and Tigrai) before the decree of April 8, 1937?

[9] "De Sacrae Congregationis pro Ecclesia Orientali competentia"—*Apollinaris*, XI (1938), 366.

[10] In order to render a speedier examination and settlement of questions

tory of Serbia and Montenegro as defined before 1915 (both are found in Jugoslavia), Galicia,[12] and the Malabarese territory.

According to Staffa's statistics[13] the jurisdiction of the Sacred Congregation for the Oriental Church was extended by the Motu proprio "*Santa Dei Ecclesia*" to the following hierarchies of the Latin Rite: the Latin Patriarchate of Jerusalem, three archdioceses (Rhodes, Smyrna, Ispahan), eight dioceses (Athens, Chius, Candia, Zacynthus and Cephalonia, Naxus-Andros-Mico, Santoria, Sira, Nicopolis), seven Apostolic Vicariates (Egypt,

---

and causes regarding the Russians living in or outside of Russia, Pope Pius XI on June 20, 1925, established within the Sacred Congregation for the Oriental Church a special Commission under the presidency of the Cardinal Secretary of that Sacred Congregation.

Later by the Motu proprio "*Inde ab inito,*" of April 6, 1930 (*AAS,* XXII [1930], 153–154), this Commission for Russia was separated from the Sacred Congregation for the Oriental Church and became *sui iuris* and independent of any authority save that of the pope. Thus this Commission in regard to Russians replaced the Sacred Congregation for the Oriental Church. Then by the Motu proprio "*Quam sollicita,*" of December 21, 1934, Pope Pius XI decreed that henceforth only those matters which pertain to Russians living in their own country were to be reserved and entrusted to the special Commission for Russia, without prejudice to the authority and right of the Sacred Congregation for the Oriental Church according to canon 257. Moreover this Commission for Russia was annexed to the Sacred Congregation for Extraordinary Ecclesiastical Affairs, and the Secretary of the latter Sacred Congregation became the President of the Commission.

Staffa (*loc. cit.*) explains the Motu proprio "*Quam sollicita*" as follows: the affairs and causes of Russians of the Latin Rite living in Russia are reserved to the special Commission for Russia; the Russian faithful of the Latin Rite living outside of Russia are subjects of the Ordinary of the place where they are; the Russians who belong to the Oriental Rite, whether they be in or outside of Russia, depend on the Sacred Congregation for the Oriental Church. Cf. also *infra,* p. 142.

[11] In the Concordat between the Holy See and Rumania it is stated that in regard to the Latin Rite the archdiocese of Bucharest with its four suffragan sees passed from the jurisdiction of the Sacred Congregation of the Propagation of the Faith to that of all the other Sacred Congregations for the Latin Church. Cf. *AAS,* XXI (1929), 442.

[12] The faithful of the Latin Rite were not under the jurisdiction of the Sacred Congregation of the Propagation of the Faith; they were under the jurisdiction of all the other Sacred Congregations for the Latin Rite.

[13] Cf. "De Sacrae Congregationis pro Ecclesia Orientali competentia"—*Apollinaris,* XI (1938), 366–369.

Nile Delta, Suez Canal, Constantinople, Thessalonica, Sophia and Philoppopolis, Aleppo), and the Apostolic Mission *sui iuris* of Trebizond (Trabzon).

Article II. Contents

The first four articles of the dispositive part of the Motu proprio "*Sancta Dei Ecclesia,*" of March 25, 1938, are as follows:[14]

> I. The Sacred Congregation for the Oriental Church, which is presided over by the Sovereign Pontiff himself, has full and exclusive jurisdiction over the following countries: Egypt and the Peninsula of Sinai, Eritrea and Northern Ethiopia, Southern Albania, Bulgaria, Cyprus, Greece, the Dodecanese Islands, Iran, Iraq, Lebanon, Palestine, Syria, Transjordan, Asiatic Turkey, and Thrace subject to Turkey.
>
> II. Consequently, in the above mentioned regions the Sacred Congregation for the Oriental Church possesses —not only for the faithful of the Oriental Rite but also for the faithful of the Latin Rite, and for their hierarchy, works, institutes, and pious associations—all the faculties which the other Sacred Congregations possess for the faithful of the Latin Rite outside these territories, without prejudice, however, to the right of the Holy Office, and without diminution of the reservations which have hitherto been made to the Sacred Congregation of the Discipline of the Sacraments, to the Sacred Congregation of Sacred Rites, to the Sacred Congregation of Studies for Seminaries and Universities, and to the Sacred Penitentiaria.
>
> III. As regards the faithful of the Oriental Rite who reside outside the places mentioned above, the competency of the Sacred Congregation for the Oriental Church remains in all respects intact. To it, therefore, are reserved all matters of whatever kind which concern either the persons or the discipline or the rites of the Oriental Church, even though they be mixed, that is, though they also touch the Latins either by reason of the thing or of the person concerned; and for these

[14] Bouscaren, *The Canon Law Digest,* II, 111–112; *AAS,* XXX (1938), 157–158.

> faithful it has all the faculties which, for faithful of the Latin Rite, belong to other Sacred Congregations, always without prejudice to the right of the Holy Office, and without diminution of the reservations which have hitherto been made to the Sacred Congregation of Studies for Seminaries and Universities and the Sacred Penitentiaria.
>
> IV. The Sacred Congregation for the Oriental Church decides controversies in a disciplinary manner; but those which, as it will have judged, need to be decided in a judicial manner, it shall refer to the tribunal which the Sacred Congregation itself shall have designated.

The first observation to be made is that the faithful of the Latin Rite in most of the above named regions [15] up to the time of this Motu proprio were under the jurisdiction of the Sacred Congregation of the Propagation of the Faith in accordance with the norms of canon 252, while the faithful of the Oriental Rite in these very same regions were under the jurisdiction of the Sacred Congregation for the Oriental Church in accordance with the norms of canon 257. On the dates specified in this document of Pope Pius XI,[16] the faithful of the Latin Rite who were subject to the Sacred Congregation of the Propagation of the Faith came under the jurisdiction of the Sacred Congregation for the Oriental Church so that this latter Sacred Congregation alone was placed in charge of all the faithful of the Catholic Church in those regions. This fact, i. e., that all the faithful in these regions were to be governed by this one Sacred Congregation, is the meaning to be attached to the following words of

[15] The two exceptions are Eritrea and Northern Ethiopia—cf. *supra*, p. 127.

[16] On June 1, 1938: Palestine, Transjordan, Egypt, the Peninsula of Sinai, and the island of Cyprus.

On January 1, 1939: Greece, the Dodecanese Islands, Southern Albania, Bulgaria, Asiatic Turkey, and Thrace subject to Turkey.

On June 1, 1939: Syria, Lebanon, Iraq, and Iran.—*AAS*, XXX (1938), 158; Bouscaren, *The Canon Law Digest*, II, 112.

Let it be noticed that no date is given for Eritrea and Northern Ethiopia, since both these regions were already under the jurisdiction of the Sacred Congregation for the Oriental Church.

Article I of the Motu proprio: " The Sacred Congregation for the Oriental Church . . . has *full and exclusive* jurisdiction . . ." But the jurisdiction of this one Sacred Congregation in regard to the faithful of the Latin Rite is not in all respects the same as its jurisdiction in regard to the faithful of the Oriental Rite in these same regions. In regard to the latter, the Sacred Congregation for the Oriental Church has the same powers which it enjoys for faithful of the Oriental Rite everywhere. In regard to the faithful of the Latin Rite in the territories named above, the Sacred Congregation for the Oriental Church has inherited all the faculties which the Sacred Congregation of the Propagation of the Faith formerly possessed for them, and which the Sacred Congregation of the Propagation of the Faith still possesses in accordance with the prescriptions of canon 252 for the faithful of the Latin Rite who are within its jurisdiction and live outside the regions named in the Motu proprio; accordingly, some of the Sacred Congregations, which had jurisdiction for those who were subject to the Sacred Congregation of the Propagation of the Faith, retain those very same faculties towards them even though they have come under the jurisdiction of the Sacred Congregation for the Oriental Church.[17]

The following summarizes concretely the powers or the absence of powers of the Sacred Congregation for the Oriental Church for the faithful of the Latin Rite who are under its jurisdiction according to the regulations of the motu proprio "*Sancta Dei Ecclesia*"; at the same time the faculties of the other Sacred Congregations in regard to this same group are noted.

(a) Whatever pertains to the jurisdiction of the Holy Office is excluded from the jurisdiction of the Sacred Congregation for the Oriental Church;[18] the jurisdiction of the Holy Office is universal.

(b) The Sacred Congregation for the Oriental Church has the same faculties for the faithful of the Latin Rite under its juris-

---

[17] Motu proprio "*Sancta Dei Ecclesia,*" art. II—*AAS,* XXX (1938), 157; Bouscaren, *The Canon Law Digest,* II, 111.

[18] Motu proprio "*Sancta Dei Ecclesia,*" art. II—*supra,* p. 130. Cf. canon 247.

diction as the Sacred Consistorial Congregation [19] and the Sacred Congregation of the Council [20] have, according to canons 248 and 250 respectively of the Code, for the faithful of the Latin Rite under their jurisdiction.

(c) The Sacred Congregation of the Propagation of the Faith, whose jurisdiction in these regions passed to the Sacred Congregation for the Oriental Church, in regard to the faithful of the Latin Rite under its jurisdiction possesses all the faculties of the Sacred Congregation of the Discipline of the Sacraments with two exceptions.

(1) The first of these exceptions concerns matrimonial cases (*causae matrimoniales*). Canon 252, § 4,[21] of the Code expressly states that the Sacred Congregation *de Propaganda Fide* is bound to refer all affairs concerning matrimonial cases to the competent Sacred Congregations—that is, either to the Sacred Congregation of the Discipline of the Sacraments or to the Holy Office.[22] With the exception of the universal jurisdiction of the Holy Office for whatever pertains to the Pauline Privilege, mixed religion, disparity of cult,[23] and all cases involving a Catholic and non-Catholic brought in any way whatsoever before the Holy See,[24] the Sacred Congregation of the Discipline of the Sacraments handles all other matrimonial cases of the external forum which are to be treated in a disciplinary way, including cases concern-

---

[19] Staffa, "De Sacrae Congregationis pro Ecclesia Orientali competentia"—*Apollinaris,* XI (1938), 369.

[20] *Ibid.*, pp. 370–371.

[21] "Haec autem Congregatio tenetur ad competentes Congregationes deferre negotia quae aut fidem attingunt, aut causas matrimoniales, aut generales normas circa sacrorum rituum disciplinam tradendas vel interpretandas." Let it be noticed that this law is not as general as it was under the Constitution "*Sapienti consilio*" (I, 6º, 4), which read: "Nihilominus . . . volumus ut Congregatio de Propaganda Fide ad peculiares alias Congregationes deferat quaecumque aut fidem attingunt, aut matrimonium aut sacrorum rituum disciplinam."

[22] The Sacred Congregation of the Propagation of the Faith, however, received power to grant faculties for certain matrimonial dispensations and radical sanations. Cf. Staffa, "De Sacrae Congregationis pro Ecclesia Orientali competentia"—*Apollinaris,* XI (1938), 370.

[23] Canon 247, § 3.

[24] *Supra,* pp. 104–105.

ing the process of a ratified and non-consummated marriage of Catholics of the Latin Rite and all matters connected therewith. It is especially to be noted that since the Sacred Congregation for the Oriental Church has fallen heir to the faculties of the Sacred Congregation of the Propagation of the Faith, it cannot handle cases on ratified and non-consummated marriage of fatihful of the Latin Rite [25]—it must remit them to the Sacred Congregation of the Discipline of the Sacraments; but the Sacred Congregation for the Oriental Church can handle such cases if one of the parties is a Catholic of the Oriental Rite and the other is a Catholic of the Latin Rite.

(2) The other exception is in reference to matters reserved to the Sacred Congregation of Sacred Rites. For whereas, on the one hand, the Sacred Congregation of the Discipline of the Sacraments has no jurisdiction whatever in regard to the rites and ceremonies which ought to be observed in the confection, administration and reception of the sacraments—these affairs belong to the jurisdiction of the Sacred Congregation of Sacred Rites in regard to faithful of the Latin Rite, except for those who are under the Sacred Congregation of the Propagation of the Faith,—the Sacred Congregation of the Propagation of the Faith, on the other hand, must refer to the Sacred Congregation of Sacred Rites *only* those affairs pertaining to the discipline of sacred rites which require the establishment, determination or interpretation of *general* norms [26] (i. e., general liturgical laws).[27]

What has been said of the Sacred Congregation of the Propagation of the Faith in the preceding paragraphs is to be attributed likewise to the Sacred Congregation for the Oriental Church in regard to the faithful of the Latin Rite entrusted to its jurisdiction according to the Motu proprio "*Sancta Dei Ecclesia.*"

---

[25] Staffa (*loc. cit.*) indicates that it can handle such cases between Latins in Eritrea and Northern Ethiopia: ". . . easdem tamen causas inter latinos iam ante Litteras Apostolicas *Sancta Dei Ecclesia* sibi subiectos potest S. C. pro Ecclesia Orientali cognoscere, quia absque exclusione istarum causarum eos S. C. pro Ecclesia Orientali sub sua iurisdictione receperat." Cf. also *supra*, p. 128, footnote 8.

[26] Canon 252, § 4.

[27] Toso, *Commentaria Minora,* 63.

With the exception of what has been mentioned above everything else designated under the jurisdiction of the Sacred Congregation of the Discipline of the Sacraments in canon 249 also pertains to the Sacred Congregation for the Oriental Church.

(d) In regard to the sacred rites and ceremonies the Sacred Congregation for the Oriental Church takes care, on the one hand, that the sacred rites and ceremonies are diligently observed in the celebration of Mass, in the administration of the sacraments, in the performance of divine offices, and in everything pertaining to the divine worship of the Latin Church; it grants opportune dispensations from the observance of these rites and ceremonies; it gives insignia and honorary privileges (both personal and temporary, as well as local and perpetual) which are connected with the sacred rites and ceremonies; it safeguards sacred rites and ceremonies from abuses.[28] It also handles whatever in any way refers to sacred relics.[29]

On the other hand, the Sacred Congregation of Sacred Rites alone both gives and interprets the *general norms* concerning the discipline of the sacred rites of the Latin Church.[30] Hence not only does the Sacred Congregation of Sacred Rites watch over, examine and correct the liturgical books of the Latin Church (all matters, however, pertaining to faith or dogma are reserved to the Holy Office), but it also approves and rejects new divine offices, and judges and settles doubts about rites.[31] Moreover, since whatever pertains to the beatification and canonization of the Servants of God is to be decided "*ordine iudiciario*," such matters are not treated by the Sacred Congregation for the Oriental Church in accordance with article IV of the Motu proprio "*Sancta Dei Ecclesia*"[32] but by the Sacred Congregation of Sacred Rites.[33]

---

[28] Canon 253, § 1 and § 2. Staffa, "De Sacrae Congregationis pro Ecclesia Orientali competentia"—*Apollinaris*, XI (1938), 372.

[29] Canon 253, § 3. Staffa, *loc. cit.*

[30] Canons 253, § 3, and 252, § 4.

[31] Staffa, "De Sacrae Congregationis pro Ecclesia Orientali competentia"—*Apollinaris*, XI (1938), 372. Cf. also "*Normae Peculiares*," cap. VIII, art. 8, n. 2—*AAS*, I (1909), 99.

[32] "Haec Sacra Congregatio controversias dirimit via disciplinari; quas

(e) In reference to the religious and their missions erected for Orientals the Sacred Congregation for the Oriental Church has jurisdiction in all matters which concern these religious as missionaries, whether individually or collectively.[34] Wherefore this Sacred Congregation grants them faculties, imparts to them instructions and norms, governs their work through Apostolic Delegates, warns the slothful, orders the recall of the inept, permits or forbids the founding of new missions, suppresses or changes places of missions already existing, or commits those places to other religious.[35] But the Sacred Congregation for the Oriental Church refers or leaves to the Sacred Congregation of Religious whatever concerns the religious of the Latin Rite as religious either individually or collectively (e. g., their vows, government and discipline, rules and constitutions, admission and dismissal, studies, goods and property, privileges, dispensations, etc.), since the Sacred Congregation of Religious has exclusive jurisdiction in such matters.[36]

(f) Staffa states contrary to those who claim that the jurisdiction of the Sacred Ceremonial Congregation has no territorial limits[37] that what is attributed to the Sacred Ceremonial Congregation in canon 254 of the Code[38] is not excluded according to canon 252 from the jurisdiction of the Sacred Congregation *de Propaganda Fide,* and it also is not excluded according to the

---

vero ordine iudiciario dirimendas iudicaverit, ad tribunal remittet quod ipsa Congregatio designaverit."—*AAS,* XXX (1938), 158.

[33] Cf. *supra,* pp. 120–123.

[34] Canon 252, § 5; Staffa, "De Sacrae Congregationis pro Ecclesia Orientali competentia"—*Apollinaris,* XI (1938), 371.

[35] Staffa, *loc. cit.*

[36] Canons 251, § 1, § 3, and 252, § 5. Staffa, *loc. cit.*

[37] For instance, Maroto, *Institutiones,* II (1919), 259; De Meester, *Juris Canonici et Juris Canonico-civilis Compendium,* II (1923), 66; Bouuaert-Simenon, *Manuale Juris Canonici* (Vols. I and III, 3. ed., 1930; Vol. II, 1931, Gandae et Leodii: Apud Auctores in Seminariis Gandavensi et Leodiensi), I, 231, 232 footnote 1.

[38] "Ad Congregationem Caeremonialem pertinet moderatio caeremoniarum in Sacello Aulaque Pontificali servandarum et sacrarum functionum quas Patres Cardinales extra pontificale sacellum peragunt; itemque eadem Congregatio cognoscit quaestiones de praecedentia tum Patrum Cardinalium tum Legatorum quos variae Nationes ad Sanctam Sedem mittunt."

Motu proprio *"Sancta Dei Ecclesia"* from the jurisdiction of the Sacred Congregation for the Oriental Church. However, he states, the Sacred Congregation for the Oriental Church, just as the Sacred Congregation of the Propagation of the Faith, refers matters mentioned in canon 254 to the Sacred Ceremonial Congregation.[39]

(g) As to the functions reserved to the Sacred Congregation for Extraordinary Affairs in the first part of canon 255 of the Code (namely, to establish or divide dioceses, and to promote suitable priests to vacant dioceses whenever in these matters the civil governments must be considered),[40] there can be no doubt that in accordance with canon 252 such matters fall within the jurisdiction of the Sacred Congregation of the Propagation of the Faith and therefore within the jurisdiction of the Sacred Congregation for the Oriental Church in accordance with the Motu proprio *"Sancta Dei Ecclesia"*; but, according to Staffa,[41] as often as the civil government must be dealt with in regard to the above named affairs, these matters are referred by the Sacred Congregation for the Oriental Church to the Sacred Congregation for Extraordinary Ecclesiastical Affairs.

(h) The Sacred Congregation for the Oriental Church watches over all that pertains to the government, discipline, temporal administration, alienation of property, and studies of the seminaries and the ecclesiastical colleges of the Latin Rite.[42] But, after the Constitution *"Deus scientiarum Dominus,"* the canonical erection and supreme control of every university and faculty of ecclesiastical studies, wherever they may exist, are reserved to the Sacred Congregation of Studies for Seminaries and Universities. However, for the period between the Constitution *"Sancta Dei Ecclesia"* and the Constitution *"Deus scientiarum Dominus"* the Sacred Congregation for the Oriental Church did have within

[39] Staffa, "De Sacrae Congregationis pro Ecclesia Orientali competentia" —*Apollinaris,* XI (1938), 372.

[40] The second part of this canon, as previously stated, obviously is special to the Sacred Congregation for Extraordinary Ecclesiastical Affairs alone. Cf. *supra,* p. 108.

[41] "De Sacrae Congregationis pro Ecclesia Orientali competentia"—*Apollinaris,* XI (1938), 369, 370, 372.

[42] Canon 256.

its jurisdiction the canonical erection and supreme control of the universities and faculty of ecclesiastical studies dependent on the authority of the Church, including those entrusted to religious communities.[43]

(i) It is evident from what has been said in chapter III of this work[44] and as specifically mentioned in article II of the Motu proprio "*Sancta Dei Ecclesia*"[45] that what pertains to the internal forum belongs exclusively to the Sacred Penitentiaria. Staffa, however, mentions that just as the Sacred Congregation of the Propagation of the Faith could grant indulgences to its subjects, so also the Sacred Congregation for the Oriental Church can grant indulgences to the faithful of the Latin Rite in the territories designated in the Motu proprio "*Sancta Dei Ecclesia*"; yet, according to the present legislation, the Sacred Congregation for the Oriental Church cannot grant indulgences to its subjects of the Oriental Rite wherever they may be.[46]

Since the remaining articles (VI–XI) of the Motu proprio "*Sancta Dei Ecclesia*" need no explanation, it is sufficient simply to relate them:[47]

> VI. From the date of the promulgation of this Motu Proprio to the day of the passing over of the respective regions to the exclusive jurisdiction of the Sacred Congregation for the Oriental Church, no works or institutions shall be founded nor any change made in the present state of things without the previous consent of the Sacred Congregation for the Oriental Church.
>
> VIII. When the countries of the Christian East will have passed under the exclusive jurisdiction of the Sacred Congregation for the Oriental Church, the documents regarding these countries, which are kept in the archives of the Sacred Congregation of the Propagation

---

[43] Canon 256. Staffa, "De Sacrae Congregationis pro Ecclesia Orientali competentia"—*Apollinaris,* XI (1938), 373, footnote 25.

[44] *Supra,* pp. 113–116.

[45] *Supra,* p. 130.

[46] Staffa, "De Sacrae Congregationis pro Ecclesia Orientali competentia" —*Apollinaris,* XI (1938), 376.

[47] Bouscaren, *The Canon Law Digest,* II, 112–113; *AAS,* XXX (1938), 158–159.

of the Faith, shall be transferred and delivered to the archives of the Sacred Congregation for the Oriental Church, as far as this is possible and according to the mutual agreement of those entrusted with these two Offices.

VIII. The Sacred Congregation of the Propagation of the Faith will hand over to the Sacred Congregation for the Oriental Church all funds which are destined for works and institutions of those countries which have been assigned to the exclusive jurisdiction of the latter. In case no such distinct funds exist, the Sacred Congregation of the Propagation of the Faith shall make up from its own funds a revenue equivalent to the amount of all ordinary and extraordinary subsidies which this Sacred Congregation was accustomed to send every year to the aforesaid countries for their respective works and institutions. The extraordinary subsidies should be calculated on the average amount sent yearly to these countries in the course of the last three years, that is 1935 to 1937.

IX. The Pontifical Work of the Propagation of the Faith will yearly remit to the Sacred Congregation for the Oriental Church a sum which will maintain a fixed comparative ratio and proportion between the total amount of the subsidies, both ordinary and extraordinary, which have been sent in the last three years, as has been stated, in favor of the Orientals and Latins in those countries, and the grand total of the receipts and revenues which the said Work of the Propagation of the Faith has received during the same period.

X. The Pontifical Work of St. Peter the Apostle for the Native Clergy will yearly remit to the Sacred Congregation for the Oriental Church an amount equal to two per cent of all the revenues and receipts of the said Pontifical Work.

XI. The *Substitute* of the Sacred Congregation for the Oriental Church is *ex iure* a member of the Supreme General Council of the Pontifical Works of the Propagation of the Faith and of Saint Peter the Apostle for the Native Clergy.

CHAPTER V

MISCELLANEA

ARTICLE I. THE POWERS OF THE SACRED CONGREGATION DURING THE VACANCY OF THE APOSTOLIC SEE

The Sacred Congregation for the Oriental Church, just as is the case with all the other Sacred Congregations, possesses ordinary power of jurisdiction in matters committed to its care by the law of the Code; but this is vicarious ordinary power since it is exercised in the name of the pope.[1] The report that must be made to the pope and the approbation that must be received according to the prescriptions of canon 244, § 1 and § 2, in no way detract from the nature of this jurisdiction.[2]

As to the existence and exercise of this power during the vacancy of the Apostolic See, Pope Pius X in the Constitution "*Vacante Sede Apostolica,*" of December 25, 1904, makes mention and gives certain definite norms.[3] From the very nature of the matter and the contents of the Constitution it is obvious that the Sacred Congregation for the Oriental Church is governed by it. In the first paragraph of chapter IV of title I—which chapter is devoted to the Sacred Roman Congregations and their faculties during the vacancy of the Apostolic See—it is stated that the following norms are to be observed by all the Sacred Congregations notwithstanding any privileges whatsoever:

(a) The Sacred Congregations have no power in those matters which during the occupancy of the Apostolic See they are not able to handle unless *facto verbo cum SSmo* or *ex audientia*

[1] Canon 197, § 1 and § 2. Cf. also Reilly, *The General Norms of Dispensation,* The Catholic University of America Canon Law Studies, n. 119 (Washington, D. C.: The Catholic University of America Press, 1939), pp. 58-59.

[2] Monin, *De Curia Romana,* p. 198.

[3] Constitution "*Vacante Sede Apostolica,*" tit. I, cap. IV—*Codex Iuris Canonici,* Documentum I.

SSmi or by virtue of special and extraordinary faculties which the Roman Pontiffs are accustomed to grant to the Prefects or Secretaries of these Sacred Congregations.

(b) The faculties which are attributed to the Sacred Congregations through the Apostolic Letters, and hence are had as ordinary and proper faculties of these Sacred Congregations, are not extinguished by the death of the Roman Pontiff.

(c) However, the Sacred Congregations are to use these ordinary faculties freely *pro rei opportunitate,* but only in granting those favors (*gratiae*) which are of minor importance. In expediting and deciding matters which seem to be more serious or controverted, the urgency of the matter must be considered, for: (1) if the matter is such that it can be deferred to a later time, it is to be reserved to the future pope; (2) if the matter cannot be deferred, then the Sacred College of Cardinals can commit the affair to the Prefect and some of the other cardinals of that Sacred Congregation to which the pope most likely would have committed the examination of that business. This selected Sacred Congregation, after having discussed the matter, can give a provisional solution. As Cappello rightly states,[4] this decision of the chosen Sacred Congregation neither is nor can be called definitive since the confirmation or perhaps reprobation of the same is reserved to the future pope.

Article II. Special Sections of the Sacred Congregation for the Oriental Church

In order to execute effectively and speedily the expedition of certain matters the Sacred Congregation for the Oriental Church has special sections—that is, set committees—devoted to those affairs. One of these special sections is the Special Commission for the handling of matrimonial cases, which resulted from the papal audiences of March 24 and May 5 of the year 1928.[5] Similarly another special section, the Liturgical Section, resulted from the papal audience of February 8, 1930.[6]

---

[4] *De Curia Romana,* II (1912), 84.

[5] *Annuario Pontificio* for the year 1933, p. 529.

[6] *Annuario Pontificio* for the year 1933, p. 530.

In the Motu proprio "*Quam sollicita,*" of December 21, 1934, Pope Pius XI decreed that only business and causes which pertained to Russians living in Russia were to be reserved and entrusted henceforth to the Commission for Russia, without prejudice to the authority and right of the Sacred Congregation for the Oriental Church according to canon 257; and this Commission was attached to the Sacred Congregation for Extraordinary Ecclesiastical Affairs.[7] Then, he decreed that there be established in the Sacred Congregation for the Oriental Church a special Section which would be devoted to all those throughout the world who professed the so-called Slavonic-Byzantine rite, and thus including those Russians living outside of Russia who hitherto had been subject to the Commission for Russia. Moreover some of the bishops of those dioceses in which the Slavonic-Byzantine rite was in use could be attached to this Section in the capacity of Consultors, if there was need of their service.

In his concern for those of the Slavonic-Byzantine rite who have returned to the fold and at the same time for those who have remained in schism and may some day return to the One Church of Jesus Christ, Pope Pius XI committed to the Sacred Congregation for the Oriental Church the task of editing without delay liturgical books of this rite. Thus the rite would be integrally and safely preserved. In the preparation of this matter the Sacred Congregation could receive for counsel and labor those who manifested a strong desire to help and possessed knowledge in this field.[8]

ARTICLE III. THE CODIFICATION OF CANON LAW OF THE ORIENTAL CHURCH

Since the codification of Canon Law of the Oriental Church has been closely related to the Sacred Congregation for the Oriental Church and some of its members, it is proper to consider this subject in this work.

The utility and need of a Code of Canon Law for the Oriental Church was adverted to and expressed by some—among whom

[7] *AAS,* XXVII (1935), 65–66; *supra,* p. 129, footnote 10.

[8] *AAS,* XXVII (1935), p. 66; Bouscaren, *The Canon Law Digest,* II, 111.

were Gregory Iussef, Melkite Patriarch of Antioch,[9] and Joseph Audo, Chaldean Patriarch of Babylon,[10]—in the early part of the second half of the nineteenth century.[11] As time passed, this need was felt more and more by the prelates and the increasing number of the clergy working among the Orientals, and correspondingly their expressed desires for a Code multiplied. It naturally followed that after the appearance of the *Codex Iuris Canonici* in 1917 under Pope Benedict XV, they sent innumerable requests to the Holy See for a similar Code for the Oriental Church.[12]

Finally Pope Pius XI in 1929 took the initial steps towards this work. Under his order the Sacred Congregation for the Oriental Church in a circular letter of January 5, 1929, to the patriarchs, metropolitans, archbishops and bishops of the Oriental Church requested them: (a) after having consulted whomever they willed, to indicate freely what they thought of a codification of Canon Law for the Oriental Church; (b) having in mind the discipline, traditions, privileges, necessities of each Oriental rite, to give their ideas on the preparation of so great a work and the practical way of putting this into execution so that the codification would be of a real utility to the Oriental rites; (c) to inform the Sacred Congregation for the Oriental Church of capable persons to help in this work.[13] The responses to this circular letter were enthusiastic in confirming the need of codification; they stated that such an undertaking was not only opportune, but necessary indeed,[14] and they directed attention to the necessity of gathering the sources or "*Fonti*" of the Oriental rites into a collection (or

---

[9] Mansi, *Sacrorum Conciliorum Nova et Amplissima Collectio* (53 vols. in 60, Vols. I-XXXI, Florentiae, Venetiis, Parisiis, 1759-1798; Vols. XXXIb-LIII, Parisiis, Leipzig, Arnhem, 1901-1927), XLIX, 200.

[10] Mansi, *op. cit.*, L, 515 C. D.

[11] Cf. Congressus VI Commissionis Orientalis, 4 decembris 1868—Mansi, *op. cit.*, XLIX, 1012.

[12] Coussa, "De Codificatione Canonica Orientali"—*Acta Congressus Iuridici Internationalis* (Romae: Apud Custodiam Librariam Pont. Instituti Utriusque Iuris, 1935-), IV (1937), 495.

[13] *AAS*, XXI (1929), 669; Coussa, *loc. cit.*

[14] Coussa, "De Codificatione Canonica Orientali"—*Acta Congressus Iuridici Internationalis*, IV, 525-526.

corpus iuris), in which ancient and modern documents of the different disciplines should be orderly arranged.[15]

Pope Pius XI towards the end of 1929 instituted a Commission of cardinals to direct studies preparatory to the codification. This Commission had as its President the very capable, erudite and experienced Pietro Cardinal Gasparri (1852–1934), who had borne a very heavy share of the labor and at the same time had been a central figure in directing the successful issue of the Code of Canon Law.[16] The other members of this Commission were Luigi Cardinal Sincero (1870–1936), who at that time was Secretary of the Sacred Congregation for the Oriental Church, Bonaventura Cardinal Cerretti (1872–1933) and Francesco Cardinal Ehrle (1845–1934), both attached to the Sacred Congregation for the Oriental Church; the Secretary was Amleto Cicognani,[17] who at that time occupied the position of Assessor in the Sacred Congregation for the Oriental Church. This Commission was charged with the direction of the threefold task decreed by the pope, namely: (a) that the preparatory historical-canonical studies concerning the laws and customs of each of the Oriental rites should be made by the priests whom the bishops had delegated; (b) that the drafts of canons redacted by these delegated priests should be sent to the Ordinaries in order that the latter might make animadversions about them; (c) that juridical, especially canonical, sources of all the Oriental rites should be compiled by scholars possessed of knowledge of Canon Law and skilled in history.[18]

This program was carried out with the aid of two special committees which were formed:

(a) One was for canonical studies, i. e., to draft canons or

---

[15] *Ibid.*, p. 496.

[16] Cicognani, *Canon Law*, p. 421.

[17] Since 1933 Amleto Giovanni Cicognani, Titular Archbishop of Laodicea, has been the Apostolic Delegate to the United States of America.

[18] *AAS*, XXVII (1935), 306-307; Coussa, *ibid.*, p. 529; Bergh, "Constitution d'une Commission pontificale pour la redaction du 'Code de droit canonique oriental'"—*Nouvelle Revue Théologique* (Tournai, 1869–), LXII (1935), 864–865.

laws,[19] and was under the direction of Cardinal Gasparri. In addition to fourteen Oriental delegates, there were five Consultors of the Sacred Congregation for the Oriental Church assigned by that Sacred Congregation.[20]

(b) The other was for historical studies, i. e., to compile source materials,[21] and was under the direction of Cardinal Sincero; it consisted mainly of Orientals.

The procedure in the committee for drafting the canons was as follows. Cardinal Gasparri assigned beforehand a certain number of canons concerning which each one of the delegated Oriental members of the committee[22] was to make a complete preparatory study within a certain time limit. In making this study, the delegated member was entirely free to write and propose whatever he wished or whatever consulted bishops suggested to him; he was also free to prove his assertion in the way he considered more efficacious: be it by documents, by arguments, etc. Then, each one submitted his study on the same topic to one of the four or five selected Consultors of the Sacred Congregation for the Oriental Church, whose task it was to draft a canon from these. This draft, in turn, was printed and distributed to all the delegated members a certain number of days before a full session of all was held. In this session the draft of the canon was read and everyone was free to make animadversions concerning it. If any of these animadversions was judged to be right by the cardinals of the Commission, the text of the draft was amplified, diminished, or modified accordingly. Upon the insistence of a

---

[19] Cicognani, *Canon Law,* p. 459, footnote 31; Coussa, "De Codificatione Canonica Orientali"—*Acta Congressus Iuridici Internationalis,* IV, 529.

[20] Dausend ("Das interrituelle Recht im Codex Iuris Canonici"—Görres-Gesellschaft, LXXIV [1939], 170) mentions 5 Latin canonists who take part in this work, whereas Coussa (*ibid.,* p. 530) mentions only 4 Latin Consultors. Cf. Appendix of this work on p. 227 where 5 Latin Consultors are listed.

[21] Cicognani, *loc. cit.;* Coussa, *ibid.,* p. 529.

[22] In this group of 14 there were an Ethiopian, Armenian, Bulgarian, Chaldean, Copt, Greek, Italo-Greek, Malabar, Melkite, Rumanian, Russian, Ruthenian, Syrian, Syro-Maronite. All lived at Rome except for the Ethiopian, Bulgarian, Copt, and Malabar. Cf. Coussa, *ibid.,* p. 530, footnote 108; cf. also the Appendix of this work on pp. 158–159.

delegate or upon the order of the Cardinal President, many doubts or queries were noted, and later proposed to the bishops. After a second reading of the draft some time later, once again the draft was printed and sent to all the Ordinaries of the Oriental Rite, to Latin Ordinaries either in the Orient or in the Occident who had in their diocese a body of faithful of the Oriental Rite, to Superiors of Orders, Religious Congregations, to Universities, etc., so that they might give their own opinion about each and everything contained in the draft. When the opinions of the bishops and the others were returned, they were given to one of the five Consultors, whose function it was to coordinate after each respective canon the proposals of the bishops. This new draft was finally submitted to the examination of the cardinals of the Commission. The Roman Pontiff himself then saw the proposals and arguments of the bishops and the decisions of the cardinals.[23]

The committee for the compilation of the sources ("*Fonti*") proceeded in a different manner—each member of the committee was assigned to the collection of general sources or else of sources of his own rite. When their labors are entirely completed there will be three series of sources. One series, which is known as Series III, consists of 16 fascicles or volumes.[24]

---

[23] Coussa, "De Codificatione Canonica Orientali"—*Acta Congressus Iudicii Internationalis,* IV, 529–530.

[24] They are listed in the following order:

Fascicolo I: Testi Vari di Diritto Nuovo (1550–1902).
" II: Testi Vari di Diritto Nuovo (1550–1902).
" III: Disciplina Antiochena (Siri).
" IV: Discipline Chaldéenne (Chaldéens).
" V: Testi di Diritto Antichi e Moderni Riguardenti gli Etiopi.
" VI: Testi di Diritto Antichi Riguardanti gli Etiopi.
" VII: Disciplina Armena. Testi Vari di Diritto Canonico Armeno (Secoli IV–XVII).
" VIII: Studi Storici Sulle Fonti del Diritto Canonico Orientale.
" IX: Disciplina Generale Antica (Sec. II–IX).
" X: Disciplina Byzantina. Rumeni. Testi di Diritto Particolare dei Rumeni.
" XI: Jus Particulare Ruthenorum.
" XII: Jus Particulare Maronitarum. Textus Juris Approbati.
" XIII: Maroniti. Diritto dei Religiosi.

In this series the sources are arranged under headings or titles of the subject matter, and these titles follow in alphabetic order—for example, the successive titles for numbers 198–201 in the fascicle for the Particular Law of the Ruthenians follows: n. 198—*Diebus sacris prohibentur spectacula, ludi;* n. 199—*Differentia inter Ruthenos et Latinos et Graeco-Russos;* n. 200—*Dimissoriales litterae in Ordinatione alieni subditi;* n. 201—*Dispositio et cura sacerdotis in administrandis Sacramentis.*[25] When it was discovered that this alphabetic arrangement of titles embodied the repetition of sources, it was decided to change to the systematic-chronological method (in this method all texts pertaining to an object or institute—such as, On the Roman Pontiff, On Patriarchs, On Metropolitans, etc.—are arranged into chapters and titles, and these texts are coordinated in a chronological order). Thus all the completed fascicles and those under press at the time of this decision to change methods were placed in what is known as Series III. All others follow the systematic-chronological order and are in either Series I or Series II. Series I embraces volumes which contain the Acts of the Roman Pontiffs, whether already published or not, which in any way whatsoever pertain to the canonical law of the Oriental Rite, whereas Series II contains the sources of individual rites as well as sources common to all or several Oriental rites (as for instance, texts from the Acts of the Ecumenical Councils, Commentators of Byzantine Law, etc.).[26] At the end of both Series

---

" XIV: Maroniti. Diritto non approvato.

" XV: Droit Particulier des Melkites. Textes du droit Approuvé.

" XVI: Melchiti. Diritto non approvato.

Cf. also Cicognani, *Canon Law*, p. 207, footnote 35: Cicognani-Staffa, *Commentarium ad Librum Primum Codicis Iuris Canonici*, p. 15, footnote 1.

[25] *Codificazione Canonica Orientale, Fonti*, fascicolo XI (*Jus Particulare Ruthenorum*), pp. 237–243.

[26] Cicognani-Staffa (*Commentarium ad Librum Primum Codicis Iuris Canonici*, p. 15, footnote 1) lists some of the works in that series: "Serie II—*Fascicolo* I: Textes Législatifs touchant Le Cénobitisme égyptien (F. Kozman)—*Fascicolo* VI: De fontibus iuris ecclesiastici Russorum (Ae. Herman S. I.)—*Fascicolo* VIII: De Fontibus iuris ecclesiastici Syro-Malankarensium (Placidus a S. Joseph, T. O. C. D.)."

I and II there is a very useful analytical index which refers to marginal numbers alongside the texts of the fascicle.[27]

When the threefold task assigned by Pope Pius XI had been completed (except for some source collections), a notification dated July 17, 1935, of the Sacred Congregation for the Oriental Church announced that the pope had decided to proceed to the redaction of the Code of Oriental Canon Law, and that he had erected a pontifical Commission to direct this work. This Commission was directed to examine the animadversions and opinions of the Ordinaries about the preparatory drafts of the canons, to determine the structure of the text of the canons, and finally to proceed to the redaction of the Code. But since this Code, not only as to its laws, but also as to the manner of its formulation, ought to be expressed in a manner characteristic of the people to whose rule it is destined, the pope decided that the cardinals of the Commission should be aided in the redaction of this Code by a group of Consultors chosen especially from among Oriental clerics. Finally, he ordered that the redaction of each title or book be submitted to examination by the Oriental patriarchs, archbishops and bishops.[28]

The personnel of this pontifical Commission was as follows:[29]

Cardinal Luigi Sincero, *President*
" Eugenio Pacelli (who is at present Pope Pius XII)
" Giulio Serafini
" Pietro Fumasoni-Biondi [30]
Very Rev. Acacio Coussa, B. A., *Secretary*

CONSULTORS

Francesco Agagianian, Titular Bishop of Comana in Armenia

[27] Cf. Kozman, *Textes Législatifs Touchant Le Cénobitisme Egyptien,* Codificazione Canonica Orientale Fonti Serie II—Fascicolo I (Romae: Typographe Polyglotte Vaticane, 1935), pp. 3–4.

[28] *AAS,* XXVII (1935), 306–307; Bergh, "Constitution d'une Commission pontificale pour la rédaction du 'Code de droit canonique oriental'"—*Nouvelle Revue Théologique,* LXII (1935), 865–866.

[29] *AAS,* XXVII (1935), 307. All the Christian names are given in the Italian language.

[30] He was the Apostolic Delegate to the United States of America from 1922–1933.

Very Rev. Francesco Gozman
" " Giovanni Balan
" ' Pietro Dib
" ' Pietro Sfair
" " Cirillo Korolevskij
Paolo Hindo
Garabed Amaduni
Giuseppe Zajackivskyj, O.S.B.M.
Romualdo Souarn, A.A.
Arcadio Larraona, C.M.F.
Ippolito della Sacra Famiglia, O.C.D.
Emil Herman, S.J.

Article IV. Letters Addressed to the Congregation

In a *Monitum* of August 10, 1933, the Sacred Congregation for the Oriental Church stated that all letters to this Sacred Congregation are to be addressed only (*unice*) in the following manner:[31]

> A Sua Eminenza Revm̃a, il. Sig. Cardinale Segretario della Sacra Congregazione Orientale.—Città del Vaticano.

Let it be noted, however, that this in no way affects the customary salutation ("*Beatissime Pater,*" i. e., the Pope) of the letter or petition directed to the Sacred Congregation.

[31] *AAS,* XXV (1933), 346.

CONCLUSIONS

(1) According to Pope Gregory XV's Constitution "*Inscrutabili divinae providentiae*," of June 22, 1622, the Sacred Congregation of the Propagation of the Faith supplied the function of the other Sacred Congregations (the Sacred Congregation of the Holy Office included) in regard to matters pertaining to missionary regions subjected to it; whether it supplied the functions of the Sacred Penitentiaria in all or in some respects is not definitely determined. The more serious (*graviora*) matters, however, were to be referred to the pope, after having been treated by the Sacred Congregation of the Propagation of the Faith. But in practice the Sacred Congregation of the Propagation of the Faith did not decide all these matters by itself; it did remit affairs to the other Sacred Congregations for solution.

(2) The Sacred Congregation of the Propagation of the Faith for affairs of the Oriental Rite (the *Sacra Congregatio de Propaganda Fide pro negotiis ritus orientalis*), instituted on January 6, 1862, possessed the very same vast powers bestowed previously upon the Sacred Congregation of the Propagation of the Faith by Pope Gregory XV and his successors.

(3) Although the Sacred Congregation of the Propagation of the Faith was limited in its powers by the provisions of the Constitution "*Sapienti consilio*," I, 6°, 4–5,—wherein it was stated that the Sacred Congregation of the Propagation of the Faith even within its territory was not to decide business which related to faith, or matrimony, or the discipline of the sacred rites, and that it was to remit or leave to the Sacred Congregation for Affairs of Religious whatever concerned Religious as Religious, whether considered individually or collectively—the Sacred Congregation of the Propagation of the Faith for affairs of the Oriental Rite was not affected by any of the above noted provisions.

(4) There can be no doubt that it was within the jurisdiction of the Sacred Congregation of the Propagation of the Faith

for affairs of the Oriental Rite to decide matters *in linea disciplinari* under the Constitution "*Sapienti consilio*"; but it is not definitely determined whether or not its jurisdiction was limited in cases to be decided *ordine iudiciario*.

(5) Although the Code was to go into effect and have the force of law on May 19, 1918, the provisions of Canon 257 regarding the Sacred Congregation for the Oriental Church really went into effect with the establishment of that Sacred Congregation on December 1, 1917.

(6) By the law of canon 257, § 2, it is within the jurisdiction of the Sacred Congregation for the Oriental Church in regard to the Orientals to erect and divide dioceses and to propose to the Supreme Pontiff for election or confirmation—according to the laws proper to each Oriental rite—suitable ecclesiastics for vacant sees even when civil governments have to be dealt with in doing these things; however, it can defer them to the Sacred Congregation for Extraordinary Ecclesiastical Affairs, as is its practice according to Staffa. Of course, as particular cases present themselves, the pope himself can assign them to the Sacred Congregation for Extraordinary Ecclesiastical Affairs.

(7) It is not within the jurisdiction of the Sacred Congregation for the Oriental Church to handle affairs which refer to the beatification and canonization of Servants of God, whether these matters concern Orientals or whether they concern Latins in the regions placed under the full and exclusive jurisdiction of the Sacred Congregation for the Oriental Church by the Motu proprio "*Sancta Dei Ecclesia.*"

APPENDIX

CHRONOLOGICAL LISTS[1]

Cardinal Prefects of the "Sacra Congregatio de Propaganda Fide" (1622–1861)

Sauli, Antonio Maria	1622
Ludovisi, Luigi [Ludovico]	1622–1632
Barberini, Antonio senior	1632–1644
Capponi, Luigi	1644–1659
Barberini, Antonio senior (second time)	1659–1671
Altieri, Paoluzzo	1671–1698
Barberini, Carlo	1698–1704
Sacripanti, Giuseppe	1704–1727
Petra, Vincenzo	1727–1747
Valenti-Gonzaga, Silvio	1747–1756
Spinelli, Giuseppe	1756–1763
Castelli, Giuseppe Maria	1763–1780
Antonelli, Leonardo	1780–1795
Gerdil, Sigismondo Giacinto	1795–1800
Borgia, Stefano	1800–1804
Dugnani, Antonio, *Pro-Prefect*	1804–1806
Di Pietro, Michele	1806–1814
Litta, Lorenzo	1814–1818
Fontana, Francesco	1818–1822
Consalvi, Ercole	1823–1824
Della Somaglia, Giulio Maria, *Pro-Prefect*	1824–1826
Cappellari, Mauro	1826–1831
Pedicini, Carlo Maria	1831–1834
Fransoni, Filippo	1834–1856
Barnabó, Alessandro	1856–(1874)

Cardinal Prefects of the "Sacra Congregatio pro negotiis ritus orientalis"

Barnabó, Alessandro	1862–1874
Franchi, Alessandro	1874–1878
Simeoni, Giovanni	1878–1892
Ledochowski, Miecislao	1892–1902
Gotti, Girolamo	1902–1916
Serafini, Domenico	1916–1917

(Suppressed, November 30, 1917)

[1] *Statistica,* pp. 17–23.

CARDINAL PREFECTS OF THE "SACRA CONGREGATIO SUPER CORRECTIONE LIBRORUM ORIENTALIUM"

Della Mirandola, Ludovico Pico 1722–1743
Tamburini, Fortunato 1743–1761
Antonelli, Niccolo 1761–1767
Boschi, Giovanni Carlo 1769–1788
Antonelli, Leonardo 1796–1811
Litta, Lorenzo .... –1820
Pacca, Bartolomeo 1826–

(Suppressed, January 6, 1862)

SECRETARIES OF THE "SACRA CONGREGATIO DE PROPAGANDA FIDE" (1622–1861)

Ingoli, Francesco 1622–1649
Massari, Dionisio 1649–1657
Alberici, Mario 1657–1664
Corsi, Domenico Maria, *Pro-Secretary* ....
Casanate, Girolamo 1667–1668
Ubaldi-Baldeschi, Federico 1668–1673
Ravizza, Francesco 1673–1675
Cerri, Urbano 1675–1679
Cibo, Edoardo 1680–1695
Fabroni, Carlo Agostino 1695–1706
Gozzadini, Ulisse Giuseppe, *Pro-Secretary* ....
Banchieri, Antonio 1706–1707
Collicola, Carlo, *Pro-Secretary* ....
De'Cavalieri, Silvio 1707–1717
Carafa, Luigi 1717–1724
Ruspoli, Bartolomeo 1724–1730
Fortiguerra, Nicola 1730–1735
Monti, Filippo Maria 1735–1743
Lercari, Nicola 1744–1757
Antonelli, Nicola 1757–1759
Marefoschi, Mario 1759–1770
Borgia, Stefano 1770–1789
Rinuccini, Giovanni, *Pro-Secretary* ....
Zondadari, Antonio 1789–1795
Brancadoro, Cesare 1796–1801
Coppola, Domenico 1802–1807
Quarantotti, Giovanni 1807–1816
Pedicini, Carlo Maria 1816–1823
Caprano, Pietro 1823–1828
Castracane, Castruccio 1828–1833
Mai, Angelo 1833–1838

Cadolini, Ignazio 1838–1843
Brunelli, Giovanni 1843–1847
Barnabo, Alessandro 1848–1856
Bedini, Caietano 1856–1861
Capalti, Annibale 1861–

Secretaries of the "Sacra Congregatio pro negotiis ritus orientalis"

Simeoni, Giovanni 1862–1868
Iacobini, Ludovico 1868–1874
Aloisi-Masella, Gaetano 1874–1877
Rampolla del Tindaro, Mariano 1877–1880
Cretoni, Serafino 1880–1889
Persico, Ignazio, Titular Archbishop of Damiata 1889–1891
Aiuti, Andrea, Titular Archbishop of Acrida 1891–1893
Veccia, Luigi 1893–1899
Savelli-Spinola, Antonio 1899–1906
Rolleri, Girolamo 1906–1917

Cardinal Secretaries of the Sacred Congregation for the Oriental Church

Marini, Niccolo 1917–1922
Tacci, Giovanni 1922–1926
Sincero, Luigi 1926–1936
(Pro-Secretary, February 6, 1926; Secretary, January 26, 1927)
Tisserant, Eugenio 1936–

Assessors of the Sacred Congregation for the Oriental Church

Papadopoulos, Isaia, Titular Bishop of Grazianopoli... 1917–1928
Cicognani, Amleto Giovanni 1928–1933
Cesarini, Giuseppe 1933–1941
Antonio, Arata 1941–

The Sacred Congregation for the Oriental Church for the year 1945[2]

His Holiness, Pope Pius XII, *Prefect*

Cardinals

Tisserant, Eugenio, *Secretary*
Gasparri, Enrico, Bishop of Velletri
Marchetti-Selvaggiani, Francesco, Bishop of Frascati
Salotti, Carlo, Bishop of Palestrina

[2] *Annuario Pontificio* for the year 1945, pp. 667–670.

Dougherty, Dionisio
Hlond, Augusto
Lavitrano, Luigi
Fumasoni-Biondi, Pietro
Innitzer, Teodoro
Tappouni, Ignazio Gabriele
Marmaggi, Francesco
Boetto, Pietro
Caccia-Dominioni, Camillo
Canali, Nicola
Jorio, Domenico
Massimi, Massimo
Mercati, Giovanni
Most Rev. Arata Antonino, Titular Archbishop of Sàrdi, *Assessor*
Msgr. Giovanni Rosso, *Substitute*

CONSULTORS

(The asterisk indicates that the Consultor lives outside of Rome.)

Rossi, Antonio Anastasio, Patriarch of Consantinople
*Agagianian, Gregorio Pietro XV, Patriarch of Cilicia, of the Armenians
Pisani, Pietro, Titular Archbishop of Constanza in Scythia (Tomi)
Constantini, Celso, Titular Archbishop of Theodosiopolis in Arcadia
Smets, Adriano, Titular Archbishop of Gangra
*Margotti, Carlo, Archbishop of Gorizia
Der Abrahamian, Sergio, Titular Archbishop of Chalcedon, of the Aremenians
*Kiley, Mosè, Archbishop of Milwaukee
*Della Pietra, Marco Giovanni, Archbishop of Ancona
*Szelażek, Adolfo, Bishop of Luceoria
*Besson, Mario, Bishop of Lausanne, Geneva and Fribourg
Bucys, Pietro, Titular Bishop of Olympus (of the Byzantine rite)
Evreinoff, Alessandro, Titular Bishop of Pionia (of the Byzantine rite)
Ottaviani, Alfredo
Tardini, Domenico
Msgr. Eras, Bernardo
" Roberti, Francesco
" Luttor, Francesco
" Teodori, Giovanni
" Canestri, Alberto
" Sacco, Giuseppe

Msgr. Giobbe, Filippo
" Cercone, Leonardo
" de Angelis, Serafino
" O'Reilly, Giacomo
" Dell'Acqua, Angelo
" Bartoccetti, Vittorio
Rev. Korolevskij, Cirillo (of the Byzantine rite)
Very Rev. *Torossian, Giovanni, of the Mechitarists of Venice (of the Armenian rite)
" " Filograssi, Giuseppe, of the Society of Jesus
" " Hudecek, Giovanni, of the Congregation of the Most Holy Redeemer
" " de Meester, Placido, of the Belgian Benedictine Congregation
" " Souarn, Romualdo, of the Augustinians of the Assumption
" " Kandjuk, Pancrazio, of the Order of the Basilians of St. Josaphat (of the Byzantine rite)
" " d'Ambrosio, Francesco Saverio, of the Friars Minor Conventuals
" " Cappello, Felice M., of the Society of Jesus
" " Vosté, Giacomo M., of the Order of Preachers
" " Mills, Antonio Maria, of the Servants of Mary
" " *Ippolito della S. Famiglia, of the Discalced Carmelites
" " Leduc, Agostino, of the Order of Preachers
" " Larraona, Arcadio, of the Missionary Sons of the Immaculate Heart of Mary
" " Suarez, Emanuele, of the Order of Preachers
" " Herman, Emil, of the Society of Jesus
" " Scartabelli, Marcello, of the Friars Minor
" " Goyenèche, Servo, of the Missionary Sons of the Immaculate Heart of Mary
" " Jugie, Martino, of the Augustinians of the Assumption
" " Janin, Raimondo, of the Augustinians of the Assumption
" " Quénard, Gervasio, of the Augustinians of the Assumption
" " Coussa, Acacio, of the Basilian Order of Aleppo (of the Byzantine rite)
" " Salaville, Severiano, of the Augustinians of the Assumption
" " van Lantschoot, Arnoldo, of the Premonstratensians

Very Rev. Vailhé, Simeone, of the Augustinians of the Assumption
" " Raes, Alfonso, of the Society of Jesus

SPECIAL COMMISSIONS FOR THE HANDLING OF MATRIMONIAL CASES

"Commissarii" deputed for the decision:

Msgr. Theodori, Giovanni
" Canestri, Alberto
Very Rev. Mills, Antonio Maria
" " Suarez, Emanuele
" " Goyenèche, Servo
" " Coussa, Acacio

"Commissarii" deputed for the defence of the bond:

Msgr. Bartoccetti, Vittorio
Very Rev. Souarn, Romualdo
" " Kandjuk, Pancrazio
" " Cappello, Felice M.
" " Leduc, Agostino
" " Larraona, Arcadio

SPECIAL SECTION FOR LITURGY

Consultors

Msgr. *Dib, Pietro (of the Antiochene rite)
Rev. Korolevskij, Cirillo (of the Byzantine rite)
Very Rev. de Meester, Placido
" " Vosté, Giacomo
" " Hanssens, Giovanni Michele, of the Society of Jesus
" " Raes, Alfonso

Officials

Msgr. Melilli, Ignazio (Minutante)
" Giovanelli, Amerigo "
" Terzariol, Adone "
" Mojoli, Giuseppe "
" Pappalardo, Paolo "
" Gragnani, Angelo "
Mr. Mosca, Stanislao "
Msgr. Spina, Antonio "
" Bruning, Giacomo (Minutante with the duty of Archivist)
" McGeough, Giuseppe (Minutante)

Rev. Onofri, Michele (Minutante with the duties of Master of Protocol)
" .... (Minutante)
.... "
Msgr. Ponte, Tommaso (Scrittore)
Mr. Scudellari, Elio "
Rev. .... "
Mr. Ceccopieri Maruffi, Conte Riccardo (Cashier and Collector of Taxes)

Interpreter

Msgr. Sfair, Pietro

COMMISSION OF THE DELEGATED ORIENTAL MEMBERS FOR THE CODIFICATION OF CANON LAW OF THE ORIENTAL CHURCH

Armenian: Rev. Garabed Amaduni
Bulgarian: Rev. Clemente Pascaleff
Chaldean: Rev. Paolo David
Copt: Rev. Francesco Gozman
Ethiopian: Most Rev. Chidane-Maryam Kassa, Titular Bishop of Tibari
Greek: Rev. Cirillo Korolevskij
Italo-Albanian: Rev. Ieromonaco Isidoro Croce
Malabar: Rev. Zaccaria Vachaparambil
Maronite: Rev. Paolo Sfair
Melkite: Rev. Ieromonaco Acacio Coussa
Rumanian: Rev. Giovanni Balan
Russian: Msgr. Alessandro Sipiaguine
Ruthenian: Rev. Ieromonaco Dionisio Holoveckyj
Syrian: Msgr. Tomasso Halabai

The Latin Consultors of This Commission

Rev. Felice Maria Cappelo
" Emilio Herman
" Ippolito della S. Famiglia
" Arcadio Larraona
" Romualdo Souarn

COMMISSION FOR THE COLLECTION OF THE "FONTI" OF ORIENTAL LAW

Rev. Carlo Abela
" Giovanni Batan
" Doroteo Calavassy
" Ieromonaco Isidoro Croce
Pietro Dib, Corepiscopo Maronita

Msgr. Silvano Grebaut
Rev. Vartan Hatzuni
" Enrico Hyvernat
" Cirillo Korolevskij
" Clemente Pascaleff
" Giuseppe Ricciotti
Msgr. Eugenio Tisserant
Rev. Giacomo Vosté

BIBLIOGRAPHY

SOURCES

Acta Apostolicae Sedis, Commentarium Officiale, Romae, 1909–

Annuario Pontificio, Roma: Typografia Poliglotta Vaticana, 1912–. Formerly entitled *Notizie,* 1716(?)–1858; *Annuario Pontificio,* 1860–1871; *La Gerarchia Cattolica,* 1872–1911; and again *Annuario Pontificio* from 1912 on. None was published for 1813–1814, 1848–1850, 1859(?).

Benedicti XIV Pont. Opt. Max. olim Prosperi Cardinalis De Lambertinis Bullarium (commencing with tome III the title is *Bullarii Romani Continuatio Summorum Pontificum Benedicti XIV, Clementis XIII, Clementis XIV, Pii VI, Pii VII, Leonis XII et Pii VIII*), 9 tomes in 14, Prati: In Typographia Aldina, 1845–1856.

Bouscaren, T. Lincoln, *The Canon Law Digest,* 2 vols., and Supplement—1941, Milwaukee: Bruce, 1934–1941.

Bullarium Pontificium Sacrae Congregationis de Propaganda Fide, Romae: Typis Collegii Urbani, 1859–

Bullarum Diplomatum et Privilegiorum Sanctorum Romanorum Pontificum Taurinensis Editio, 24 vols. et Appendix, Augustae Taurinorum, 1857–1872.

Codex Iuris Canonici Pii X Pontificis Maximi iussu digestus, Benedicti Papae XV auctoritate promulgatus, Westminster, Maryland: The Newman Book Shop, 1942.

Codicis Iuris Canonici Fontes cura Emi Petri Card. Gasparri editi, 9 vols., Romae (postea Civitate Vaticana); Typis Polyglottis Vaticanis, 1923–1939. (Vols. VII–IX ed. cura et studio Emi Iustiniani Card. Serédi.)

Codificatione Canonica Orientale, Fonti, Typografia Poliglotta Vaticana, 1930–

Collectanea S. Congregationis de Propaganda Fide seu Decreta Instructiones Rescripta Pro Apostolicis Missionibus, 2 vols., Romae: Ex Typographia Polyglotta S. C. de Propaganda Fide, 1907.

Leonis XIII Pontificis Maximi Acta, 23 vols., Romae: Ex Typographia Vaticana, 1881–1905.

Mansi, Ioannes Dominicus, *Sacrorum Conciliorum Nova et Amplissima Collectio,* 53 vols. in 60, Paris, Arnhem, Leipzig, 1901–1927.

Statistica con Cenni Storici della Gerarchia e dei Fedeli di Rito Orientale, published by Sacra Congregazione Orientale, Tipografia Poliglotta Vaticana, 1932.

Sylloge praecipuorum documentorum recentium Summorum Pontificum et S. Congregationis de Propaganda Fide necnon aliarum SS. Congregationum Romanorum ad usum missionariorum, Typis Polyglottis Vaticanis, 1939.

REFERENCE WORKS

Attwater, Donald, *The Catholic Eastern Churches,* revised ed., Milwaukee, Wisconsin: The Bruce Publishing Company, 1937.

Ayrinhac, H. A., *Constitution of the Church in the New Code of Canon Law,* London, New York, Toronto: Longmans, Green and Co., 1930.

Baart, Peter A., *The Roman Court,* 4. ed., New York: Fr. Pustet & Co., 1899.

[Bachofen], Charles Augustine, *A Commentary on the New Code of Canon Law,* 8 vols., St. Louis: Herder & Co., 1921-1938. Vol. I, 6. ed., 1931; Vol. II, 6. ed., 1936; Vol. III, 5. ed., 1938; Vol. IV, 3. ed., 1925; Vol. V, 5. ed., 1935; Vol. VI, 3. ed., 1931; Vol. VII, 3. ed., 1930; Vol. VIII, 3. ed., 1931.

Bargilliat, M., *Praelectiones Juris Canonici,* 22. ed., 2 vols., Parisiis: Apud Berche et Tralin, 1905.

Beste, Udalricus, *Introductio in Codicem,* Collegeville, Minn.: St. John's Abbey Press, 1938.

Blat, Albertus, *Commentarium Textus Codicis Iuris Canonici,* 6 vols., Romae: Libreria del Collegio "Angelico," 1920-1927. Vol. II, 2. ed., 1921.

Bouix, D., *Tractatus de Curia Romana seu de Cardinalibus, Romanis Congregationibus, Legatis, Nuntiis, Vicariis et Protonotariis Apostolicis,* Parisiis, 1859.

Bouuaert, F.-Simenon, G., *Manuale Juris Canonici,* Vols. I and III, 3. ed., 1930; Vol. II, 1931, Gandae et Leodii: Apud Auctores in Seminariis Gandavensi et Leodiensi.

Cance, Adrien, *Le Code de Droit Canonique,* 3 vols., Paris: J. Gabalda et Fils, 1927-1929. Vol. I, 6. ed., 1930.

Cappello, Felix M., *De Curia Romana Juxta Reformationem a Pio X Sapientissime Inductam,* 2 vols., Romae, Ratisbonae, Neo-Eboraci, Cincinnati: Fridericus Pustet. 1911-1912.

——, *Praxis Processualis,* Taurini-Romae: Domus Editorialis Marietti, 1940.

Catholic Encyclopedia, The, 15 vols., and 2 supplements, New York, 1907-1922.

Chelodi, Joannes, *Ius de Personis iuxta Codicem Iuris Canonici,* ed. altera a Sac. Ernesto Bertagnolli recognita et aucta, Tridenti: Libr. Edit. Tridentum, 1927.

Choupin, Lucien, *Valeur des Décisions Doctrinales et Disciplinaires du Saint-Siège,* 3. ed., Paris: Gabriel Beauchesne, 1928.

Cicognani, Amleto G., *Canon Law,* 2. ed., authorized English version by J. O'Hara and F. Brennan, Philadelphia: Dolphin Press, 1935.

Cicognani, Amleto G.-Staffa, Dino, *Commentarium ad Librum Primum Codicis Iuris Canonici,* Romae: Ex Officina Typographica Romana "Buona Stampa," 1939.

Coronata, Matthaeus Conte a, *Institutiones Iuris Canonici ad Usum Utriusque Cleri et Scholarum,* 5 vols., Taurini (Italia): Marietti, 1928–1936.

Craisson, D., *Manuale Juris Canonici,* 5. ed., 3 vols., Pictavii: Ex Typis H. Oudin, 1877.

Dausend, Hugo, *Das interrituelle Recht im Codex Iuris Canonici,* heft 79, *Görres-Gesellschaft* (Koln: J. P. Bachem, 1908; Paderborn, Ferdinand Schoningh, 1909–), 1939.

De Luca, Joannes, *Theatrum Veritatis et Justitiae sive Decisivi Discursus, ad Veritatem Editi in Forensibus, Controversiis, Canonicis, et Civilibus, in Quibus, in Urbe Advocatus, pro Una Partium Scripsit, vel Consultus Respondit,* 16 tomes in 9, Coloniae Agrippae: Apud Henricum Rommerskirchen, 1706.

De Meester, Alphonsus, *Juris Canonici et Juris Canonico-civilis Compendium,* nova ed., 3 vols. in 4, Brugis: Desclée, De Brouwer & S[i], 1921–1928.

Deshayes, F., *Memento Juris Ecclesiastici,* Parisiis: Apud Berche et Tralin, 1895.

De Smet, Aloysius, *De Sponsalibus & Matrimonio Tractatus Canonicus & Theologicus,* Brugis: Car. Beyaert, 1909.

Dictionnaire de Théologie Catholique, 14 vols. in 26, Paris: Letouzey et Ané, 1903–1939.

Doheny, William, *Canonical Procedure in Matrimonial Cases,* 2 vols., Milwaukee: The Bruce Publishing Company, 1938–1944.

Duskie, John Aloysius, *Canonical Status of the Orientals in the United States,* The Catholic University of America Canon Law Studies, n. 48, Washington, D. C.: The Catholic University of America, 1928.

Eubel, Conradus, *Hierarchia Catholica Medii Aevi sive Summorum Pontificum, S.R.E. Cardinalium, Ecclesiarum Antistitum Series,* 4 vols., Vols. I (1913) and II (1914) in 2. ed. edited by Gulielmus Van Gulik-Conradus Eubel, Vol. IV (1935) edited by Patritius Gauchat under the title of *Hierarchia Catholica Medii et Recensioris Aevi sive Summorum Pontificum, S.R.E. Cardinalium, Ecclesiarum Antistitum Series,* Monasterii: Sumptibus et Typis Librariae Regensburgianae.

Ferreres, Joannes, *Institutiones Canonicae,* 2. ed., 2 vols., Barcinone: Eugenius Subirana, 1920.

Fortescue, Adrian, *The Lesser Eastern Church,* London: Catholic Truth Society, 1913.

———, *The Orthodox Eastern Church,* 3. ed., London: Catholic Truth Society, 1929.

———, *The Uniate Eastern Churches,* edited by George D. Smith, New York, Cincinnati, Chicago: Benziger Brothers, 1923.

Gérin, Marcel, *Le Gouvernement des Missions,* Les Thèses Canoniques de Laval, n. 1, Québec, Canada: Université Laval, 1944.

Goyau, G.-Pératé, A.-Fabre, P., *Le Vatican, les Papes et la Civilisation,* Paris: Librairie de Firmin-Didot et Cie, 1895.

Haine, A. J. J. F., *De la Cour Romaine,* Louvain: Typographie de Vanlinthout et Cie, 1859.

Hefele, C. J.-Leclercq, H., *Histoires des Conciles,* 10 vols. in 19, Paris: Letouzey et Ané, 1907-1938.

Hilling, Nicholas, *Procedure at the Roman Curia,* New York: Joseph F. Wagner, 1907.

Hurter, H., *Nomenclator Literarius Recentioris Theologiae Catholicae Theologos Exhibens qui inde a Concilio Tridentino Floruerunt Aetate, Natione, Disciplinis Distinctos,* 2. ed., 3 vols., Oenipotente: Libraria Academica Wagneriana, 1892-1895.

Kay, Thomas Henry, *Competence in Matrimonial Procedure,* The Catholic University of America Canon Law Studies, n. 53, Washington, D. C.: The Catholic University of America, 1929.

Kennedy, Edwin J., *The Special Matrimonial Process in Cases of Evident Nullity,* The Catholic University of America Canon Law Studies, n. 93, Washington, D. C.: The Catholic University of America, 1935.

Kozman, François, *Textes Législatifs Touchant Le Cénobitisme Egyptien,* Codificazione Canonica Orientale Fonti, Serie II—Fascicolo I, Romae: Typographe Polyglotte Vaticane, 1935.

Kubelbeck, William, *The Sacred Penitentiaria and Its Relations to Faculties of Ordinaries and Priests,* The Catholic University of America Canon Law Studies, n. 5, Washington, D. C.: The Catholic University of America, 1918.

Laurentius, Ios., *Institutiones Iuris Ecclesiastici,* Friburgi Brisgoviae: Sumptibus Herder, 1903.

Lega, Michael, *Praelectiones in Textum Iuris Canonici de Iudiciis Ecclesiasticis,* 4 vols., Romae, 1896-1901.

Lemmens, Leonardus, *Acta S. Congregationis de Propaganda Fide pro Terra Sancta, Biblioteca Bio-Bibliografica della Terra Sancta e dell' Oriente Francescano,* 14 vols., edited by Girolamo Golubovitch, Quaracchi presso Firenze, 1921-1936.

Lexikon für Theologie und Kirche, 10 vols., edited by Michael Buchberger, Frieburg im Breisgau: Herder & Co.: 1930-1938.

Maroto, Philippus, *Institutiones Iuris Canonici ad Normam Novi Codicis,* 2 vols., Matriti: Typis "Imprenta Ibérica" Stanislai Maestre, 1919.

Martin, Michael, *The Roman Curia,* New York: Benziger Brothers, 1913.

Martin, Victor, *Les Congrégations Romaines,* Paris: Librairie Bloud & Gay, 1930.

Meehan, Andreas, *Compendium Juris Canonici,* Roffae: Ex Typographia Joannis P. Smith, 1899.

Meier, Carl Anthony, *Penal Administrative Procedure Against Negligent Pastors,* The Catholic University of America Canon Law Studies, n.

140, Washington, D. C.: The Catholic University of America Press, 1940.

Michiels, Gommarus, *Principia Generalia de Personis in Ecclesia,* Lublin, Polonia: Universitas Catholica, 1932.

Monin, Arthur, *De Curia Romana,* Lovanii: Josephus Van Linthout, 1912.

Moroni, Cavaliere Gaetano, *Dizionario di Erudizione Storico-Ecclesiastica,* 103 vols., Venezia: Della Tipografia Emiliana, 1840-1861.

Noval, Joseph, *Commentarium Codicis Iuris Canonici,* lib. IV, *De Processibus,* 2 vols., Pars I, *De Iudiciis,* 1920; Pars II, *De Causis Beatificationis Servorum Dei et Canonizationis Beatorum,* 1932; Pars IV, *De Modo Procedendi in Nonnullis Expediendis Negotiis vel Sanctionibus Poenalibus Applicandis,* 1932; Augustae Taurinorum-Romae: Marietti.

Oesterle, Gerardus, *Praelectiones Iuris Canonici,* Romae: In Collegio S. Anselmi, 1931.

Ojetti, Benedictus, *De Romana Curia,* Romae: Ex Cooperativa Typographia Manuzio, 1910.

Pastor, Ludwig, *The History of the Popes,* 34 vols., Vols. I-VI edited by Frederick Ignatius Antrobus, Vols. VII-XXIV edited by Ralph Francis Kerr, Vols. XXV-XXXIV edited by Dom Ernest Graf, St. Louis: B. Herder, 1898-1941.

Phillips, Georg, *Kirchenrecht,* 7 vols., Regensburg, 1845-1872; Vol. VIII, Part I, ed. by Friedrich Vering [1833-1896], Regensburg, 1889.

Pirhing, Ernricus, *Jus Canonicum in V Libros Decretalium Distributum Nova Methodo Explicatum,* 4 vols., Dilingae, 1674-1677.

Prümmer, Dominicus, *Manuale Iuris Canonici in Usum Scholarum,* 5. ed., Friburgi Brisgoviae: Herder & Co., 1927.

Reiffenstuel, Anacletus, *Ius Canonicum Universum,* 5 vols. in 7, Parisiis, 1864-1882.

Reilly, Edward Michael, *The General Norms of Dispensation,* The Catholic University of America Canon Law Studies, n. 119, Washington, D. C.: The Catholic University of America Press, 1939.

Rice, Patrick W., *Proof of Death in Pre-Nuptial Investigation,* The Catholic University of America Canon Law Studies, n. 123, Washington, D. C.: The Catholic University of America Press, 1940.

Roberti, Franciscus, *De Processibus,* 2 vols., Romae: Apud Aedes Facultatis Iuridicae ad S. Apollinaris, 1926.

Sägmüller, J. B., *Lehrbuch des katholischen Kirchenrechts,* Freiburg im Breisgau: Herdersche Verlagshandlung, 1930.

Sarti, Franciscus-Leitner, Martinus, *Praelectiones Juris Canonici,* 4. ed., 3 vols., Ratisbonae, Romae, Neo-Eboraci et Cincinnati: Sumptibus et Typis Friderici Pustet, 1904-1905.

Schmidt, John Rogg, *The Principles of Authentic Interpretation in Canon 17 of the Code of Canon Law,* The Catholic University of America

Canon Law Studies, n. 141, Washington, D. C.: The Catholic University of America Press, 1941.

Sebastianelli, Guilelmo, *Praelectiones Iuris Canonici,* 3 vols., Romae, Ratisbonae, Neo-Eboraci, Cincinnati: Fridericus Pustet, 1905–1906. Vol. I (*De Personis*), 2. ed., 1905; Vol. II (*De Rebus*), 2. ed., 1905; Vol. III (*De Iudiciis Ecclesiasticis*), 1906.

Simier, Jules, *La Curie Romaine,* Paris: Editions de la "Revue Augustinienne," 1909.

Sipos, Stephanus, Enchiridion Iuris Canonici, 3. ed., Pécs: Ex Typographia "Haladás R. T.," 1936.

Smith, S. B., *Elements of Ecclesiastical Law,* 3 vols., New York, Cincinnati, Chicago: Benziger Brothers, 1877–1888. Vol. I, 9. ed., 1893.

Streit, Carolus, *Atlas Hierarchicus,* Paderbonae in Guestfalia: Sumptibus Typographiae Bonifacianae, 1913. (Pro terris externis, extra Germaniam, Austriam-Hungariam, opus praestat apud B. Herder, Typographum Editorem Pontificium, Friburgi Brisgoviae.)

Toso, Albertus, *Ad Codicem Iuris Canonici Benedicti XV Pont. Max. Auctoritate Promulgatum Commentaria Minora,* 5 vols. in 2, Tiferni Tiberini: Ex Offic. Typogr. Vinciana, 1921–1927.

Vermeersch, A.–Creusen, J., *Epitome Iuris Canonici,* 3 vols., Mechlinae-Romae: H. Dessain, 1934–1937. Vol. I, 6. ed., 1937; Vol. II, 5. ed., 1934; Vol. III, 5. ed., 1936.

Vromant, G., *Ius Missioniariorum,* Louvain: Librairie E. Desbarax, 1929.

Wernz, Franciscus X., *Ius Decretalium,* 6 vols., Romae et Prati, 1898–1905.

Wernz, Franciscus X.–Vidal, Petrus, *Ius Canonicum,* 7 vols. in 8, Romae: Apud Aedes Universitatis Gregorianae, 1923–1943. Vol. II, 3. ed., 1943, recognita A. P. Philippo Aguirre.

Woywod, Stanislaus, *A Practical Commentary on the Code of Canon Law,* 6. ed., 2 vols., New York: Joseph F. Wagner, 1941.

ARTICLES

Anonymous, "Des Congrégations Romaines et de Leur Pratique"—*Analecta Juris Pontificii,* II (1857), 2230–2282; 2364–2424.

Arendt, G., "De Exclusiva S. Officii Competentia circa Matrimonium Mixtum (Can. 247)"—*Jus Pontificium,* VII (1927), 120–137.

Benigni, U., "Sacred Congregation of Propaganda"—*The Catholic Encyclopedia,* XII, 456–461.

Bergh, E., "Constitution d'une Commission pontificale pour la rédaction du 'Code de droit canonique oriental'"—*Nouvelle Revue Théologique,* LXII (1935), 864–865.

Besse, J. M., "Rule of Saint Basil"—*The Catholic Encyclopedia,* II, 322–324.

Boudinhon, A., "La Commission pour l'Interpretation Officielle du Code"—*Le Canoniste Contemporain,* XL (1917), 397–400.

Brems, A., "De Interpretatione Authentica Codicis I. C. Per Pont. Commissionem"—*Jus Pontificium,* XVI (1936), 78–105.

Choupin, Lucien, "La Constitution 'Sapienti consilio' de Pie X et la Réorganisation de la Curie Romaine"—*Etudes Religieuses,* CXVII (1908), 308–320, 642–658.

Coussa, A., "De Codificatione Canonica Orientali"—*Acta Congressus Iuridici Internationalis,* IV (1937), 493–532.

Cugnoni, G., "Autobiografia del Card. G. A. Santori"—*Archivio della R. Società Romana di Storia Patria,* XII (1889), 327–372.

Forget, J., "Congrégations Romaines"—*Dictionnaire de Théologie Catholique,* III (1931), 1103–1119.

Goyau, Georges, "Les Initatives Belges dans la Fondation de la Propagande"—*La Revue Générale,* CXII (1924), 1–23.

Herman, E., "De 'Ritu' in Iure Canonico"—*Orientalia Christiana,* XXXII (1933), 96–158.

Heteren, Willibrordo Van, "Progetto di fondazione di un Collegio di rito greco nell' isola di Candia verso la fine del XVI secolo"—*Bessarione,* Anno IV (1899–1900), Vol. VII, pp. 600–608.

Hilling, Nikolaus, "Die gesetzgeberische Tätigkeit Benedikts XV seit der Promulgation des Codex iuris canonici"—*Archiv für katholisches Kirchenrecht,* CIII (1923), 5–36.

———, "Die Entscheidung des Hl. Offiziums vom 18. Januar 1928 über seine Kompetenz in Ehesachen"—*Archiv für katholisches Kirchenrecht,* CVIII (1928), 536–549.

Korolevskij, Cirillo, "L'Istruzione di Clemente VIII 'Super Aliquibus Ritibus Graecorum' (1595) e le Congregazioni per la Riforma dei Greci (1593)"—*Bessarione,* Anno XVII (1913), Vol. XXIX, pp. 466–481.

Petrani, Alexius, "De Sacra Congregatione pro Ecclesia Orientali eiusque facultatibus"—*Apollinaris,* X (1937), 28–46.

Salaville, S., "Un Théoricien de l'Apostolat Catholique au XVIIe Siècle"—Echoes d'Orient, XIX (1920), 129–152.

Schmidlin, "Die Gründung der Propagandakongregation (1622)"—*Zeitschrift für Missionswissenschaft,* XII (1922), 1–14.

———, "Eine Vorläuferin der Propaganda unter Klemens VIII"—*Zeitschrift für Missionswissenschaft,* XI (1921), 232–234.

Staffa, D., "De Sacrae Congregationis pro Ecclesia Orientali competentia"—*Apollinaris,* XI (1938), 358–376.

Tacchi Venturi, "Diario Concistoriale di Antonio Santori di S. Severina"—*Studi e documenti di Storia e Diritto,* XXIV (1903), 73–142; 205–272.

Toso, A., "De competentia S. Poenitentiariae Ap. circa negotia fori interni Orientalium"—*Jus Pontificium,* X (1930), 243.

Villien, A., "L'Institut Pontifical pour l'Etude des Questions Orientales"—*Le Canoniste Contemporain,* XL (1917), 502–505.

Villien, A., "Le Saint-Office et la Suppression de la Congrégation de l'Index"—*Le Canoniste Contemporain*, XL (1917), 98–111.

PERIODICALS

Acta Congressus Iuridici Internationalis, Romae: Apud Custodiam Librariam Pont. Instituti Utriusque Iuris, 1935–

Analecta Juris Pontificii, Romae, 1855–1868; Parisiis, 1869–1890; later *Analecta Ecclesiastica*, 1893–1911.

Apollinaris, Romae, 1928–

Archiv für katholisches Kirchenrecht, Innsbruck, 1857–1861; Mainz, 1862–

Archivio della R. Società Romana di Storia Patria, Roma, 1877–

Bessarione, Roma, 1896–

Canoniste Contemporain, Le, 45 vols., Paris: P. Lethielleux, 1878–1922; from 1924–1926: *Le Canoniste.*

Echos D'Orient, Paris, 1897–

Irish Ecclesiastical Record, The, Dublin, 1864–

Jus Pontificium, Romae, 1921–

Nouvelle Revue Théologique, Tournai, 1869–

Orientalia Christiana, Roma, 1923–

Periodica de Re Canonica et Morali Utili praesertim Religiosis et Missionariis, Brugis, 1905–; ab anno 1927: *Periodica de Re Canonica, Morali, Liturgica.*

Revue des Questions Historiques, Paris, 1866–

Revue Générale (later *La Revue Générale*), Bruxelles, 1865–

Studi e Documenti di Storia e Diritto, Roma, 1880–

Theologisch-praktische Quartalschrift, Linz, 1832–

Zeitschrift für Missionswissenschaft, Münster: Aschendorffsche Verlagsbuchhandlung, 1911–

ALPHABETICAL INDEX

BIOGRAPHICAL NOTE

Michael Walter Dziob was born on December 9, 1917, in Woonsocket, R. I. After completing his elementary education at McFee School and the parochial school of St. Stanislaus Kostka in that city, he attended the Woonsocket Junior High School and Senior High School. From the fall of 1934 to 1936 he pursued the pre-ecclesiastical course at Providence College, Providence, Rhode Island. In 1936 he entered the seminary of the American College of the Immaculate Conception at Louvain, Belgium, where he completed his philosophical studies and commenced his theological course. After the outbreak of World War II he returned to the U. S. A., and finished his theology at St. Mary's Seminary, Baltimore, Maryland. He was ordained to the priesthood on May 20, 1942. In the fall of the same year he enrolled in the School of Canon Law at the Catholic University of America, where he received the degree of the Baccalaureate in Canon Law in May, 1943, and the degree of the Licentiate in Canon Law in May, 1944.

CANON LAW STUDIES*

1. Freriks, Rev. Celestine A., C.PP.S., J.C.D., Religious Congregations in Their External Relations, 121 pp., 1916.
2. Galliher, Rev. Daniel M., O.P., J.C.D., Canonical Elections, 117 pp., 1917.
3. Borkowski, Rev. Aurelius L., O.F.M., J.C.D., De Confraternitatibus Ecclesiasticis, 136 pp., 1918.
4. Castillo, Rev. Cayo, J.C.D., Disertacion Historico-Canonica sobre la Potestad del Cabildo en Sede Vacante o Impedida del Vicario Capitular, 99 pp., 1919 (1918).
5. Kubelbeck, Rev. William J., S.T.B., J.C.D., The Sacred Penitentiaria and Its Relation to Faculties of Ordinaries and Priests, 129 pp., 1918.
6. Petrovits, Rev. Joseph J. C., S.T.D., J.C.D., The New Church Law on Matrimony, X-461 pp., 1919.
7. Hickey, Rev. John J., S.T.B., J.C.D., Irregularities and Simple Impediments in the New Code of Canon Law, 100 pp., 1920.
8. Klekotka, Rev. Peter J., S.T.B., J.C.D., Diocesan Consultors, 179 pp., 1920.
9. Wanenmacher, Rev. Francis, J.C.D., The Evidence in Ecclesiastical Procedure Affecting the Marriage Bond, 1920 (Printed 1935).
10. Golden, Rev. Henry Francis, J.C.D., Parochial Benefices in the New Code, IV-119 pp., 1921 (Printed 1925).
11. Koudelka, Rev. Charles J., J.C.D., Pastors, Their Rights and Duties According to the New Code of Canon Law, 211 pp., 1921.
12. Melo, Rev. Antonius, O.F.M., J.C.D., De Exemptione Regularium, X-188 pp., 1921.
13. Schaaf, Rev. Valentine Theodore, O.F.M., S.T.B., J.C.D., The Cloister, X-180 pp., 1921.
14. Burke, Rev. Thomas Joseph, S.T.D., J.C.D., Competence in Ecclesiastical Tribunals, IV-117 pp., 1922.
15. Leech, Rev. George Leo, J.C.D., A Comparative Study of the Constitution "Apostolicae Sedis" and the "Codex Juris Canonici," 179 pp., 1922.
16. Motry, Rev. Hubert Louis, S.T.D., J.C.D., Diocesan Faculties According to the Code of Canon Law, II-167 pp., 1922.
17. Murphy, Rev. George Lawrence, J.C.D., Delinquencies and Penalties in the Administration and the Reception of the Sacraments, IV-121 pp., 1923.

* Below n. 100 only numbers 25 and 57 are still available. Beginning with n. 100 only the following numbers are unavailable: Nos. 100–118 inclusive, and also n. 122.

18. O'Reilly, Rev. John Anthony, S.T.B., J.C.D., Ecclesiastical Sepulture in the New Code of Canon Law, II-129 pp., 1923.
19. Michalicka, Rev. Wenceslas Cyrill, O.S.B., J.C.D., Judicial Procedure in Dismissal of Clerical Exempt Religious, 107 pp., 1923.
20. Dargin, Rev. Edward Vincent, S.T.B., J.C.D., Reserved Cases According to the Code of Canon Law, IV-103 pp., 1924.
21. Godfrey, Rev. John A., S.T.B., J.C.D., The Right of Patronage According to the Code of Canon Law, 153 pp., 1924.
22. Hagedorn, Rev. Francis Edward, J.C.D., General Legislation on Indulgences, II-154 pp., 1924.
23. King, Rev. James Ignatius, J.C.D., The Administration of the Sacraments to Dying Non-Catholics, V-141 pp., 1924.
24. Winslow, Rev. Francis Joseph, O.F.M., J.C.D., Vicars and Prefects Apostolic, IV-149 pp., 1924.
25. Correa, Rev. Jose Servelion, S.T.L., J.C.D., La Potestad Legislativa de la Iglesia Catolica, IV-127 pp., 1925.
26. Dugan, Rev. Henry Francis, A.M., J.C.D., The Judiciary Department of the Diocesan Curia, 87 pp., 1925.
27. Keller, Rev. Charles Frederick, S.T.B., J.C.D., Mass Stipends, 167 pp., 1925.
28. Paschang, Rev. John Linus, J.C.D., The Sacramentals According to the Code of Canon Law, 129 pp., 1925.
29. Piontek, Rev. Cyrillus, O.F.M., S.T.B., J.C.D., De Indulto Exclaustrationis necnon Saecularizationis, XIII-289 pp., 1925.
30. Kearney, Rev. Richard Joseph, S.T.B., J.C.D., Sponsors at Baptism According to the Code of Canon Law, IV-127 pp., 1925.
31. Bartlett, Rev. Chester Joseph, A.M., LL.B., J.C.D., The Tenure of Parochial Property in the United States of America, V-108 pp., 1926.
32. Kilker, Rev. Adrian Jerome, J.C.D., Extreme Unction, V-425 pp., 1926.
33. McCormick, Rev. Robert Emmett, J.C.D., Confessors of Religious, VIII-266 pp., 1926.
34. Miller, Rev. Newton Thomas, J.C.D., Founded Masses According to the Code of Canon Law, VII-93 pp., 1926.
35. Roelker, Rev. Edward G., S.T.D., J.C.D., Principles of Privilege According to the Code of Canon Law, XI-166 pp., 1926.
36. Bakalarczyk, Rev. Richardus, M.I.C., J.U.D., De Novitiatu, VIII-208 pp., 1927.
37. Pizzuti, Rev. Lawrence, O.F.M., J.U.L., De Parochis Religiosis, 1927. (Not Printed.)
38. Bliley, Rev. Nicholas Martin, O.S.B., J.C.D., Altars According to the Code of Canon Law, XIX-132 pp., 1927.
39. Brown, Mr. Brendan Francis, A.B., LL.M., J.U.D., The Canonical Juristic Personality with Special Reference to its Status in the United States of America, V-212 pp., 1927.

40. Cavanaugh, Rev. William Thomas, C.P., J.U.D., The Reservation of the Blessed Sacrament, VIII-101 pp., 1927.
41. Doheny, Rev. William J., C.S.C., A.B., J.U.D., Church Property: Modes of Acquisition, X-118 pp., 1927.
42. Feldhaus, Rev. Aloysius H., C.PP.S., J.C.D., Oratories, IX-141 pp., 1927.
43. Kelly, Rev. James Patrick, A.B., J.C.D., The Jurisdiction of the Simple Confessor, X-208 pp., 1927.
44. Neuberger, Rev. Nicholas J., J.C.D., Canon 6 or the Relation of the Codex Juris Canonici to the Preceding Legislation, V-95 pp., 1927.
45. O'Keefe, Rev. Gerald Michael, J.C.D., Matrimonial Dispensations, Powers of Bishops, Priests, and Confessors, VIII-232 pp., 1927.
46. Quigley, Rev. Joseph A. M., A.B., J.C.D., Condemned Societies, 139 pp., 1927.
47. Zaplotnik, Rev. Johannes Leo, J.C.D., De Vicariis Foraneis, X-142 pp., 1927.
48. Duskie, Rev. John Aloysius, A.B., J.C.D., The Canonical Status of the Orientals in the United States, VIII-196 pp., 1928.
49. Hyland, Rev. Francis Edward, J.C.D., Excommunication, Its Nature, Historical Development and Effects, VIII-181 pp., 1928.
50. Reinmann, Rev. Gerald Joseph, O.M.C., J.C.D., The Third Order Secular of Saint Francis, 201 pp., 1928.
51. Schenk, Rev. Francis J., J.C.D., The Matrimonial Impediments of Mixed Religion and Disparity of Cult, XVI-318 pp., 1929.
52. Coady, Rev. John Joseph, S.T.D., J.U.D., A.M., The Appointment of Pastors, VIII-150 pp., 1929.
53. Kay, Rev. Thomas Henry, J.C.D., Competence in Matrimonial Procedure, VIII-164 pp., 1929.
54. Turner, Rev. Sidney Joseph, C.P., J.U.D., The Vow of Poverty, XLIX-217 pp., 1929.
55. Kearney, Rev. Raymond A., A.B., S.T.D., J.C.D., The Principles of Delegation, VII-149 pp., 1929.
56. Conran, Rev. Edward James, A.B., J.C.D., The Interdict, V-163 pp., 1930.
57. O'Neill, Rev. William H., J.C.D., Papal Rescripts of Favor, VII-218 pp., 1930.
58. Bastnagel, Rev. Clement Vincent, J.U.D., The Appointment of Parochial Adjutants and Assistants, XV-257 pp., 1930.
59. Ferry, Rev. William A., A.B., J.C.D., Stole Fees, V-136 pp., 1930.
60. Costello, Rev. John Michael, A.B., J.C.D., Domicile and Quasi-Domicile, VII-201 pp., 1930.
61. Kremer, Rev. Michael Nicholas, A.B., S.T.B., J.C.D., Church Support in the United States, VI-136 pp., 1930.
62. Angulo, Rev. Luis, C.M., J.C.D., Legislation de la Iglesia sobre la intencion en la application de la Santa Misa, VII-104 pp., 1931.

63. Frey, Rev. Wolfgang Norbert, O.S.B., A.B., J.C.D., The Act of Religious Profession, VIII-174 pp., 1931.
64. Roberts, Rev. James Brendan, A.B., J.C.D., The Banns of Marriage, XIV-140 pp., 1931.
65. Ryder, Rev. Raymond Aloysius, A.B., J.C.D., Simony, IX-151 pp., 1931.
66. Campagna, Rev. Angelo, Ph.D., J.U.D., Il Vicario Generale del Vescovo, VII-205 pp., 1931.
67. Cox, Rev. Joseph Godfrey, A.B., J.C.D., The Administration of Seminaries, VI-124 pp., 1931.
68. Gregory, Rev. Donald J., J.U.D., The Pauline Privilege, XV-165 pp., 1931.
69. Donohue, Rev. John F., J.C.D., The Impediment of Crime, VII-110 pp., 1931.
70. Dooley, Rev. Eugene A., O.M.I., J.C.D., Church Law on Sacred Relics, IX-143 pp., 1931.
71. Orth, Rev. Clement Raymond, O.M.C., J.C.D., The Approbation of Religious Institutes, 171 pp., 1931.
72. Pernicone, Rev. Joseph M., A.B., J.C.D., The Ecclesiastical Prohibition of Books, XII-267 pp., 1932.
73. Clinton, Rev. Connell, A.B., J.C.D., The Paschal Precept, IX-108 pp., 1932.
74. Donnelly, Rev. Francis B., A.M., S.T.L., J.C.D., The Diocesan Synod, VIII-125 pp., 1932.
75. Torrente, Rev. Camilo, C.M.F., J.C.D., Las Procesiones Sagradas, V-145 pp., 1932.
76. Murphy, Rev. Edwin J., C.PP.S., J.C.D., Suspension Ex Informata Conscientia, XI-122 pp., 1932.
77. MacKenzie, Rev. Eric F., A.M., S.T.L., J.C.D., The Delict of Heresy in its Commission, Penalization, Absolution, VII-124 pp., 1932.
78. Lyons, Rev. Avitus E., S.T.B., J.C.D., The Collegiate Tribunal of First Instance, XI-147 pp., 1932.
79. Connolly, Rev. Thomas A., J.C.D., Appeals, XI-195 pp., 1932.
80. Sangmeister, Rev. Joseph V., A.B., J.C.D., Force and Fear as Precluding Matrimonial Consent, V-211 pp., 1932.
81. Jaeger, Rev. Leo A., A.B., J.C.D., The Administration of Vacant and Quasi-Vacant Episcopal Sees in the United States, IX-229 pp., 1932.
82. Rimlinger, Rev. Herbert T., J.C.D., Error Invalidating Matrimonial Consent, VII-79 pp., 1932.
83. Barrett, Rev. John D. M., S.S., J.C.D., A Comparative Study of the Third Plenary Council of Baltimore and the Code, IX-221 pp., 1932.
84. Carberry, Rev. John J., Ph.D., S.T.D., J.C.D., The Juridical Form of Marriage, X-177 pp., 1934.
85. Dolan, Rev. John L., A.B., J.C.D., The Defensor Vinculi, XII-157 pp., 1934.

86. HANNAN, REV. JEROME D., A.M., S.T.D., LL.B., J.C.D., The Canon Law of Wills, IX-517 pp., 1934.
87. LEMIEUX, REV. DELISE A., A.M., J.C.D., The Sentence in Ecclesiastical Procedure, IX-131 pp., 1934.
88. O'ROURKE, REV. JAMES J., A.B., J.C.D., Parish Registers, VII-109 pp., 1934.
89. TIMLIN, REV. BARTHOLOMEW, O.F.M., A.M., J.C.D., Conditional Matrimonial Consent, X-381 pp., 1934.
90. WAHL, REV. FRANCIS X., A.B., J.C.D., The Matrimonial Impediments of Consanguinity and Affinity, VI-125 pp., 1934.
91. WHITE, REV. ROBERT J., A.B., LL.B., S.T.B., J.C.D., Canonical Ante-Nuptial Promises and the Civil Law, VI-152 pp., 1934.
92. HERRERA, REV. ANTONIO PARRA, O.C.D., J.C.D., Legislacion Ecclesiastica sobra el Ayuno y la Abstinencia, XI-191 pp., 1935.
93. KENNEDY, REV. EDWIN J., J.C.D., The Special Matrimonial Process in Cases of Evident Nullity, X-165 pp., 1935.
94. MANNING, REV. JOHN J., A.B., J.C.D., Presumption of Law in Matrimonial Procedure, XI-111 pp., 1935.
95. MOEDER, REV. JOHN M., J.C.D., The Proper Bishop for Ordination and Dimissorial Letters, VII-135 pp., 1935.
96. O'MARA, REV. WILLIAM A., A.B., J.C.D., Canonical Causes for Matrimonial Dispensations, IX-155 pp., 1935.
97. REILLY, REV. PETER, J.C.D., Residence of Pastors, IX-81 pp., 1935.
98. SMITH, REV. MARINER T., O.P., S.T.Lr., J.C.D., The Penal Law for Religious, VII-169 pp., 1935.
99. WHALEN, REV. DONALD W., A.M., J.C.D., The Value of Testimonial Evidence in Matrimonial Procedure, XIII-297 pp., 1935.
100. CLEARY, REV. JOSEPH F., J.C.D., Canonical Limitations on the Alienation of Church Property, VIII-141 pp., 1936.
101. GLYNN, REV. JOHN C., J.C.D., The Promoter of Justice, XX-337 pp., 1936.
102. BRENNAN, REV. JAMES H., S.S., M.A., S.T.B., J.C.D., The Simple Convalidation of Marriage, VI-135 pp., 1937.
103. BRUNINI, REV. JOSEPH BERNARD, J.C.D., The Clerical Obligations of Canons 139 and 142, X-121 pp., 1937.
104. CONNOR, REV. MAURICE, A.B., J.C.D., The Administrative Removal of Pastors, VIII-159 pp., 1937.
105. GUILFOYLE, REV. MERLIN JOSEPH, J.C.D., Custom, XI-144 pp., 1937.
106. HUGHES, REV. JAMES AUSTIN, A.B., A.M., J.C.D., Witnesses in Criminal Trials of Clerics, IX-140 pp., 1937.
107. JANSEN, REV. RAYMOND J., A.B., S.T.L., J.C.D., Canonical Provisions for Catechetical Instruction, VII-153 pp., 1937.
108. KEALY, REV. JOHN JAMES, A.B., J.C.D., The Introductory Libellus in Church Court Procedure, XI-121 pp., 1937.

109. McMANUS, REV. JAMES EDWARD, C.SS.R., J.C.D., The Administration of Temporal Goods in Religious Institutes, XVI-196 pp., 1937.
110. MORIARTY, REV. EUGENE JAMES, J.C.D., Oaths in Ecclesiastical Courts, X-115 pp., 1937.
111. RAINER, REV. ELIGIUS GEORGE, C.SS.R., J.C.D., Suspension of Clerics, XVII-249 pp., 1937.
112. REILLY, REV. THOMAS F., C.SS.R., J.C.D., Visitation of Religious, VI-195 pp., 1938.
113. MORIARTY, REV. FRANCIS E. C.SS.R., J.C.D., The Extraordinary Absolution from Censures, XV-334 pp., 1938.
114. CONNOLLY, REV. NICHOLAS P., J.C.D., The Canonical Erection of Parishes, X-132 pp., 1938.
115. DONOVAN, REV. JAMES JOSEPH, J.C.D., The Pastor's Obligation in Prenuptial Investigation, XII-322 pp., 1938.
116. HARRIGAN, REV. ROBERT J., M.A., S.T.B., J.C.D., The Radical Sanation of Invalid Marriages, VIII-208 pp., 1938.
117. BOFFA, REV. CONRAD HUMBERT, J.C.D., Canonical Provisions for Catholic Schools, VII-211 pp., 1939.
118. PARSONS, REV. ANSCAR JOHN, O.M.Cap., J.C.D., Canonical Elections, XII-236 pp., 1939.
119. REILLY, REV. EDWARD MICHAEL, A.B., J.C.D., The General Norms of Dispensation, XII-156 pp., 1939.
120. RYAN, REV. GERALD ALOYSIUS, A.B., J.C.D., Principles of Episcopal Jurisdiction, XII-172 pp., 1939.
121. BURTON, REV. FRANCIS JAMES, C.S.C., A.B., J.C.D., A Commentary on Canon 1125, X-222 pp., 1940.
122. MIASKIEWICZ, REV. FRANCIS SIGISMUND, J.C.D., Supplied Jurisdiction According to Canon 209, XII-340 pp., 1940.
123. RICE, REV. PATRICK WILLIAM, A.B., J.C.D., Proof of Death in Prenuptial Investigation, VIII-156 pp., 1940.
124. ANGLIN, REV. THOMAS FRANCIS, M.S., J.C.D., The Eucharistic Fast, VIII-183 pp., 1941.
125. COLEMAN, REV. JOHN JEROME, J.C.D., The Minister of Confirmation, VI-153 pp., 1941.
126. DOWNS, REV. JOSEPH EMMANUEL, A.B., J.C.D., The Concept of Clerical Immunity, XI-163 pp., 1941.
127. ESSWEIN, REV. ANTHONY ALBERT, J.C.D., Extrajudicial Penal Powers of Ecclesiastical Superiors, X-144 pp., 1941.
128. FARRELL, REV. BENJAMIN FRANCIS, M.A., S.T.L., J.C.D., The Rights and Duties of the Local Ordinary Regarding Congregations of Women Religious of Pontifical Approval, V-195 pp., 1941.
129. FEENEY, REV. THOMAS JOHN, A.B., S.T.L., J.C.D., Restitutio in Integrum, VI-169 pp., 1941.
130. FINDLAY, REV. STEPHEN WILLIAM, O.S.B., A.B., J.C.D., Canonical

Norms Governing the Deposition and Degradation of Clerics, XVII-279 pp., 1941.

131. Goodwine, Rev. John, A.B., S.T.L., J.C.D., The Right of the Church to Acquire Property, VIII-119 pp., 1941.
132. Heston, Rev. Edward Louis, C.S.C., Ph.D., S.T.D., J.C.D., The Alienation of Church Property in the United States, XII-222 pp., 1941.
133. Hogan, Rev. James John, A.B., S.T.L., J.C.D., Judicial Advocates and Procurators, XIII-200 pp., 1941.
134. Kealy, Rev. Thomas M., A.B., Litt.B., J.C.D., Dowry of Women Religious, IX-152 pp., 1941.
135. Keene, Rev. Michael James, O.S.B., J.C.D., Religious Ordinaries and Canon 198, V-164 pp., 1942.
136. Kerin, Rev. Charles A., S.S., M.A., S.T.B., J.C.D., The Privation of Christian Burial, XVI-279 pp., 1941.
137. Louis, Rev. William Francis, M.A., J.C.D., Diocesan Archives, X-101 pp., 1941.
138. McDevitt, Rev. Gilbert Joseph, A.B., J.C.D., Legitimacy and Legitimation, X-247 pp., 1941.
139. McDonough, Rev. Thomas Joseph, A.B., J.C.D., Apostolic Administrators, X-217 pp., 1941.
140. Meier, Rev. Carl Anthony, A.B., J.C.D., Penal Administrative Procedure Against Negligent Pastors, XI-240 pp., 1941.
141. Schmidt, Rev. John Rogg, A.B., J.C.D., The Principles of Authentic Interpretation in Canon 17 of the Code of Canon Law, XII-331 pp., 1941.
142. Slafkosky, Rev. Andrew Leonard, A.B., J.C.D., The Canonical Episcopal Visitation of the Diocese, X-197 pp., 1941.
143. Swoboda, Rev. Innocent Robert, O.F.M., J.C.D., Ignorance in Relation to the Imputability of Delicts, IX-271 pp., 1941.
144. Dubé, Rev. Arthur Joseph, A.B., J.C.D., The General Principles for the Reckoning of Time in Canon Law, VIII-299 pp., 1941.
145. McBride, Rev. James T., A.B., J.C.D., Incardination and Excardination of Seculars, XX-585 pp., 1941.
146. Król, Rev. John T., J.C.D., The Defendant in Contentious Trials, XII-207 pp., 1942.
147. Comyns, Rev. Joseph J., C.SS.R., A.B., J.C.D., Papal and Episcopal Administration of Church Property, XIV-155 pp., 1942.
148. Barry, Rev. Garrett Francis, O.M.I., J.C.D., Violation of the Cloister, XII-260 pp., 1942.
149. Bolduc, Rev. Gatien, C.S.V., A.B., S.T.L., J.C.D., Les Études dans les Religions Cléricales, VIII-155 pp., 1942.
150. Boyle, Rev. David John, M.A., J.C.D., The Juridic Effects of Moral Certitude on Pre-Nuptial Guarantees, XII-188 pp., 1942.
151. Canavan, Rev. Walter Joseph, M.A., Litt.D., J.C.D., The Profession of Faith, XII-143 pp., 1942.

152. **Desrochers, Rev. Bruno, A.B., Ph.L., S.T.B., J.C.D., Le Premier Concile Plénier de Québec et le Code de Droit Canonique, XIV-186 pp., 1942.**
153. Dillon, Rev. Robert Edward, A.B., J.C.D., Common Law Marriage, X-148 pp., 1942.
154. **Dodwell, Rev. Edward John, Ph.D., S.T.B., J.C.D., The Time and** Place for the Celebration of Marriage, X-156 pp., 1942.
155. Donnellan, Rev. Thomas Andrew, A.B., J.C.D., The Obligation of the Missa pro Populo, VII-131 pp., 1942.
156. Eltz, Rev. Louis Anthony, A.B., J.C.D., Cooperation in Crime, XII-208 pp., 1942.
157. Gass, Rev. Sylvester Francis, M.A., J.C.D., Ecclesiastical Pensions, XI-206 pp., 1942.
158. Guiniven, Rev. John Joseph, C.SS.R., J.C.D., The Precept of Hearing Mass, XIV-188 pp., 1942.
159. Gulczynski, Rev. John Theophilus, J.C.D., The Desecration and Violation of Churches, X-126 pp., 1942.
160. Hammill, Rev. John Leo, M.A., J.C.D., The Obligations of the Traveler According to Canon 14, VIII-204 pp., 1942.
161. Haydt, Rev. John Joseph, A.B., J.C.D., Reserved Benefices, XI-148 pp., 1942.
162. Huser, Rev. Roger John, O.F.M., A.B., J.C.D., The Crime of Abortion in Canon Law, XII-187 pp., 1942.
163. **Kearney, Rev. Francis Patrick, A.B., S.T.L., J.C.D., The Principles of Canon 1127, X-162 pp., 1942.**
164. Linahen, Rev. Leo James, S.T.L., J.C.D., De Absolutione Complicis In Peccato Turpi, 114 pp., 1942.
165. McCloskey, Rev. Joseph Aloysius, A.B., J.C.D., The Subject of Ecclesiastical Law According to Canon 12, XVII-246 pp., 1942.
166. O'Neill, Rev. Francis Joseph, C.SS.R., J.C.D., The Dismissal of Religious in Temporary Vows, XIII-220 pp., 1942.
167. **Prince, Rev. John Edward, A.B., S.T.B., J.C.D., The Diocesan Chan-**cellor, X-136 pp., 1942.
168. Riesner, Rev. Albert Joseph, C.SS.R., J.C.D., Apostates and Fugitives from Religious Institutes, IX-168 pp., 1942.
169. Stenger, Rev. Joseph Bernard, J.C.D., The Mortgaging of Church Property, 186 pp., 1942.
170. Waldron, Rev. Joseph Francis, A.B., J.C.D., The Minister of Baptism, XII-197 pp., 1942.
171. Willett, Rev. Robert Albert, J.C.D., The Probative Value of Documents in Ecclesiastical Trials, X-124 pp., 1942.
172. Woeber, Rev. Edward Martin, M.A., J.C.D., The Interpellations, XII-161 pp., 1942.
173. Benko, Rev. Matthew Aloysius, O.S.B., M.A., J.C.D., The Abbot *Nullius*, XIV-148 pp., 1943.

174. CHRIST, REV. JOSEPH JAMES, M.A., S.T.L., J.C.D., Dispensation from Vindicative Penalties, XIV-285 pp., 1943.
175. CLANCY, REV. PATRICK M. J., O.P., A.B., S.T.Lr., J.C.D., The Local Religious Superior, X-229 pp., 1943.
176. CLARKE, REV. THOMAS JAMES, J.C.D., Parish Societies, XII-147 pp., 1943.
177. CONNOLLY, REV. JOHN PATRICK, S.T.L., J.C.D., Synodal Examiners and Parish Priest Consultors, X-223 pp., 1943.
178. DRUMM, REV. WILLIAM MARTIN, A.B., J.C.D., Hospital Chaplains, XII-175 pp., 1943.
179. FLANAGAN, REV. BERNARD JOSEPH, A.B., S.T.L., J.C.D., The Canonical Erection of Religious Houses, X-147 pp., 1943.
180. KELLEHER, REV. STEPHEN JOSEPH, A.B., S.T.B., J.C.D., Discussions with Non-Catholics: Canonical Legislation, X-93 pp., 1943.
181. LEWIS, REV. GORDIAN, C.P., J.C.D., Chapters in Religious Institutes, XII-169 pp., 1943.
182. MARX, REV. ADOLPH, J.C.D., The Declaration of Nullity of Marriages Contracted Outside the Church, X-151 pp., 1943.
183. MATULENAS, REV. RAYMOND ANTHONY, O.S.B., A.B., J.C.D., Communication, a Source of Privileges, XII-225 pp., 1943.
184. O'LEARY, REV. CHARLES GERARD, C.SS.R., J.C.D., Religious Dismissed After Perpetual Profession, X-213 pp., 1943.
185. POWER, REV. CORNELIUS MICHAEL, J.C.D., The Blessing of Cemeteries, XII-231 pp., 1943.
186. SHUHLER, REV. RALPH VINCENT, O.S.A., J.C.D., Privileges of Regulars to Absolve and Dispense, XII-195 pp., 1943.
187. ZIOLKOWSKI, REV. THADDEUS STANISLAUS, A.B., J.C.D., The Consecration and Blessing of Churches, XII-151 pp., 1943.
188. HENEGHAN, REV. JOHN JOSEPH, S.T.D., J.C.D., The Marriages of Unworthy Catholics: Canons 1065 and 1066, XVI-213 pp., 1944.
189. CARROLL, REV. COLEMAN FRANCIS, M.A., S.T.L., J.C.L., Charitable Institutions.
190. CIESLUK, REV. JOSEPH EDWARD, Ph.B., S.T.L., J.C.L., National Parishes in the United States.
191. COBURN, REV. VINCENT PAUL, A.B., J.C.D., Marriages of Conscience, XII-172 pp., 1944.
192. CONNORS, REV. CHARLES PAUL, C.S.Sp., A.B., J.C.D., Extra-Judicial Procurators in the Code of Canon Law, X-94 pp., 1944.
193. COYLE, REV. PAUL RAYMOND, A.B., J.C.D., Judicial Exceptions, X-142 pp., 1944.
194. FAIR, REV. BARTHOLOMEW FRANCIS, A.B., S.T.L., J.C.L., The Impediment of Abduction.
195. GALLAGHER, REV. THOMAS RAPHAEL, O.P., A.B., S.T.Lr., J.C.D., The Examination of the Qualities of the Ordinand, X-166 pp., 1944.
196. GANNON, REV. JOHN MARK, S.T.L., J.C.D., The Interstices Required for the Promotion to Orders, XII-100 pp., 1944.

197. Goldsmith, Rev. J. William, B.C.S., S.T.L., J.C.D., The Competence of Church and State over Marriage—Disputed Points, X-128 pp., 1944.
198. Goodwine, Rev. Joseph Gerard, A.B., S.T.B., J.C.D., The Reception of Converts, XIV-326 pp., 1944.
199. Kowalski, Rev. Romuald Eugene, O.F.M., A.B., J.C.D., Sustenance of Religious Houses of Regulars, X-174 pp., 1944.
200. McCoy, Rev. Alan Edward, O.F.M., J.C.D., Force and Fear in Relation to Delictual Imputability and Penal Responsibility, XII-160 pp., 1944.
201. McDevitt, Rev. Vincent John, Ph.B., S.T.L., J.C.L., Perjury.
202. Martin, Rev. Thomas Owen, Ph.D., S.T.D., J.C.D., Adverse Possession, Prescription and Limitation of Actions: The Canonical "Praescriptio," XX-208 pp., 1944.
203. Miklosovic, Rev. Paul John, A.B., J.C.L., Attempted Marriages and Their Consequent Juridic Effects.
204. Mundy, Rev. Thomas Maurice, A.B., S.T.L., J.C.D., The Union of Parishes, X—164 pp., 1945.
205. O'Dea, Rev. John Coyle, A.B., J.C.D., The Matrimonial Impediment of Nonage, VIII-126 pp., 1944.
206. Olalia, Rev. Alexander Ayson, S.T.L., J.C.D., A Comparative Study of the Christian Constitution of States and the Constitution of the Philippine Commonwealth, XII—136 pp., 1944.
207. Poisson, Rev. Pierre-Marie, C.S.C., A.B., Ph.L., Th.L., J.C.L., Droits Patrimoniaux des Maisons et des Églises Religieuses.
208. Stadalnikas, Rev. Casimir Joseph, M.I.C., J.C.D., Reservation of Censures, X-141 pp., 1944.
209. Sullivan, Rev. Eugene Henry, S.T.L., J.C.D., Proof of the Reception of the Sacraments, X—165 pp., 1944.
210. Vaughan, Rev. William Edward, J.C.D., Constitutions for Diocesan Courts, X-210 pp., 1944.
211. Paro, Rev. Gino, S.T.D., J.C.L., The Right of Apostolic Legation.
212. Balzer, Rev. Ralph Francis, C.P., J.C.L., The Computation of Time in a Canonical Novitiate.
213. Dougherty, Rev. John Whelan, A.B., S.T.L., J.C.L., De Inquisitione Speciali.
214. Dziob, Rev. Michael Walter, J.C.L., The Sacred Congregation for the Oriental Church.

www.ingramcontent.com/pod-product-compliance
Lightning Source LLC
LaVergne TN
LVHW050235080826
844660LV00012B/534

* 9 7 8 0 8 1 3 2 2 3 9 8 8 *